Advance Praise for *Change for Good*

"When Jerry and I built Ben & Jerry's we had to invent a way that our company could help solve social problems and be profitable at the same time. In *Change for Good*, Paul Klein provides a roadmap to do just that. By sharing stories, examples, tools, and inspiration he shows businesses how to become more successful by taking action to change people's lives and make the world a much better place. I wish we had this book 40 years ago!"

— BEN COHEN, CO-FOUNDER, BEN & JERRY'S

"Paul Klein's *Change for Good* is an excellent guide for practitioner or student. Paul thoughtfully walks the reader through case studies, expert advice, and recent trends to provide a practical and enjoyable guide to achieving the next stage in sustainable business outcomes."

— LIZ MAW, PRESIDENT, PRESIDIO GRADUATE SCHOOL

"Guiding skittish business leaders to make a real difference is never easy, but in *Change for Good* Paul Klein asks thoughtful questions and outlines practical ways to help you come to grips with the apparent contradiction of impactful business. Rather than a contradiction, it's a path to succeed *and* make a positive impact."

— ROD LOHIN, EXECUTIVE DIRECTOR, LEE-CHIN INSTITUTE
AT THE ROTMAN SCHOOL OF MANAGEMENT

"Full of stories and simple strategies, for corporate, community, civil servants, and frontline agencies, too. Klein shows and tells how change is possible: when we act intentionally, think long term — and do so in a united way."

— DANIELE ZANOTTI, PRESIDENT AND CEO,
UNITED WAY GREATER TORONTO

CHANGE FOR GOOD

*An Action-Oriented Approach for Businesses
to Benefit from Solving the World's
Most Urgent Social Problems*

PAUL KLEIN

This book is also available as a Global Certified Accessible™ (GCA) ebook. ECW Press's ebooks are screen reader friendly and are built to meet the needs of those who are unable to read standard print due to blindness, low vision, dyslexia, or a physical disability.

Purchase the print edition and receive the eBook free. For details, go to ecwpress.com/eBook.

Published by ECW Press
665 Gerrard Street East
Toronto, Ontario, Canada M4M 1Y2
416-694-3348 / info@ecwpress.com

Editor for the Press: Jennifer Smith
Cover design: David Drummond

LIBRARY AND ARCHIVES CANADA CATALOGUING IN PUBLICATION

Title: Change for good : an action-oriented approach for businesses to benefit from solving the world's most urgent social problems / Paul Klein.

Names: Klein, Paul (Founder of impakt), author.

Description: Includes index.

Identifiers: Canadiana (print) 20210340746 | Canadiana (ebook) 20210340789

ISBN 978-1-77041-631-4 (hardcover)
ISBN 978-1-77305-931-0 (ePub)
ISBN 978-1-77305-932-7 (PDF)
ISBN 978-1-77305-933-4 (Kindle)

Subjects: LCSH: Social responsibility of business. | LCSH: Social action. | LCSH: Social change. | LCSH: Social problems.

Classification: LCC HD60 .K54 2022 | DDC 658.4/08—dc23

This book is funded in part by the Government of Canada. *Ce livre est financé en partie par le gouvernement du Canada.* We also acknowledge the support of the Government of Ontario through the Ontario Book Publishing Tax Credit, and through Ontario Creates.

PRINTED AND BOUND IN CANADA   PRINTING: FRIESENS   5 4 3 2 1

MIX
Paper from responsible sources
FSC® C016245

This book is for my mother and father,
who believed deeply in social justice and in the power of creativity.

To Joanne, Sophie, and Joshua,
who give my life purpose.

And to changemakers everywhere,
who believe it's important to make the world a better place.

CONTENTS

The Journey to Change for Good

In 1988, I was working at the Toronto Symphony Orchestra and attended a conference of the American Symphony Orchestra League in Chicago. The keynote speaker was Ben Cohen, co-founder of Ben & Jerry's. At the time, Ben & Jerry's ice cream wasn't available in Canada, and I'd never heard of them. The essence of Cohen's talk was that businesses could contribute to solving social problems in addition to making a profit. Earlier that year, Cohen had founded 1% for Peace, which advocated for 1 percent of the national defence budget to be redirected to fund peace-promoting activities and projects. In support of this campaign, Ben & Jerry's created the Peace Pop ice cream stick that spun off proceeds to the 1% for Peace campaign. At the end of the presentation, Peace Pops were passed out to the audience.

Hearing Cohen talk about business doing more than making a profit was the first time I'd heard that businesses could have a social purpose. I remember feeling incredibly inspired by Cohen's message about how the company was intentionally using its business platform to create social change. I also remember thinking that I wanted to help companies support social change.

A few years earlier, Anita Roddick created The Body Shop, a cosmetics company that produced natural beauty products in ways that reduced environmental impact such as using refillable containers and encouraged social change through campaigns that challenged societal norms on issues related to beauty. For example, in 1997 they created a size 16 doll called Ruby, to challenge that beauty is related to body size. With the exception of Ben & Jerry's and The Body Shop, I hadn't heard of any other businesses that were intentionally connecting the dots between profit and social change.

A large part of my work at the Toronto Symphony Orchestra involved finding corporations to support the organization's concerts, tours, and educational programs. It never occurred to me that helping to increase access to music was a dimension of social change. However, I was connecting businesses with a social good and starting to learn about what mattered to the corporations that were our partners at the symphony and how they made decisions about supporting social causes.

Continuing along a path that was largely serendipitous, I left the Toronto Symphony to join the Canadian Parks and Wilderness Society (CPAWS), a national charity dedicated to the protection of public land, ocean, and freshwater. The experience I had at CPAWS was also the first time I had the chance to develop programs that were designed to make Change for Good. While I was at CPAWS, I also discovered the possibility of bringing creativity and innovation to social change.

For example, we created "Banffopoly" an advocacy campaign disguised as a board game to engage and involve Canadians in understanding the impact of business development on the environment in Banff National Park. Our direct mail "game" had players considering how business decisions about real estate development in Banff might, on the one hand, create economic benefit by increasing environmental tourism and, on the other hand, harm the environment by interrupting wildlife migration and compromising other aspects of the local ecosystem. Another campaign to protect the very remote Tatshenshini River in the southwestern Yukon and the northwestern corner of British Columbia featured a map with day-by-day journal entries of a trip down the river. Our hope was to create an immersive experience that would resonate with people who would likely never have the opportunity to visit the Tatshenshini.

During the time I was at CPAWS, I had the experience of working with corporations that were being helpful and harmful at the same time.

In this case, natural resource businesses that were causing harm to the environment and supporting environmental protection. The duality of businesses that are often responsible and irresponsible is an important theme you'll see throughout this book. For most businesses, balancing profit and purpose is extremely difficult — especially in situations where shareholders' interests are prioritized over the interests of other stakeholders such as employees and local communities. The spectrum here runs from companies that are genuinely harmful and make donations to charity in order to appear less egregious, to businesses that have less negative impact and have a culture in which doing good is of great importance. In Chapter 2, I share examples of how this duality has been a part of business since antiquity. More recently, new business structures such as B Corps have made it possible for companies to give equal balance to making a profit and making a positive contribution to society and the environment.

CPAWS needed funding and our corporate partners wanted to do something good, but we had no means of assessing whether or not this was appropriate or how far we should go to build and promote these relationships.

In 1993, I got a call from John Kim Bell, an Indigenous orchestra conductor I'd met at the Toronto Symphony. Bell had founded the Canadian Native Arts Foundation, an organization that gave grants to Indigenous people to pursue studies and build careers in the arts. He had the idea of recognizing Indigenous accomplishment in other areas and developed the National Aboriginal Achievement Awards and what later became the National Aboriginal Achievement Foundation (now known as Indspire). Bell was beginning to work on the first awards program and live television broadcast, and he wanted help in securing funding from corporations. It was an incredible opportunity to learn more about how corporations invest in social change and to be immersed in a largely Indigenous organization.

Bell and I had the privilege of being invited to an Indigenous ceremony in a longhouse with local chiefs in British Columbia. Afterwards, one of the chiefs told me the difference between his people and others. He said people who weren't Indigenous walk into the future facing forward, and people from his culture walk into the future facing backward so that they don't forget the value of their culture, language, and natural environment. I've always remembered that story because, for me, it captured the dichotomy between business and social change: looking at the world through a lens of values, purpose, and meaning or focusing only on creating economic value and profit to the detriment of what really matters.

I think that story also touched on what I was trying to do but didn't realize at the time: create social change by building relationships with groups that had contradictory perspectives and priorities but needed to find a middle ground for the purpose of something more important. Helping to find the corporate funding for the first two years of the National Aboriginal Achievement Awards was an opportunity to help bring Bell's vision to life in a way that connected businesses with social change.

In the 1990s, businesses began considering how to become more strategic in why and how they supported the community. We started to see the beginning of a social responsibility ecosystem of organizations and programs designed to help corporations do well and do good at the same time.

In 1992, Business for Social Responsibility was launched, with 51 member companies and an inaugural event featuring Ben Cohen, Anita Roddick, and Stonyfield Farms' co-founder Gary Hirshberg. In 1997, President Bill Clinton and a number of prominent business leaders helped to bring more attention to the idea of corporate social responsibility with the creation of the Ron Brown Award for Corporate Leadership for companies that were good corporate citizens. In Canada, the Canadian Centre for Philanthropy launched IMAGINE, an initiative that called for corporations to contribute 1 percent of pre-tax profits to charitable organizations.

During that time, I was a senior consultant at a "social marketing" agency in Toronto called Manifest Communications that had been an early leader in harnessing communications to help drive social change. One of Manifest's most successful early initiatives was creating

ParticipACTION, a campaign originally launched by the Canadian government to promote healthy living and encourage Canadians to make physical fitness a priority.

While I was at Manifest, it started to become evident to me that donating funds to causes such as homelessness or hunger wasn't wrong, but it also wasn't helping to solve these social problems. I realized that what was important was not how much money was given, but how the money was used to create change. There were many cases where corporations contributed millions of dollars to support causes rather than help solve problems. Further, this approach didn't engage the full extent of what a corporation could bring to the table, including expertise, human capacity, and use of products or services. Manifest started to explore this potential through programs such as the Ericsson Response, a disaster relief program that leveraged Ericsson's business expertise as a multinational networking and telecommunications company. Through this program, the company's communications infrastructure was deployed to provide connectivity to humanitarian workers in disaster areas through the installation of temporary internet until local services had been recovered.

The importance of partnerships between corporations and charitable organizations for the purpose of social change was also becoming clearer to the business community. More corporations began to consider how to partner with charities in a way that linked business funding and human resources to social issue expertise and credibility.

In 2000, it occurred to me that I'd already had 15 years of experience in doing what was now being seen as a priority by businesses. The way I wanted to connect the dots between business and social change organizations was starting to crystalize and I thought I could continue this work as consultant working on my own.

At the time, consultants were positioned as the "experts" and clients were expected to listen to their advice. This approach works in some areas such as law, engineering, or medicine, where what to do and what not to do is very clear. The space I was in was very different. Business decisions about what was then called corporate citizenship were based on a combination of values, relationships, and collaborations. I found that listening to what mattered to businesses and their non-profit partners was much more important than telling them what to do. This simple observation is still the essence of how I help businesses solve social problems today.

I quit my job to start impakt. My wife and I had just purchased a house, our daughter had just been born, and I had no savings and no plan. I thought I would work from home to help large corporations solve social problems by connecting them with charitable organizations. I remember thinking that this was such a smart idea because the concept of corporate social responsibility (CSR) was gaining in importance and virtually no one else had experience in this area. I didn't realize that I was many years ahead of the curve and that very few companies were paying people to help them make the shift from corporate philanthropy to CSR.

Failure wasn't an option, and I spent hours every day calling and emailing potential clients. Mostly, I found that there was no "business case" for CSR; no one was responsible for this aspect of a company's business, and no budget was available to pay for someone like me to help them. By pure persistence, I was able to convince a few large corporations that they could benefit by improving how they contributed funds to the community, and I convinced a few charities that they could benefit from being partners with these corporations.

I was fortunate to have the support of Larry Enkin, the recently retired CEO of the Coppley Apparel Group, as an advisor and mentor. In addition to running a successful business, Larry had earned a degree in social work and been a pioneer in bringing business thinking to the social sector. His unique experience in both business and social change was so helpful as I was continuing to learn more about how to develop programs in partnership with corporations and charitable organizations.

In the early days of impakt, I had very few clients and a lot of time on my hands. Larry suggested that I use the time I had to write articles for business publications about what I was learning. I started writing about CSR for *Canadian Business* magazine and then many other publications including *Forbes*, the *Guardian*, *Advertising Age*, and the *Stanford Social Innovation Review*. Over time, sharing my experiences and ideas helped me crystalize my understanding of the role of business in society and contribute to what others in the business and social sector were doing to demonstrate the value of corporate investments in the community.

In the 2000s, corporations began to be more strategic in considering why and how to invest in society, and the lexicon of related terms expanded to include corporate community investment, sustainability, corporate citizenship, business ethics, stakeholder management, corporate responsibility, shared value, and corporate social performance. At the same time as businesses were beginning to formalize their work in this area, much of the discussion focused on making the business case for corporate social responsibility. This meant identifying the tangible benefits that businesses derived from investing in initiatives designed to help society.

At the time, most people in business still believed in economist Milton Friedman's argument that the social responsibility of business was to increase profits.[1] Others were looking for reliable evidence that businesses could benefit financially from being socially responsible and that Friedman's argument was not necessarily correct.

Increasingly, a base of academic and industry-specific research helped to demonstrate to skeptics that a business case for corporate social responsibility could be made.[2] The specific benefits of investing in society were starting to be backed up by data and examples of companies that were contributing to social change and benefiting from doing so. These benefits included improved recruitment and retention, reducing costs as a result of saving energy, reducing the risk of not complying with current and future environmental regulation, building positive relationships with local communities, gaining competitive advantage in the minds of consumers, and helping to strengthen a company's reputation by aligning business activities with the goals and values of society.[3] The increasing validation of corporate social responsibility also contributed to a growing marketplace of advisory services, conferences, and newsletters.

For me, the gradual legitimization of the social purpose of business helped underscore what I'd believed since I heard Ben Cohen's talk in

1988. In retrospect, I don't think I was saying anything different than I'd been saying before, but people were starting to listen differently. I also saw that the business leaders I worked with fell into two camps: those who required quantitative evidence of the value of investing in social change, and others who simply believed it was the right thing to do for their companies and that they would derive benefit as a result. In the cases where "proof" of the value of investing in social change was required, very little happened. It was only in cases where leaders believed that this was the right thing to do, and believed that the business value would emerge over time, that building amazing social change programs was possible.

I also observed that corporations, such as large financial institutions, which measure success based mostly (or solely) on profitability and shareholder return were least likely to prioritize social change. At the other end of the spectrum were companies with entrepreneurial leaders for whom social change was personally important. These leaders built their businesses in a way that reflected their values and had an inherent social purpose. For example, Howard Schultz made what he called "scale for good" central to Starbucks' social purpose, and the company's work on creating employment opportunities for youth was groundbreaking.

L'Oréal's 2006 purchase of The Body Shop for $1.14 billion was another indication that companies with a social purpose were being seen as valuable. It was also cause for controversy and a demonstration of the importance of leadership. L'Oréal was known to test its products on animals, and the company was part-owned by Nestlé, which had been criticized for its treatment of producers in developing countries — two things that were anathema to The Body Shop's brand and purpose. In defence of the sale of her company, Anita Roddick made the case that working with a large corporation would help to increase the company's social impact. In an interview with the *Guardian*, it was reported that "she sees herself as a kind of 'Trojan Horse' who by selling her business to a huge firm will be able to influence the decisions it makes. Suppliers who had formerly worked with The Body Shop will in future have contracts with L'Oréal, and whilst working with the company 25 days a year Roddick was able to have an input into decisions."[4]

Even though The Body Shop has continued to prioritize social change and environmental responsibility, I don't think the company ever recaptured the commitment to advocacy and social change that was so important to Roddick. The Body Shop was a revolutionary business. Today, it's simply a responsible business.

Despite the growing acceptance of corporate social responsibility as a priority and an increase in financial and human resources available to make this happen, I felt that the business and social performance of most programs were underwhelming. I think this was because CSR had become something that corporations needed to be seen as doing rather something that was backed up by a genuine commitment to social change. It was easy for corporations to create a communications narrative about their contributions to charities, but very few businesses made a real commitment to meaningful and measurable social change. This has been described by many as the "rhetoric and reality gap" or as *Peanuts* creator, Charles M. Schulz, once observed, "There's a big difference between a bumper sticker and a philosophy." I call this CSR Lite, and I'll be referencing this phenomenon throughout the book.

The 2008 financial crisis has been described as the worst economic disaster since the Great Depression of 1929. I think it was also the awakening of the social purpose of business. The fact that this crisis was caused by the uncontrolled self-interest of some of the world's largest financial institutions, and was completely avoidable, was a clear signal that Friedman's argument that the "business of business was business" was no longer valid. For the first time, success in business began to be equated with the social welfare of employees, customers, and communities.

I think of the 2010s as the decade of social purpose. It was the beginning of businesses starting to close the rhetoric and reality gap by shifting social responsibility from being largely an exercise in optics to something more meaningful. One important global initiative helped to accelerate this shift: the 17 Sustainable Development Goals (SDGs) that were established in 2015 by the United Nations General Assembly as a "blueprint to achieve a better and more sustainable future for all."[5]

The questions that became most important for businesses included:

- What is the social purpose of our business?

- How do we balance our business objectives with helping to achieve the SDGs?

- How do we shift from philanthropic "investments" in charities to driving innovation that results in social change?

- How do we measure performance in ways that link the traditional metrics of business with helping to solve social problems?

During this time, our work at impakt began to shift from solely providing advice to help corporations and civil society organizations improve the social impact of their programs to actually creating our own social change programs. This began with the development of HireUp, a social enterprise platform with the mission of helping to end youth homelessness by connecting youth who had experienced homelessness with entry-level employment at large corporations.

Much of what made HireUp possible was having an ambitious idea and being completely committed to making it happen. At the beginning, we didn't even ask our corporate partners for financial support — we just told them what we were doing and why it mattered. In the end, we got funding from the Government of Canada and built partnerships with a number of large corporations including Home Depot Canada, Scotiabank, TD, Walmart Canada, FirstService, and Nordstrom.

I think people in business who acknowledged the lack of effectiveness of most social responsibility programs recognized that taking business and social change to the next level would require genuine commitment from influential business leaders along with collective action among businesses, NGOs, civil society, aid agencies, and governments. In the last few years, this has started to happen in earnest.

"The private sector is understanding that no business can succeed in societies that fail. And increasingly, [they] not only see an economic opportunity to get involved — creating livelihoods, making these economies work — but they also see that if business doesn't actively start owning or addressing some of the issues that are out there in society, then society won't let them be around," said Paul Polman, former CEO of Unilever. In 2019, Larry Fink, chairman and CEO of BlackRock Inc. wrote, "Unnerved by fundamental economic changes and the failure of government to provide lasting solutions, society is increasingly looking to companies, both public and private, to address pressing social and economic issues. These issues range from protecting the environment to retirement to gender and racial inequality, among others."

When people like Polman and Fink started to advocate for the importance and value of businesses to have a social purpose and be agents of social change, the ground shifted in a way that I don't think would have happened otherwise. Shortly after Fink's letter was released, I was at a global business event called the Gathering Summit and his message was mentioned in virtually every discussion among the brand and business leaders in attendance.

The impact of COVID-19 on society's most vulnerable exposed the size of the gap between those with a lot of privilege and those with very little. In addition to the immediate priorities of keeping people healthy and keeping the economy functioning to the extent it was possible to do so, the coronavirus crisis reinforced the need to accelerate and improve social change for racialized people, for people living on low incomes and in crowded living conditions, for people experiencing homelessness, and for those dealing with mental health and addiction issues.

Sadly, many of the charitable organizations that provide help to the most vulnerable faced a drastic reduction in donations. This drop, in combination with the need for social distancing, limited their ability to provide essential programs and services. In the short term, governments provided emergency relief and the business response was mixed. On the one hand, corporations such as Four Seasons Hotels and Resorts collaborated with Johns Hopkins Medicine International to validate an innovative new global health and safety program, Lead with Care.[6] On the other hand, it was reported that Cargill endangered the lives of its employees by continuing to operate its meat-packing plant in High River, Alberta, despite the fact that 935 of the plant's two thousand workers had already been infected by COVID-19.[7]

WHAT IS CHANGE FOR GOOD?

Shortly after the onset of the COVID-19 pandemic, it became clear that the progress that had been made on addressing the SDGs was in jeopardy. I started to think about how our team at impakt could help, and we came up with the idea of starting a weekly series of conversations with social change leaders from around the world. The plan was simply to talk about what these leaders were experiencing themselves, what they were doing differently to contribute to social change during such a difficult time, and how the pandemic was starting to shape their ideas about what would need to be different post-pandemic.

My colleague and friend Rem Langan suggested that we call these conversations "Change for Good" to reflect the importance of doing things differently to have more social impact, and the reality that how social change happens was never going to be the same.

These Change for Good conversations revealed a number of consistent themes, including the role businesses must play in helping employees who had become caregivers and who need mental health support, the need to get philanthropic funding to front-line organizations as quickly as possible, the need for more effective collaboration between corporations and governments, and the importance of recognizing and supporting small and medium-sized businesses that contribute most to the GDP and were most impacted during the pandemic. Of particular importance was the need for businesses to take action to reduce systemic racism affecting Black and Indigenous people and people of colour.

One of the Change for Good conversations that meant most to me was with Tabatha Bull, president and chief executive of the Canadian Council for Aboriginal Business. Tabatha told me what Indigenous people do to consider their impact on the world: they think seven generations ahead. Businesses that do this will be more sustainable, have better social change outcomes, and help prevent another coronavirus crisis in the future.

I realized that Change for Good was about more than just these remarkable conversations. The term "Change for Good" really represented a new approach for how businesses could shift from taking passive corporate social responsibility to helping to make active and intentional social change. Sometimes, doing this involves helping corporations overcome the inertia that causes them to operate in ways that aren't sustainable or that are causing harm to society or to the environment. Other times, it involves helping charitable organizations shift from measuring success based on their ability to stay in operation to measuring their success relative to their ability to improve social outcomes. In all cases, the common denominators for Change for Good are listening to people with lived experience of the issues being addressed, using the principles of innovation (the fastest, least expensive way to solve a problem), and having the belief that this is the right thing to do, even if there is no "proof."

Change for Good was a new system for effecting social change in the context of business that reflected what I'd been doing over the last 20 years and was central to how our team at impakt approached solving social problems. For instance, impakt helped Petro-Canada develop and launch the Petro-Canada CareMakers Foundation, a national charitable organization that creates awareness and understanding of the issue of family caregiving and inspires Canadians to help. The need to support family and other informal caregivers was important before COVID-19, and it has become even more of a priority during the pandemic. This initiative demonstrates how solving social problems can be tackled at scale.

During 2020 we also launched the Impakt Foundation for Social Change, a charitable organization with the mission of creating pathways to employment for vulnerable people. Initially, the Impakt Foundation will be focused on new research to understand how to better connect newcomers to Canada with meaningful employment in the apparel industry. The Impakt Foundation was inspired by our work on the Tailor Project, a social innovation from 1948 spearheaded by Larry Enkin's father that gave twenty-five hundred refugees, mostly Jewish tailors and their families displaced by the Holocaust, a chance at a new life in Canada.

I believe that corporate social responsibility as it is practised today isn't effective enough to help solve the problems that the United Nations has targeted in the 17 Sustainable Development Goals. To move the needle towards solving these problems requires a new approach: Change for Good.

Change for Good is an action-oriented strategy for businesses to solve specific social problems. It works by creating opportunities for the people with the most knowledge about social issues to establish a common understanding of the problem, identify promising solutions, and collaborate to bring these ideas to life through pilot projects. The Change for Good methodology is a reflection and culmination of the ideas I will share throughout this book: the need to first address what matters most to employees, the importance of involving people with lived experience in understanding and addressing social issues, the importance of making use of opportunities to use capital in new ways for the purpose of social change, the importance of being innovative and taking risks, and the importance of moving quickly and taking action.

WHAT YOU'LL FIND IN THIS BOOK

I wrote this book to share what I've learned from being at the front lines of business and social change for most of my working life. My intention isn't to showcase only best practices or to overly simplify work that is most often slow and complex. Making social change happen in a business context isn't easy, and most programs I've been a part of developing haven't actually worked nearly as well as I'd expected. I've also come to recognize that most corporations are responsible and irresponsible at the same time, and this is a recurring theme in this book.

I recognize that this duality isn't acceptable to many people. I've been called out many times for working with companies in sectors such as mining and oil and gas that are seen by advocates as being unethical.

In my experience, the people working in these companies are genuinely committed to improving their impact on society, and I've chosen to work within large organizations that have the potential to make Change for Good — despite being in areas of business where improving social outcomes and reducing environmental impact is very difficult. I also believe that unethical behaviour isn't limited to the business sector; I've seen lots of examples of bad behaviour in charitable organizations.

Writing this book has revealed something that's been underlying and often unconscious in the work I do to help businesses solve social problems. I have a fundamental belief that finding common ground for mutual benefit is more important, and more impactful, than acting unilaterally.

In this book, you'll find a collection of my personal experiences plus examples and tools that I hope will inspire you to help your company or organization make the shift from a passive approach to social responsibility to taking action to help solve a social problem. I'll start with sharing the context for business and social change today and then look at how businesses have always had a social purpose — as far back as antiquity. From there, I'll discuss why listening to the social priorities of employees and involving them in developing social change programs is the best way to begin making Change for Good. In Chapter 4, I explore why many businesses see making social change as a risk, and I provide ways for companies to move out of what I call the "Twilight Zone" of CSR Lite. Chapter 5 looks at why it's important for companies to pick up the pace of change and shows how it's possible to accelerate — even in large corporations. Next, I discuss why Change for Good means shifting from being "socially responsible" to actually taking responsibility for people and the planet. In Chapter 7, I explore how capital can be used differently to solve social problems. Next, I'll discuss why Change for Good depends on involving people with lived experience in developing and implementing social change programs. In Chapter 9, I share why hiring people with barriers to employment is a moral imperative, a civic responsibility, and also a business advantage. Chapter 10 features a discussion about why four globally significant turning points — the Great Recession, the Trump presidency, Black Lives Matter, and COVID-19 — have led to a watershed moment for businesses to Change for Good. In conclusion, I'll share how my personal experiences have led me to be involved in social change and how the principles of Change for Good can help bring meaning and purpose to your life too.

Despite the imperative to stop global warming, I haven't addressed this urgent priority in this book. This is partly because the aspects of social change that I know best are the ones that deal directly with human inequity, and these include interrelated issues such as hunger, poverty, good health and well-being, and access to decent work. It's also because so much important writing has been done that's specific to climate change. I'd point to Bill Gates's superb 2021 book, *How to Avoid a Climate Disaster*.

Beyond the specifics about why social change has become so central to business success, I believe that working with purpose is incredibly rewarding on a very personal level. I've been very fortunate to have created a space where what I do for work and how I live my life is almost indivisible. I hope the personal stories I've included in this book will make the Change for Good mantra something that's even more meaningful for you.

I hope this book will help give you new ideas, inspire you to take action, and help you change for good.

CHAPTER 1

Change for Good Today

The time difference between West Tennessee and Kathmandu is 11 hours and 45 minutes. That's why I was in the lobby of the La Quinta Inn in Memphis at 2:15 a.m. having a conversation with Nepal's sole billionaire, Binod Chaudhary, the chairman and president of the Chaudhary Group, a conglomerate that owns businesses operating in categories ranging from finance to consumer goods to hospitality. "We believe that the biggest reward is when we see a man in a simple village or mountain become an entrepreneur, start employing people, start producing goods or services, that's all we want," Chaudhary told me.[1]

A few years ago, David Patchell-Evans, founder and CEO of GoodLife Fitness and a global health and fitness entrepreneur, told me that having a successful business is difficult, creating social change is difficult, and doing both at the same time is extremely difficult. However, despite the challenge, that's exactly what Change for Good is all about.

As we'll see throughout this book, the intersection of business and social change is a space that is inherently filled with contradictory behaviour and questions that are difficult to answer. To what degree can, and should, a company's contributions to society be independent of its financial objectives? What about companies that are being responsible and irresponsible at the same time? How do we know if companies are genuinely committed to social change or are only interested in creating a positive impression to help drive sales or mitigate criticism?

In this chapter, I'll be sharing why businesses today need to deliver value to consumers at the same time as helping to solve social problems. I'll also introduce the concept of "CSR Lite," which is when businesses are socially involved only for the purpose of being seen to do something rather than actually committing to a specific social change goal. Plus, you'll find the first in a series of practical tools and advice on how to take action that I've included in each chapter. These are based on my experience in helping businesses improve their impact on society, and they are approaches that can be adapted for use by businesses in any sector. Finally, I'll begin to discuss a paradox that has characterized the relationship between business and society from antiquity to today: contributing to positive social change and being socially irresponsible at the same time.

IDENTIFYING AND SOLVING SOCIAL PROBLEMS

In the past, businesses became successful because they helped their customers solve practical problems or fulfill unmet needs or desires. That meant having a deep understanding or insight about what people needed or wanted that they didn't already have. People paid for goods and services, whether that was purchasing a dependable toaster or finding an experienced accountant. Beyond this basic exchange were variables in quality and convenience that influenced the price consumers were willing to pay. While this still holds true for business to be successful today, they now also need to understand the social circumstances and concerns of their customers and demonstrate that they are helping to solve these problems too.

Recently, I needed to purchase a new winter jacket and looked at many brands including Canada's Mountain Equipment Co-op (MEC), which is modelled after US-based REI. MEC has built its reputation on selling exceptional products at fair prices, having the smallest possible environmental footprint, conserving the outdoors, and helping Canadians get active outside. For someone like me, this is a perfect combination. MEC could help solve my problem of needing a new winter jacket in a way that would also help to protect the environment, which is a personal priority of mine.

I almost bought the MEC jacket but then decided to have a closer look at Patagonia, a company that's consistently referenced as one of the world's most responsible and sustainable businesses. Comparing these two companies, both of which have a reputation for being socially and environmentally responsible, was revealing. Both are socially responsible companies that offer similar high-quality products at comparable prices. However, Patagonia has made it virtually impossible to purchase its products without knowing the problems caused by the clothing industry and what the company is doing about these problems.

Before clicking through to purchase my jacket, I got this message: "Everything we make has an impact on people and the planet. So does everything you buy. The clothing industry contributes up to 10% of the pollution driving the climate crisis. And apparel workers are among the lowest paid in the world. That's why we make high-quality clothes with recycled materials and promote fair and safe labour conditions for workers. There are some things you can do, too. Buy less. Buy used. Repair what you wear out. Buy from brands that care for their people and the planet. Your purchases are your demands."

The difference in how each company is being socially responsible is reflected in their mission statements. MEC's mission is to inspire and enable everyone to lead active outdoor lifestyles by selling outdoor gear, clothing, and services. The last line of Patagonia's mission statement is "to use business to inspire and implement solutions to the environmental crisis." I bought the Patagonia jacket because I felt like doing this would contribute to solving problems that I think are important — climate change, low wages and poor working conditions in developing countries, and excess and unnecessary consumption by consumers.

(In 2020, MEC was sold to private equity firm Kingswood Capital Management and is no longer a cooperative social enterprise. I think part of the organization's business challenges had to do with losing its connection to its roots as a cooperative organization and being run like a private enterprise. Ironically, the organization lost its social purpose at a time when this could have contributed to a significant competitive advantage. Today, MEC is just another business that sells outdoor gear.)

Change for Good starts with companies asking themselves: Do we make our employees and our customers feel like they are making the world a much better place? Today, understanding what needs to be changed to make the world better is grounded in the United Nations Sustainable Development Goals (SDGs).

In 2015, the 2030 Agenda for Sustainable Development was adopted by all United Nations Member States. It provides a shared blueprint for peace and prosperity for people and the planet, now and into the future. The 17 SDGs that are central to the 2030 Agenda recognize that "ending poverty and other deprivations must go hand-in-hand with strategies that improve health and education, reduce inequality, and spur economic growth — all while tackling climate change and working to preserve our oceans and forests."[2]

The SDGs for 2030 are:

1. **No Poverty:** Access to basic human needs of health, education, and sanitation.

2. **Zero Hunger:** Providing food and humanitarian relief and establishing sustainable food production.

3. **Good Health and Well-being:** Better, more accessible health systems to increase life-expectancy.

4. **Quality Education:** Inclusive education to enable upward social mobility and end poverty.

5. **Gender Equality:** Education regardless of gender, advancement of equality laws, and fair representation of women.

6. **Clean Water and Sanitation:** Improving access for billions of people who lack these basic facilities.

7. **Affordable and Clean Energy:** Access to renewable, safe, and widely available energy sources for all.

8. **Decent Work and Economic Growth:** Creating jobs for all to improve living standards and providing sustainable economic growth.

9. **Industry, Innovation and Infrastructure:** Generating employment and income through innovation.

10. **Reduced Inequality:** Reducing income and other inequalities, within and between countries.

11. **Sustainable Cities and Communities:** Making cities safe, inclusive, resilient, and sustainable.

12. **Responsible Consumption and Production:** Reversing current consumption trends and promoting a more sustainable future.

13. **Climate Action:** Regulating and reducing emissions and promoting renewable energy.

14. **Life Below Water:** Conservation, promoting marine diversity, and regulating fishing practices.

15. **Life on Land:** Reversing man-made deforestation and desertification to sustain all life on Earth.

16. **Peace and Justice and Strong Institutions:** Inclusive societies, strong institutions, and equal access to justice.

17. **Partnerships to Achieve the Goals:** Revitalizing strong global partnerships for sustainable development.

The SDGs are overlapping, but most are built off goal number one: no poverty. Prior to the pandemic, the world was already off track by 6 percent in ending poverty by 2030. As a result of COVID-19, global poverty increased for the first time in decades: over seventy-one million people were pushed into extreme poverty.[3] The likelihood of achieving the first SDG goal by 2030 was low and is now even more remote. Not just that, the intersectionality between poverty and most of the other SDGs means we're now far from where we need to be in areas that the United Nations has determined are critically important for the future of humanity.

Pre-COVID-19, there was a growing imperative for businesses to help solve social problems. However, as a result of COVID-19, social problems have been exacerbated, and businesses now have an even more important societal role to play with respect to issues that are related to their operations. These include work-life balance, mental health, sustainable transportation, diversity and inclusion, and climate change.

For example, owning a bicycle became more of a priority when taking public transit was seen as risky. Not having a suitable home office wasn't a problem until going to work at an office wasn't possible in the same way. Remote learning became ubiquitous for children in elementary schools, for youth in secondary and post-secondary schools, and for others in adult learning programs. Shifts such as these propelled an unprecedented growth in bicycle sales,[4] a surge in goods and services needed for home offices,[5] and a massive spike in the e-learning industry that saw growth of more than 36 percent as schools migrated to new learn-at-home technologies.[6]

In addition to having more sales, some companies became leaders by helping to solve practical problems in order to increase sustainability in cities and communities, improve good health and well-being, and increase access to quality education — all of which are SDG priorities. For example, prior to the pandemic, Cadillac Fairview, a Canadian company that owns and manages commercial real estate around the world, had identified social detachment as the focus of its corporate purpose, "Transforming Communities for a Vibrant Tomorrow." As a result of the pandemic, Cadillac Fairview's purpose and focus on social detachment became even more important and the company recognized the need to look more closely at how this issue was impacting communities where it had operations in Canada. This led to the development of new partnerships with community organizations that are addressing the root causes of social detachment and developing new solutions to this problem. Jason Anderson, senior vice-president Brand, Marketing, Communication, had this to say about the company's actions during the pandemic: "Despite our industry being hit hard by the pandemic, our Purpose became a great filter by which we could make decisions quickly during such an intense time. We made a commitment to our more than 3,000 employees and third-party contractors that we would not lay them off. We worked individually with our hundreds of clients on rent deferrals and navigating government assistance programs. We also supported front line health care workers across Canada with hand sanitizer, PPE, and even free parking spots."

Similar to Cadillac Fairview, many companies complement business activities that contribute to social change with community programs. For example, Trek, one of the world's leading bicycle manufacturers and distributors, has an initiative called #GoByBike that is designed to fight climate change by encouraging people to choose bikes over cars and normalize bike transportation for the health of the planet. Trek is also a partner of World Bicycle Relief, an organization that increases access to sustainable transportation in developing countries.

CSR LITE

In 2011, I wrote an article for *Forbes* about the absence of social purpose at Apple.[7] I wondered how the world's most valuable company could be missing in action in the area of social change at a time when this had become a priority for employees and consumers.

At the time, the company's primary social responsibility focus was on stopping unethical practices among its suppliers. These practices were revealed in Apple's 2011 *Supplier Responsibility Progress Report* as including the use of underage labour at 10 facilities, dangerous working conditions at two facilities, falsification of audit materials at four facilities, and bribery at one facility. It was obvious that these actions were irresponsible and also clear to me that simply eliminating these problems wouldn't demonstrate leadership at the level that I'd expect from such a successful company.

I felt that being the most valuable company also meant that its leaders had a responsibility to help change the world, and I suggested some ideas for actions that Apple could take to elevate its social purpose:

- Support the development of technology that contributes to and measures social change in areas including fighting disease, distributing food, and improving education.

- Support innovative design for other products that contribute to social change such as assistive devices for the aging population, bicycles and alternative transportation, and renewable energy.

- Use its platforms to disseminate the most credible research, tools, and program information relating to social change.

Apple remains at the top of the *Forbes'* list of the world's most valuable brands,[8] and now seems like a good time to revisit what this company is doing to help change the world for the better. According to a December 2020 article in *Computerworld*, which calls itself "the Voice of Business Technology," Apple's COVID-19 response helped the world's leading technology firm become a "poster child for corporate social responsibility."[9]

Apple CEO Tim Cook was quoted in the article as saying, "This quarter and throughout the year, our response to this crisis has been to ask, how can we help? In terms of COVID-19 response, that has meant sourcing and donating millions of face masks, designing and manufacturing millions of face shields and scaling the production of millions of test kits."[10]

The company also harnessed its various divisions to develop Apple-designed masks for health care workers, a handwashing app for iPhones and a collaboration with Google on a potentially life-saving COVID-19 contact-tracing app. Also in 2020, the company offered more ways to support the fight against HIV/AIDS in Africa while simultaneously protecting those communities from COVID-19, and it marked World AIDS Day in December with fundraising opportunities and providing free access to TV shows, films, and music that show the human impact of AIDS.

"So, is Apple simply shrouding itself in values in a cynical attempt to progress its brand?" asked *Computerworld* contributor Jonny Evans. "While I'm certain there are some critics who make such claims, I tend to believe the company is growing to meet the needs of its times."

On October 29, 2020, in the midst of the COVID-19 crisis, the company posted record revenue of $64.7 billion. "Apple capped off a fiscal year defined by innovation in the face of adversity with a September quarter record, led by all-time records for Mac and Services," said Cook. "Despite the ongoing impacts of COVID-19, Apple is in the midst of our most prolific product introduction period ever, and the early response to all our new products, led by our first 5G-enabled iPhone lineup, has been tremendously positive. From remote learning to the home office, Apple products have been a window to the world for users as the pandemic continues, and our teams have met the needs of this moment with creativity, passion, and the kinds of big ideas that only Apple can deliver."[11]

This very positive announcement came just a few weeks after CNN reported that more than twenty-two million jobs had vanished and that, at 7.9 percent, the unemployment rate was the highest it had ever been ahead of a presidential election since the government started tracking the monthly rate in 1948.[12] It would have been an appropriate time to share what the company was doing to help the millions of people who didn't have such a successful year.

Has Apple changed for good since I first wrote about them in 2011? The ongoing ambiguity about whether or not they are socially responsible tells me this is a company that is practising what I call "CSR Lite" — wanting to be seen to have a social purpose but not backing this up with substantive actions that contribute to solving social problems. Perhaps this is because, despite the evidence that social responsibility has become a differentiator that helps drive sales, their products are so good that they don't believe they'll lose any customers.

Amazon is another corporation where public opinion about its commitment to society is polarized. Ranked at number four on the *Forbes* list of the world's most responsible brands, Amazon states that it has "created more jobs in the past decade than any US company, and we have invested more than $270 billion in the US over the last decade. Beyond our own workforce, Amazon's investments have created nearly 700,000 indirect jobs in fields like construction and hospitality. We also actively work to help communities by responding to the urgent needs of reducing hunger and homelessness and investing in education for children and young adults."[13]

During the first year of the COVID-19 crisis, Amazon's net sales increased 37 percent to $96.1 billion in the third quarter compared to the same period in 2019,[14] and *Forbes* reported that Chief Executive Officer Jeff Bezos became the first person ever worth $200 billion.[15] For his part, Bezos touts the company's industry-leading pay ($15/hour for all full-time, part-time, temporary, and seasonal employees across the US) and has challenged other large employers to step up to the $15/hour mark. "Now would be a great time," said Bezos. "Offering jobs with industry-leading pay and great healthcare, including to entry-level and front-line employees, is even more meaningful in a time like this, and we're proud to have created over 400,000 jobs this year alone. We're seeing more customers than ever shopping early for their holiday gifts, which is just one of the signs that this is going to be an unprecedented holiday season. Big thank you to our employees and selling partners around the world who've been busy getting ready to deliver for customers this holiday."

When Bezos launched Amazon in 1994 out of the garage of his house, few would have expected it to become the world's third-largest company by market capitalization.[16] Even fewer people would have anticipated that influential institutional investors would be calling out Amazon because of its failure to make social change enough of a priority. "Amazon has developed a reputation for running workers ragged, leaving hourly associates — disproportionately people of color — overworked and underpaid," said Sarah Zoen, senior policy advisor at Oxfam America's private-sector department. Further, the New York State Common Retirement Fund has cited "alleged discrimination of the company's Black and Latinx workers, their low wages and exposure to dangerous working conditions, including COVID-19, as well as the air pollution from distribution facilities located in minority neighborhoods." In December 2020, the Fund filed a shareholder resolution calling on the company to assess its impact on civil rights, racial equity, diversity, and inclusion, and suggesting that Amazon solicits input from employees and civil rights groups for the report and post it on the company website.[17]

SOCIAL CHANGE AS A BUSINESS OPPORTUNITY

As Amazon and other enormous retailers such as Walmart and Costco continued to thrive during the pandemic lockdowns, Canadian Ali Haberstroh developed an innovative alternative that may have the potential to disrupt Amazon by creating economic benefit and helping to solve social problems.

Haberstroh recognized that companies such as Amazon were turning online shopping from a convenience into a necessity and growing their businesses exponentially during a time that many small, local businesses were shutting their doors. As reported in the *New York Times*,[18] small and medium-sized businesses contribute more than 50 percent to Canada's gross domestic product. But during the pandemic lockdowns, 40 percent of small businesses reported layoffs while 20 percent had deferred rent payments, according to government data.

In response, Haberstroh created Not-amazon.co, a directory of locally owned businesses, to help keep small local businesses alive and, as she shared on Instagram, "so you don't have to give any money to Amazon this year!" By early 2021, Not Amazon had grown to include four thousand businesses across Toronto, Calgary, Halifax, and Vancouver and had attracted more than half a million page views. In addition to helping thousands of businesses compete with outsized competitors, Not Amazon made social change a priority by boosting businesses with Black, Indigenous, or queer owners.

Not Amazon is hardly a threat to Amazon's global dominance. However, a company that is an entirely free, volunteer-based social change endeavour is a type of competitor that Mr. Bezos could never have imagined. My hunch is that we're going to see many more versions of Not Amazon. Collectively, these socially minded start-ups might just put a dent in the profitability of much larger companies for whom social change is mostly an exercise in optics.

I think that, more than ever, companies will be judged by the degree to which what they do and how they act are genuinely in the best interests of the planet, of employees, and of vulnerable people. Not Amazon is a great example of a new company that's doing this really well. In writing this book, I had the opportunity to discover many inspiring examples of businesses that have long recognized that prioritizing the needs of people is the right thing to do.

One example is the Erreka Group, a company founded in 1961 and based in the Basque region of Spain, which produces a variety of goods including sliding doors, plastic parts used in cars, and medical devices sold around the world. It is part of Mondragon Corporation, which consists of over one hundred autonomous and independent cooperatives, employs more than seventy thousand people, and is one of the most important business groups in Europe. In a highly competitive marketplace, Erreka Group's defining purpose is grounded in its people. As their website states: "People are the most important 'differential value' for ERREKA. People considered as individuals with their own identity, with hopes, feelings, aspirations, needs, capacities, abilities and wishes."[19] The priority that Erreka places on people is reflected in its structure, as most of its workers are also owners of the company.

According to the Economic Policy Institute in Washington, the chief executives of the country's largest companies are paid approximately 320 times as much as their workers. The *New York Times* reported that at Mondragon, salaries for executives are capped at six times the lowest wage.

Today, the gap between the economically privileged and the precarious has become impossible to ignore. The ability of workers to feed their families is in doubt and the likelihood of achieving the first two SDGs, No Poverty and Zero Hunger, seems remote. In this context, Erreka's commitment to the welfare of its employees, rather than the financial interests of executives and shareholders, seems particularly important. "We have the philosophy of not firing people," said Antton Tomasena, Erreka Group's chief executive officer. "We wanted people to not have too many worries."

It's revealing that one of the largest and most progressive business groups in Europe, and a model for businesses to help solve social problems, is virtually unknown in North America. (I would never have known about Erreka Group if I hadn't come across them in an article in the *New York Times*.[20])

QUESTIONS TO ASK WHEN STARTING TO CHANGE FOR GOOD: HOW TO TAKE ACTION

Most companies aren't cooperatives and don't have the social purpose "DNA" of a company like Erreka. Few businesses are as polarizing as Amazon, which is hugely profitable and at the same time seen to be irresponsible in its treatment of employees and insensitive to broader societal concerns. How many people are as entrepreneurial and audacious as Ali Haberstroh — someone who is standing up for local retailers whose livelihoods are being threatened by global retail platforms?

Making the Change for Good shift from being in business for the sole purpose of being profitable to being profitable because you are helping to change the world starts with considering a number of guiding questions.

1. **Have we made employees the common denominator of our commitment to change?**
   Mother Teresa said, "If you want to change the world, go home and love your family." For businesses, this means going above and beyond providing fair compensation, a safe work environment, and health insurance benefits to employees. It means starting with putting a priority on diversity hiring to address, and wherever possible, prevent biases related to age, race, gender, religion, sexual orientation, and other personal characteristics that are unrelated to a person's job performance. It also means creating an inclusive culture where people of diverse backgrounds are able to thrive. Companies must provide employees with the training they need to be successful at work and with the social support they need for personal health and well-being. They must also strive to emulate companies such as Erreka that are committed to ensuring the difference in compensation between its executives and workers is not egregious.

2. **In what ways is our business contributing to social change just by doing what we're already doing?**
   For example, producing products or offering services that are themselves contributing to achieving the SDGs. By manufacturing and selling bicycles, Trek is helping to improve their customers' health and well-being, creating sustainable cities and communities, and taking action against climate change.

3. **Are our actions aligned with our words?**
   In 2018, iconic baby food brand Gerber appointed its first "spokesbaby" with Down syndrome and created a significant degree of awareness about the issue. However, it was revealed that Gerber's sister company, Gerber Life, was denying life insurance for children with Down syndrome. This serves as a good example of what *not* to do if you want your company's actions to be aligned with its words.

4. **Are we making change with the same urgency that we apply to making a profit?**

   In my experience, not surprisingly, businesses that find opportunities to improve revenue or reduce costs act very quickly. On the other hand, most of these same businesses approach supporting their communities and addressing other social concerns at a speed which I'd call glacial. The TD Bank Group's ability to launch its $25 million Community Resilience Initiative just a few weeks after the onset of the COVID-19 crisis is a great example of what's possible — even in a very large global corporation.

5. **Are we taking responsibility for people's lives?**

   There's a big difference between companies that have made social responsibility an operational business priority and those, such as Erreka Group, that actually take responsibility for their impact on employees, communities, and others impacted by their operations. Companies that want to make meaningful change need to know that making a commitment to solving a social problem and deciding how to take action is much different than most other business decisions, which are largely based on cost-benefit.

6. **Are we mobilizing capital for the purpose of social change?**

   Providing donations and grants to help charitable organizations address urgent needs such as COVID-19 and bring about longer-term change is vitally important. However, there is simply not enough philanthropic capital available to solve social problems. Doing this requires combining philanthropic funds with investment capital. In Nepal, The Chaudhary Group and The Chaudhary Foundation are investing in youth-initiated micro enterprises that have great potential but lack collateral and capital.

7. **Have we included people with lived experience?**

   When impakt started to develop social change programs, while I recognized how important this was, I also saw how we weren't really in a position to do this in a responsible way on our own because none of us had ever experienced any of the problems that impact vulnerable people. Today, too many businesses attempt to develop solutions to issues that their executives and employees have never actually experienced. Businesses can have more social impact by developing and deploying programs in collaboration with people who have themselves experienced these problems.

8. **Are we good partners?**
   Achieving SDGs such as Climate Action will require more and more meaningful collaboration between corporations, non-profit organizations, and governments. This means going beyond the rhetoric of partnerships — most of which are simply transactional relationships that deliver some degree of mutual benefit. It will require collaborative relationships with organizations in other sectors (and sometimes with competitors) that are co-created for the purpose of achieving a common good, addressing the inherent power imbalance between businesses and not-for-profit organizations. It is also important to establish a common language for effective communication and have clearly defined indicators to assess business and social outcomes.

9. **Are we prepared to take action?**
   In the aftermath of protests over the death of George Floyd, who died in May of 2020 after being restrained by a police officer in Minneapolis, Nike CEO John Donahoe took to social media with a message of activism: "For once, just don't do it." Shortly after the MAGA insurrection in Washington in early 2021, the Business Roundtable issued this statement: "The chaos unfolding in the nation's capital is the result of unlawful efforts to overturn the legitimacy of a democratic election. Business Roundtable calls on the President and all relevant officials to put an end to the chaos and to facilitate the peaceful transition of power."[21] Corporate activism has become an essential part of the

new normal, and businesses need to take action in a way that is far beyond the boundaries of corporate social responsibility.

THE IMPAKT MODEL

Beginning the journey to having more impact starts with positioning what your business is currently doing with respect to social change and determining what would be optimal in the future — this is what Rick Wolfe from PostStone Corporation calls your "preferred reality." To help businesses self-assess their current position and see how they can begin to Change for Good, I developed a tool called the impakt model, which is shown in Figure 1.1.

The model is based on three axes, each of which prompts a set of questions for consideration:

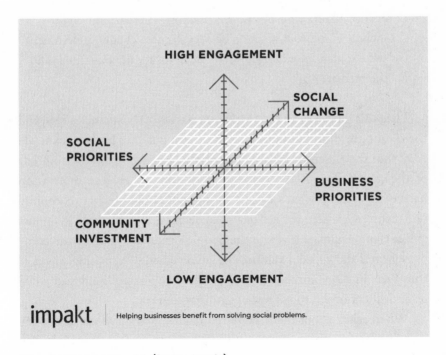

Figure 1.1: The impakt model. (Source: impakt)

1. **Social Priority vs. Business Priorities:** Why is social change important to your business? Is your company motivated by altruism and interested in making a difference to society? Are executives only interested in what will help the bottom line? Is a combination of both most important?

2. **Community Investment vs. Social Change:** How can your company approach having an impact and assessing performance toward that goal? Are investments based on inputs (donating money and time towards a social issue or organization) or outcomes (helping to solve a social problem that is aligned with your company's values and products or services?) Which of the two would your company's leadership see as most important?

3. **Low Engagement vs. High Engagement:** Who is most important to your business, and how aware are they of the social change efforts your business is making? These people could include employees, shareholders, customers/clients, government stakeholders, community partners, advocacy organizations, and the media.

I use this model in an interactive exercise with business leaders, and the results are almost always the same. Most business leaders acknowledge that their companies are currently positioned in the bottom left of the model. This is the place of CSR Lite, where the motivation has been based on what's easiest to implement and report (corporate philanthropy), where the actions have been measurable only by inputs rather than results, and where the people inside and outside the company have little to no awareness or involvement. Surprisingly, this is true even in large corporations that have well-established and well-resourced corporate social responsibility programs.

When asked about their "preferred reality," almost all executives say that they believe the optimal positioning for their companies is in the upper-right position of the model — the space where solving social problems, engaging the people that matter most, and delivering business value becomes indivisible. This is also the space that both requires and delivers leadership. Companies that commit to moving the needle on helping to solve social problems are companies that embody leadership and deserve to be seen as leaders.

Try getting a few people together in your company and using the impakt model to spark a conversation about where your business is today and where you and your colleagues think would be optimal. The path between these two positions is your journey to Change for Good.

At the Starbucks annual meeting in 2013, shareholder Tom Strobhar (who was also the founder of the anti-gay marriage Corporate Morality Action Center) complained to CEO Howard Schultz that customers had been lost because of the company's support for gay marriage. During the previous year, Starbucks had supported a referendum in Washington state that backed gay marriage, and the National Organization for Marriage had launched a retaliatory boycott of the company in response.

Schultz's reply? "Not every decision is an economic decision. Despite the fact that you recite statistics that are narrow in time, we did provide a 38% shareholder return over the last year. The lens in which we are making that decision is through the lens of our people. We employ over 200,000 people in this company, and we want to embrace diversity. Of all kinds."[22] Schultz made a bold social commitment that was also a savvy business decision aligned with the findings of a 2013 *Washington Post* poll that found Americans' support for gay marriage had increased to 58% in favour and 36% against.

A BOLDER VIEW OF BUSINESS

The need for a new approach to business and social change isn't new. An article I wrote for the *Guardian* in 2014 pointed out the flaws of corporate social responsibility and pointed to the need for businesses to be agents of social change.[23] In that article, I asked the question "Is corporate social responsibility a casualty of the law of diminishing returns?" and observed that, despite the significant investments corporations have made in being "responsible," the benefits haven't been quantifiable and the value of increasing donations, encouraging more employees to be volunteers in the community, and producing better CSR reports is questionable.

To gain more insight for my article on what corporations should be doing differently, I got the views of four leading academics who are authorities on business and social change: Peggy Cunningham of Dalhousie University, Jay Handelman of Queen's School of Business, Peter Madsen of Carnegie-Mellon University, and Kanji Tanimoto of the School of Commerce, Waseda University.

Each of these thinkers suggested that a fundamental rethink of the social purpose of business was needed. "An enlightened corporation is one that takes a bolder view of business, where profits are not their only goal but just one among several, which includes engaging in CSR activities to address the needs of society without raising the question of what might be in it for them," said Madsen. "An ideological shift from shareholder to stakeholder primacy — and managing the firm accordingly — is another way to envision this change of attitude about CSR and make the transition from a traditional to an enlightened firm."

"Very little attention has been paid to the impact that CSR practices have had directly on society or other corporate stakeholders," said Madsen. Businesses tend to overlook their social impact for a variety of other reasons including what Handelman saw as a "short-term, quarterly-results-driven focus" and the lack of what Madsen called a "generally accepted metric by which any impact of CSR might be accurately measured" and a tendency to focus on risks rather than benefits. "The harms seem to be documented better (everything from pollution, to the creation of a materialistic society, to unfair/unsafe labour practices)," suggested Cunningham. "There are huge gaps in research around the benefits."

The views shared by these academics revealed that the reasons corporations engage in social responsibility and the ways that they measure their ROI in this area had become anachronistic and inconsistent with the imperative of making a meaningful contribution to positive social change. The situation today remains the same.

"When one's heart is glad, he gives away gifts. Our Creator gave it to us, to be our way of doing things, to be our way of rejoicing, we who are Everyone on earth is given something. The potlatch was given to us to be our way of expressing joy," said Kwakwaka'wakw Elder Agnes Axu Alfred.[24] According to Living Tradition (a program of the U'mista Cultural Society, which is an organization in Alert Bay, British Columbia, with the mandate to ensure the survival of all aspects of cultural heritage of the Kwakwaka'wakw), rich and powerful people are also people who give the most away. The word "potlatch" means "to give," and guests witnessing a potlach ceremony are given gifts. The more gifts given, the higher the status achieved by the potlatch host. Potlatch ceremonies are held for many reasons including honouring important people who have passed on, celebrating marriages and the naming of babies, and restoring one's reputation in the community after a humiliation.

For me, the ethos of Change for Good is like a potlatch. The highest status goes to corporations that do the most to make the world a better place. As I'll discuss in the next chapter, since antiquity there has been a connection between social change and business, and companies have long needed to balance doing good and causing harm at the same time.

CHAPTER 2

Change for Good History

In September 2015, the United States Environmental Protection Agency issued a notice of violation of the Clean Air Act to German automaker Volkswagen Group. The agency had discovered that Volkswagen had intentionally programmed its diesel engines to activate their emission controls *only* during laboratory emission testing required to meet US regulatory standards. In real-world driving outside the laboratory, Volkswagen's diesel engines were found to emit up to 40 times more nitrogen oxides, and the company was found to have deployed this software in approximately eleven million cars worldwide.[1]

That same month, in the corporate social responsibility section of the Volkswagen website, the company declared itself as a "good corporate citizen" that gave equal priority to social, ecological, and economic objectives. The company also communicated its responsible behaviour with leadership in international CSR indices and active participation in initiatives such as the United Nations Global Compact and the Global Reporting Initiative.[2]

Volkswagen's contradictory actions illustrate the ongoing tension in the space between business and social change. How can companies justify good and bad behaviour at the same time? Can businesses contribute to society in ways that are independent of their financial objectives? Does having a social purpose give companies a "social license" that allows them to continue doing things that are harmful?

One of the most interesting discoveries for me in writing this book has been that the role of business in society, beyond the purpose of making a profit, has been a defining characteristic of business since ancient times — and using social purpose to deflect criticism for actions that would have otherwise been seen as self-interested or irresponsible is by no means a new phenomenon. Social considerations have been important for more than two thousand years. When I did the research for this book, I found that the world's earliest businesses had a social purpose and that many of the concerns about why and how companies contributed to society remain the same today.

The history of business and social change is complex, and it isn't my intention to share a thorough and objective study on this topic in this chapter. Instead, I've focused on aspects I found to be most interesting, surprising, and relevant to how businesses contribute to social change today. I'll share examples of how, beginning in antiquity, businesses were formed for the purpose of social benefit and used the "halo" of social purpose to justify actions that were regarded as inappropriate or unethical at the time — for example, how early business leaders used philanthropic contributions to support important social issues and mitigate the risk of being seen as excessively wealthy. I'll also share early examples of authentic social purpose, such as Cadbury's practice of "Quaker capitalism" in the 19th century and more contemporary examples of businesses having an inherent social purpose, including Newman's Own and The Body Shop. I'll discuss how recent crises such as the Trump presidency have contributed to corporate stakeholders being seen as equally important as corporate shareholders. Finally, I'll provide a series of action steps for businesses to follow in order to begin shifting from passive social responsibility to active Change for Good.

If you're interested in learning more about the historical relationship between business and social change, please explore the citations included in the endnotes for this chapter at the end of the book.

ORIGINS OF THE RELATIONSHIP BETWEEN COMMERCE AND ETHICS

During the time of Ancient Rome, huge quantities of goods including cereals, wine, olive oil, precious metals, marble, and spices produced in one part of the empire were exported and traded with goods from elsewhere.[3] This was done through a mix of state control and a free-market approach, which provides one of the earliest examples of businesses making a profit in ways that also contribute to social priorities such as employment and prevention of hunger.

In his *Antiquities of Rome*, the Greek historian Dionysus of Halicarnassus (first century B.C.) mentions that for the year 493 B.C. patricians had financial partnerships with the Roman government for the purpose of building temples for the deities Demeter, Dionysus, and Kore.[4] There were other prominent examples of public services provided by *societates publicanorum* in the fourth century B.C., including the supply of circus horses and the feeding of the sacred geese of Juno at Capitoline Hill. And the management of public properties included grazing rights, mining rights, fishing activity, and other concessions for public benefit.[5] The *societates publicanorum* also issued *partes*, or shares, which could be traded in the Roman Forum. These *partes* had different prices, could fluctuate in value, and, according to the ancient Greek historian Polybius, were held by a substantial number of citizens in the second century B.C.[6]

Despite the importance of trade in their economy, Romans believed that commerce had an inherent set of ethics and that the only honourable way of acquiring wealth was through war or ownership of land.[7] Cicero is reported to have argued that the wise man would only seek fortunes in order to exercise virtues such as generosity.[8] In Roman culture, nobles were "held to be above all manners of work, with the hands or with the head, for the sake of gain."[9] Even statesmen and generals served their fellow citizens without material reward. In the third century, the Roman emperor Gratian proclaimed that a man who bought merchandise "in order that he may gain by selling it again unchanged and as he bought it, that man is of the buyers and sellers who are cast forth from God's Temple."[10]

While trade in Ancient Rome depended on money lending, this was not seen as respectable for a Roman citizen. Many respectable Roman citizens made large profits from trading and money lending, but those activities were usually assigned to others whose reputation would not be at stake.[11] This may be one of the earliest business examples of using public purpose or social benefit (such as building a temple or trading goods) to create a positive impression of an activity (making a profit through commerce) that was not seen as acceptable.

In medieval times, guilds were a type of corporation used for commercial purposes in Europe, India, Japan, China, and Persia. According to Cambridge University economic historian Sheilagh Ogilvie, people formed guilds "to pursue mutual purposes" that arose from shared occupations.[12] Guilds helped ensure the welfare of their members (such as weavers, shoemakers, and bakers) by setting standards for quality and helping train the next generation of craftsmen. Members of guilds also became pivotal to their local societies by donating to charitable trusts for hospitals and almshouses. Some guilds contributed to their members' pensions and burial expenses.

Despite these positive contributions to the social good of their members and to society, guilds were also cartels that held a monopoly over the trades. In order to perform their particular trade, individual tradesmen were required to contribute to a guild's collective finances. (The word "guild" is derived from the Saxon word *gilden*, meaning "to pay" or "to yield."[13]) Leaders of guilds justified their private gains through the ways that the public benefited from their monopoly.[14]

During the Middle Ages, Christian theological doctrine dominated economic thinking. Similar to the ancient world, medieval cultural norms praised hard work and austerity but condemned trade, material desire, and usury.[15] Life in feudal times centred on war and the church, and the acquisition of land as a result of warfare remained the most acceptable way of acquiring wealth.

The prominence of maritime trade during the Middle Ages led to the development of commercial partnerships that could outlast a single voyage. One legal solution that had limited liability for its partners and could outlive members was called the *compagnia*. The *compagnia* was usually composed of family members and used for a variety of commercial purposes and the needs of religious and cultural associations. The etymological root of *compagnia* refers to the sharing of common bread, or *cum panis*,[16] and the word "company" is derived from *compagnia*. It's interesting to consider that the word we associate with business today reflects the importance of family and togetherness — both characteristics that have become important values for many corporations that strive to be socially responsible.

For example, Salesforce has adopted *ohana*, the Hawaiian word for "intentional family" to serve as the foundation for its decisions, actions, and communication.[17] According to Salesforce, Ohana embodies working collaboratively and taking care of each other. This support system is nurtured inside the company and extends from its employees to customers, partners, and members of its communities. The values of Ohana are embodied in Saleforce initiatives, such as its Pledge 1% program, which invites all entrepreneurs and their companies to integrate philanthropy into their business from an early stage. One of the company's core values is equality for all, which means working together to create a world where everyone has equal rights, equal pay for equal work, equal access to education, and equal opportunities for success.[18]

However, like many aspects of corporate social purpose, it's important to weed out the rhetoric from the reality. As Richard Branson said in a LinkedIn article he wrote titled "Why You Should Treat Your Company Like Family," "Many a Chairman will say he looks at his company like a family and then acts in a way which makes you glad you're not related!"[19]

REDEFINING A SOCIAL PURPOSE

By the 16th century, states including Britain, the Dutch Republic, Denmark, France, Portugal, and Sweden began to grant corporate charters to ventures that could advance their global ambitions. It was during this time that the common-law joint-stock corporation, or chartered company, led to the creation of important commercial entities that were predecessors of modern global companies.[20] Prominent examples of chartered companies include the English East India Company, which by the 18th century had a private army larger than the permanent British Army. The Hudson's Bay Company (which was chartered in 1670 and remains active today as a department store in Canada) and the Dutch East India Company (formed in 1602), were the first companies to list their shares on an official stock exchange.

Chartered companies built forts, waged war, and conquered territories with private armies and fleets, and negotiated treaties with Indigenous populations. These companies controlled enormous wealth; the Dutch East India Company even minted its own corporate currency. In return for being granted the rights to trading monopolies over large territories and specific trade routes, charter companies had to have a social purpose. However, by this time, a different understanding of social purpose had developed.

While older corporate structures such as the *compagnia* continued to be used for municipal, educational, and ecclesiastical purposes, governments in the early modern period expected chartered companies to increase national prestige, defeat rival nations in trade, increase economic prosperity at home, and acquire and populate overseas territories. The expectation was that these activities would result in there being a flow of goods to home economies, huge tax revenues, and increased domestic employment — all vitally important societal priorities. Similar to what the leaders of guilds had done hundreds of years earlier, chartered companies used their contributions to the public good to justify their monopolies, accumulation of wealth, and actions such as commoditizing the slave trade — which was done by the Dutch East India Company and Royal African Company.[21]

Minutes from company meetings during this time also referred to philanthropic activities. Historians William Pettigrew and Asa Brock have argued that "the early modern corporation was an instinctively and inherently social entity."[22] The directors of the East India Company were some of largest donors to charitable causes in London and directed their funds to help relieve poverty, build hospitals, and establish schools.

Doing this demonstrated their dedication to improving society and was also a savvy way to justify the large accumulation of wealth that was seen to be inconsistent with the era's cultural norms. It is also another example of enlightened self-interest that helped address social problems in a way that made business activities more acceptable. Political scientist Sankar Muthu has argued that chartered companies could only contribute to the public interest when their commercial priorities happened to overlap with broader social needs.[23]

The British Joint Stock Companies Act of 1856 provided a simple administrative procedure by which any group of seven people could register a limited liability company for themselves. Under the new law, British businesses no longer depended on Parliament to incorporate, and business corporations were no longer required to demonstrate that they had a social purpose. Not only that, courts in Britain and the United States ruled that corporations — the entities that historically had been created to serve a social purpose — were "legally prohibited from funding charitable institutions, because doing so allegedly ran counter to the interests of its shareholders."[24]

In the United States, this law remained in place until 1953 when the Supreme Court decision of A.P Smith Manufacturing Co. v. Barlow resulted in the firm being permitted to donate funds to Princeton University. In this case, the directors of A.P. Smith Manufacturing, a New Jersey–based company that manufactured fire hydrants, wanted to make a donation of $1,500 to Princeton University. The shareholders disapproved of the gift and contended that it was a breach of a director's duty to act in the corporation's or shareholders' interests.

Despite the new legal context that allowed for unbridled pursuit of profit, businesses continued to have informal relationships with social causes and organizations and contributed to social change. For example, the legal constraints around corporate support of social causes during this time contributed to a rise in philanthropy from the founders and executives of corporations. Oil industry business magnate John D. Rockefeller donated more than half a billion dollars to religious, educational, and scientific causes. Corporate executives of the Macy's department stores contributed to orphanages and other charities, and the DuPont family, who made their fortune in explosives, provided death benefits for workers killed in industrial accidents. Industrialist Andrew Carnegie, who made most of his fortune in the steel industry, was known for donating large portions of his wealth to causes related to education and scientific research and for helping to establish universities, schools, and libraries in the United States and Great Britain. In 1889, Carnegie wrote "The Gospel of Wealth," an essay published in the *North American Review*, which called both for the reconciliation of the rich and the poor and for the spending of the great sums accumulated by the rich people for public purposes. According to Carnegie, the life of a wealthy industrialist should be divided into three periods: Getting all the education he can. Making all the money he can. Giving the money to worthwhile causes.[25]

TYING PRODUCTIVITY WITH SOCIAL PURPOSE

From the earliest days of corporations during the expansion of the British Empire to the recent global pandemic, significant social and political events have consistently influenced why and how businesses contribute to social change. The shift from home-based and agricultural businesses to the modern factory system created new opportunities for employment and also created new social problems related to unhealthy and dangerous working conditions — in particular for women and children. In response, in the mid-to-late 1800s, industrialists began to be concerned about the well-being of workers — especially as it related to productivity.

For example, as early as 1836, the large German steel manufacturer Krupp established a health insurance plan for workers, followed by a pension plan and life insurance later in the century. In 1910, the Metropolitan Life Insurance company decided to build a sanatorium for employees with tuberculosis. Interestingly, this progressive idea was challenged by the New York State Superintendent of Insurance, who questioned the right of an insurance company to purchase real estate for building a sanatorium. The dispute was settled in an appellate court ruling that stated, "The enlightened spirit of the age, based upon experiences of the past, has thrown upon the employer other duties which involve a proper regard for the comfort, health, safety and well-being of the employee."[26] At the time, addressing the health problems of employees was seen as a "combination of humanitarianism and business acumen."[27] This is an interesting example of how enlightened self-interest had to be deemed as legally acceptable. Today, I think we'd look at Metropolitan Life's action as being more innovative and progressive than what most corporations do to look after the welfare of their employees.

Cadbury is an example of a company where social change related to the welfare of employees and customers was central to why the company was started and how it operated. "The original founders were Quakers, and they were trying to come up with something that they thought would be a nutritious alternative to alcohol, which was the ruin of many poor families," said Deborah Cadbury in an interview with National Public Radio.[28] "They were trying to come up with a business idea that was actually going to help people, and cocoa was this amazing new commodity and they thought they could make a business out of this nutritious drink."

Her family started the business in the 19th century based on a concept called "Quaker capitalism." According to Cadbury, the point of having a business wasn't to make a lot of money and *then* become a philanthropist. The goal was to benefit others right from the start. "As soon as they were able," she said. "They were doing things like raising the wages of their workforce, introducing Saturdays off, introducing pensions, introducing unemployment benefits and sickness benefits, and even free doctors, free dentists and vitamin pills for staff."[29]

In her book *Chocolate Wars*, Deborah Cadbury, the great-great-great-granddaughter of founder John Cadbury, describes how two hard-working Quaker brothers combined making high-quality chocolates with building a "fairyland factory" where workers had the advantage of fresh air, space for cricket, swings for the ladies, a rose garden, and a family-friendly atmosphere. After ensuring their employees were taken care of, they started to think about how their business should benefit the entire community. That led to the creation of Quaker utopian towns like Bournville, a model village just south of Birmingham, England. In Bournville, the Cadbury family hoped to improve the lives of their workers and their families by ameliorating the unacceptable living and working conditions of the working class. In 1900, George Cadbury founded the Bournville Village Trust, a charitable trust formed to promote good quality social housing that protects the environment, to manage all the housing and estates to the highest standards, and to encourage residents to share in decisions affecting their communities.

In 2010, Cadbury was acquired by Kraft in a takeover that grandsons of founder George Cadbury described as "a tragedy." According to Deborah Cadbury, the challenge for Kraft was to see what aspects of Cadbury Quaker history could be incorporated into the business model to make sure that Kraft "really uses the business as a force for good." At the time of the takeover, Kraft pledged to maintain Cadbury's social responsibility programs. "We are not foolhardy enough to do anything to harm the history of Cadbury and the integrity of the brands," said Michael Osanloo, Kraft's executive vice-president of strategy.[30] Despite what may have been a good intention, Deborah Cadbury was disappointed by Kraft's actions. "Somewhere along the way the four-hundred-year-old English Puritanical ideal of self-denial and the Quaker vision of creating wholesome nourishment for a hungry and impoverished workforce have disappeared," said Cadbury.[31]

Today, Cadbury is owned by Mondelēz International, a company that's stated purpose is "to empower people to snack right." The company's website states that it uses a "scientific assessment of our environmental footprint, as well as insights from consumers and stakeholders, as the basis for our programming, ensuring that we focus where we can have the greatest impact."[32]

Few people today would be aware of Cadbury's remarkable history as a social change leader or believe that this has been maintained by Mondelēz in a meaningful way — despite its more recent commitments to ESG. I think Mondelēz is missing an opportunity to revisit and reflect the Cadbury legacy when the socially responsible principles of Quaker capitalism would resonate particularly well with employees, consumers, and investors today.

THE TRUE ACID TEST OF BUSINESS

I think that the magnitude of business growth during the 20th century created a context in which the impact of business on society had become so pronounced that social purpose was impossible to ignore. Enormous corporations had begun to dominate major industries in the United States and, in 1932, authors Adolf Berle and Gardiner Means observed that "the economic power in the hands of the few persons who control a giant corporation is a tremendous force which can harm or benefit a multitude of individuals, affect whole districts, shift the currents of trade, bring ruin to one community and prosperity to another. The organizations which they control have passed far beyond the realm of private enterprise — they have become more nearly social institutions."[33]

In 1931, Stanford University professor T.J. Kreps, known as the "conscience of the business school,"[34] had developed an approach to identifying, estimating, and measuring the social performance of business. Kreps called this a "social audit" and described it as "a natural evolutionary step in the concern for operationalizing corporate social responsibility and, in its essence, represents a managerial effort to develop a calculus for gauging the firm's socially oriented contributions."[35] In his opinion, the social audit was the real acid test of business, not the profit-and-loss statement.

Kreps's prescient work in this area has never been more important. Today, we're more concerned than ever about understanding the social impact of business and how it contributes to financial performance. However, correlating social change outcomes with profitability remains a challenge. I've never found an impact measurement system or approach that could be used with any degree of accuracy for companies in different sectors or even for companies in the same sector. In my experience, the most important decisions about investing in social change are made by leaders who have an inherent belief that their businesses should contribute to social change. The role of leaders was explored in 1938 by Chester Barnard in the book *The Functions of the Executive*. Barnard believed that executive decisions should be based on moral codes and that business success and longevity depended on the morality of management.[36]

One of the most interesting and inspiring examples of the role business leaders can play in contributing to social change is the Tailor Project, which I mentioned in the introduction. After World War II, leaders from Canada's garment industry recognized the opportunity to help Holocaust survivors who were languishing in displaced persons camps across Europe. Industry leaders, with the support of organized labour unions, collaborated to bring twenty-five hundred Holocaust survivors to Canada and provide them with employment for one year to help them succeed in this country. Many of these people were tailors before the war, while many others, desperate to escape from deplorable conditions in the DP camps, had never sewed but convinced the selection team that they had.

The Tailor Project was led by Max Enkin, the CEO of Hamilton-based Coppley, Noyes & Randall, more widely known as Cambridge Clothes. In addition to the Tailor Project, progressive initiatives that Enkin spearheaded included creating a welfare and pension fund for the Amalgamated Clothing Workers and creating the Industrial Standards Act for the men's clothing industry in Ontario.

Max's son Larry helped grow Coppley from 60 to more than six hundred employees and built on his father's pioneering work in ensuring that the business was successful beyond making a profit. In addition to continuing to put a priority on hiring newcomers, Larry was responsible for other progressive business initiatives, including implementing an on-site "vestibule" training program for employees new to Canada that helped them learn their trade in safe, supportive conditions at the factory in Hamilton. He provided medical and social service support for employees, and he contributed generously to the community.

Three years ago, Larry asked if I could help him find the people who came to Canada with the Tailor Project and understand how this initiative came to be and how it impacted the lives of the survivors who were brought to this country. We were able to uncover the experiences of tailors who came to Canada with the Tailor Project, and their stories are shared in *The Tailor Project: How 2,500 Holocaust Survivors Found a New Life in Canada*, a book written by Andrea Knight, Paula Draper, and Nicole Bryck.

The actions that Canadian businesses took to establish the Tailor Project helped the tailors and their families to rebuild their lives in Canada. More than 70 years ago, business leaders recognized the core elements of what we now call corporate social responsibility: providing secure employment to people in need, embracing diversity, and supporting the health and welfare of employees.

CORPORATE SOCIAL IRRESPONSIBILITY

In 1949, the same year that Holocaust survivors were coming to Canada as a result of the leadership from the country's garment industry, the *Harvard Business Review* published two articles, one titled "The Roots of Business Responsibility" by B. Dempsey and the other titled "Business Responsibilities in an Uncertain World" by D.K. David. Dempsey and David were the first academics to formally talk about the social responsibility of business in society. Their arguments for CSR were based on principles of justice: First, that people and businesses do not stand alone; they also need communities to be prosperous. Second, that businesses have the resources and competence to assist with the progress and well-being of society and the individuals within it. Third, that it was the obligation of business executives to contribute to the well-being of individuals and society and to operate in ways that respect communities.[37]

It's important to recognize that many businesses operate in ways that reflect these principles of justice and perpetuate poverty at the same time — for example, by creating a class of people known as the "working poor," a term used to describe individuals who work full time and still fall under the poverty line.[38]

Walmart employs more than two million associates around the world and has taken the top spot in the Fortune 200 list for eight years in a row. Together, Walmart and the Walmart Foundation provide more than

$1 billion to support programs that align with the company's philan-
thropic priorities and mission to create opportunity so people can live
better. Despite this compelling social purpose, for years the giant retailer
has been at the centre of controversies over its low wages, overtime pay
abuses, and meagre employee benefits. "If the average person were asked
which large company most epitomizes corporate misconduct and lack of
accountability, there is a good chance the response would be Walmart,"
wrote Philip Mattera for the Corporate Research Project.[39] To Mattera's
point, in 2012 it was revealed that Walmart associates were being paid so
poorly that a store in Canton, Ohio, held a Thanksgiving drive to collect
food for fellow Walmart employees who were unable to purchase it for
the holiday.

In the years after World War II, American economist Howard
Bowen coined the term corporate social responsibility and defined it as
"the obligations of businessmen to pursue those policies, to make those
decisions, or to follow those lines of action which are desirable in terms
of the objectives and values of our society."[40] Despite this declaration
and the positive examples of the social purpose of businesses such as
Metropolitan Life and Cadbury, and the business-led Tailor Project, the
relationship between business and social change became significantly
diminished during the 20th century when maximizing profits for shareholders became paramount. In fact, the period after World War II, when
Bowen defined CSR, has been called the era of corporate social *irresponsibility*. That period is perhaps the historical low point in terms of the
impact of business on society and the environment.

The apex of this period came on September 13, 1970, when the *New York
Times Magazine* published an essay by the economist Milton Friedman
titled "A Friedman Doctrine — The Social Responsibility of Business
Is to Increase Its Profits."[41] The Friedman Doctrine was a call to arms
for American free-market capitalism and one of the most consequential
economic ideas, for better or worse, of the latter part of the 20th century. Friedman believed that executives are sole agents for a corporation's
owners, who are its shareholders. As a result, all decisions should reflect
what is in the best interests of shareholders. This belief has come to be

known as "shareholder primacy." Friedman believed that the interest of shareholders is to make as much money as possible, and he suggested that decisions that reduce profits (such as lowering emissions more than is legally required) is the same as imposing a tax on shareholders.[42]

Nestlé's baby milk scandal in the 1970s is considered to be one of the most egregious examples of a company that prioritized profit over purpose. As documented in Peter Brabeck's report "The Baby Killer" for the charity War on Want, the company was accused of getting mothers in developing countries hooked on using formula to feed their infants, which is less healthy and more expensive than breast milk.[43] A Swiss court warned Nestlé that to avoid accusations of causing death and illness through sales practices such as dressing sales reps in nurses' uniforms, they should change the way they did business. Since the 1970s, the company's actions have been regarded as a case study in how the pure pursuit of profit can be harmful to society and can also result in long-term reputational damage that is hard to shake.

A 2019 report titled *Based on Science? Revisiting Nestlé's Infant Milk Products and Claims* by the Changing Markets Foundation found that Nestlé had violated the WHO International Code of Marketing of Breastmilk Substitutes by drawing comparisons between its products and human milk.[44] The report concluded that the company uses "science" as a marketing tool, valuing high profit over scientific credibility and healthy infant nutrition.

Nestlé has a plan for positive social change. The company's *Progress Report 2019*[45] maps out a vision for the future that includes "ensuring long-term sustainable value creation for shareholders while tackling societal issues at the same time." Nestlé's ambitions for 2030 include helping fifty million children lead healthier lives, improving thirty million livelihoods in communities directly connected to their business activities, striving for zero environmental impact in their operations, acting decisively to tackle the current plastic pollution challenge, and working to become carbon neutral. Ultimately, Nestlé needs to turn platitudes such as "tackle the current plastic pollution challenge" into action — for instance, making a commitment to ending its bottled water business.

For Nestlé to change for good in a way that's believable and that will help improve its reputation, I recommend the following word substitutions: change "ambitions" to "commitments," change "striving" to "ensuring," change "acting decisively to tackle" to "eliminating plastic pollution," and change "working to become" to "becoming."

A NOTICEABLE SHIFT

The reasons why businesses address social problems and how they do this is directly related to broader social concerns. During the 1980s, a series of events occurred that caused the business community to re-prioritize the importance and value of social purpose. These included: the creation of the European Commission's Directorate-General for Environment (1981); the Chernobyl nuclear disaster (1986); the publication of the *Our Common Future* report by the Brundtland Commission, which provided a definition of sustainable development (1987); the United Nations' adoption of the Montreal Protocol (1987) and creation of the Intergovernmental Panel on Climate Change (1988); and the outbreak of HIV and AIDS.

These events significantly increased awareness of the relationship between business and sustainable development. Corporate behaviour during this time centred on actions related to environmental pollution, employment discrimination, consumer abuses, employee health and safety, quality of work life, deterioration of urban life, and questionable/abusive practices of multinational corporations.[46] Examples include film legend Paul Newman's line of food products, Newman's Own. All of the company's after-tax profits were donated to educational and charitable organizations. By purchasing Newman's Own products, consumers were able to participate in supporting the company's social change goals. Ben & Jerry's and The Body Shop are other great examples of brands that were engaging consumers in social change at the time. As I wrote in the introduction to this book, the leadership of companies like these was what inspired me to begin working in this area.

The first Business for Social Responsibility (BSR) conference I attended was in Los Angeles in the late 1990s. By that time, BSR and similar organizations, including Business in the Community (BITC) in the UK and Forum Empresa (Empresa Privada y la Responsabilidad Social en las Américas) based in Chile, were raising the bar by advocating for socially responsible business and by sharing best practices. However, in my experience, the situation on the ground was still quite basic. I remember helping the Canadian affiliate of Pfizer, the world's largest pharmaceutical company, to develop its first community investment program. This involved helping Pfizer understand why partnering with health charities that were aligned with its therapeutic area was preferable to sponsoring local hockey and soccer teams.

On August 19, 2019, the Business Roundtable issued a statement on the purpose of a corporation that was endorsed by 181 CEOs. These CEOs of the largest corporations in the United States committed to:

- **Delivering value to our customers.** We will further the tradition of American companies leading the way in meeting or exceeding customer expectations.

- **Investing in our employees.** This starts with compensating them fairly and providing important benefits. It also includes supporting them through training and education that help develop new skills for a rapidly changing world. We foster diversity and inclusion, dignity and respect.

- **Dealing fairly and ethically with our suppliers.** We are dedicated to serving as good partners to the other companies, large and small, that help us meet our missions.

- **Supporting the communities in which we work.** We respect the people in our communities and protect the environment by embracing sustainable practices across our businesses.

- **Generating long-term value for shareholders,** who provide the capital that allows companies to invest, grow and innovate.

- **Transparency and effective engagement with shareholders.**
  Each of our stakeholders is essential. We commit to deliver
  value to all of them, for the future success of our companies, our
  communities and our country.[47]

As we've seen in the examples from as far back as Roman times,
many of these commitments aren't new. However, they are even more
fundamental today, as global business leaders grapple with how the social
purpose of their businesses needs to change in response to the most
critical and interrelated issues of the day: the business implications of
President Trump's executive order that barred immigrants from seven
Muslim-majority countries from entering the U.S., Black Lives Matter,
and the COVID-19 pandemic.

In their article "The CEO Moment: Leadership for a New Era,"
McKinsey executives write that "the COVID-19 pandemic has laid bare
the profound interconnectedness between businesses and the broader
world in which they operate. . . . Employees, customers, and stakeholders expect a CEO to articulate where the company stands on critical
issues."[48] Beyond this broad statement, COVID revealed the corporations that are leaders and also exposed the laggards.

The examples of responsible and irresponsible corporate behaviour
during the pandemic that I described in the introduction are worth
re-stating. In Canada, leaders in the real estate sector collaborated to
establish COVID-19 vaccination centres in unused space in malls, conference centres, and commercial real estate properties. Verizon, the largest
US wireless carrier by subscribers, instituted an expansive sick leave policy,
provided backup dependent care for its employees, donated more than $54
million to non-profits before the end of April 2020, and did not lay off any
of its 135,000 employees in the early days of the crisis.[49] At the bottom of
the barrel were companies such as Travelodge, which closed its premises
and threw out unhoused families in defiance of government guidance.[50]

In May 2020, the killing of George Floyd by police in Minneapolis
created an unprecedented surge of support for the Black Lives Matter
movement. In response, some businesses that had contributed to

perpetuating systemic racism began to change for good. One notable example is Morgan Stanley, a company where, according to its 2019 sustainability report, only 2.2 percent of its senior executives were Black. In the aftermath of Floyd's killing, James Gorman, chief executive officer of Morgan Stanley, announced the promotion of two Black women to positions on the company's operating and management committees. This period "will not be easily forgotten in history, and it shouldn't be. God willing, it will be seen as a turning point in race relations," said Gorman in a commitment to diversity and inclusion posted on LinkedIn.[51] The company has also established the Institute for Inclusion, which has a mission to "to catalyze and accelerate an integrated and transparent strategy around diversity, equity, and inclusion in order to deliver the full potential of Morgan Stanley and drive meaningful change within our firm and beyond."[52]

Consider the actions of social media giants Twitter and Facebook during and after the American federal election in 2020. Initially, these corporations benefited significantly by helping to spread misinformation from President Donald Trump that contributed to the attack on the US Capitol Building on January 6, 2021. It was only when the president continued to incite sedition after the riots that Twitter and Facebook banned Trump from their platforms. Moving forward, social media platforms need to maintain their commitment to free speech and act faster to shut down messages that are incendiary, such as those that contributed to the insurrection at the Capitol Building.

Beyond social media, the storming of the Capitol caused many companies to cut ties with former President Trump and stop their political contributions. Shopify, a company that provides e-commerce sites for more than one million merchants, closed two online stores tied to Mr. Trump. In the days after the Capitol riot, the PGA of America announced that its board of directors had voted to terminate its agreement to play the 2022 PGA Championship, one of golf's most prestigious events, at Trump National Golf Club in Bedminster, New Jersey. And Deutsche Bank, Trump's primary lender for decades, decided not to do business with the former president or his company in the future.

The COVID-19 crisis revealed that the public expects corporations to demonstrate social purpose leadership and will punish firms that behave badly. According to research conducted in 2020 by Porter Novelli in the UK, 71 percent of respondents said that if they learned of a company's irresponsible or deceptive business practices during the crisis, they would stop buying its products or services. The same proportion said they would remember the companies that made bad decisions in the period; for example, decisions that had a negative impact on their employees, customers, or community.[53] A March 2020 survey conducted in 12 global markets revealed that 76 percent of consumers from China and 60 percent of consumers from India were most likely to make negative reviews of brands that acted poorly in light of the COVID-19 outbreak, and "in comparison, 27 percent of Americans, 24 percent of Canadians and 16 percent of Germans said they had convinced others to stop using a brand because it was not responding well to the crisis."[54]

During the pandemic, many businesses stepped up and took action in ways that hadn't been seen since the Second World War. During 2020, JUST Capital, a non-profit that tracks how corporations perform on the public's priorities, introduced the COVID-19 Corporate Response Tracker to assess how America's one hundred largest employers were responding to the crisis.[55] Their research revealed that corporations including Walmart, Home Depot, CVS, Starbucks, and Target had implemented initiatives including community relief funds, paid sick leave, and financial assistance for employees. It remains to be seen if the degree of socially responsible activity taken by corporations in response to the novel coronavirus will be sustained.

THE BUILDING BLOCKS OF CHANGE FOR GOOD: HOW TO TAKE ACTION

In 2008, I was interviewed by Ian Portsmouth from *Canadian Business* magazine, and I told him that I defined a company's social purpose as the sum total of all the direct and indirect impacts on society beyond making money.[56] More specifically, Change for Good is based on the following principles that are the building blocks for shifting from passive social responsibility to active social change:

- The social purpose of a business should embody the purpose of its leadership, and its leadership should embody the social purpose of the business.

- The social purpose of a business should be based on the belief that social change is good for business and business is good for social change.

- The social purpose of business should speak to the end (social change) rather than the means (corporate social responsibility).

- The social purpose of business shouldn't be limited to large companies — firms of all sizes have an impact on society.

- The social purpose of a business should be integrated with, and indivisible from, everything the business does to make money.

- The social purpose of a business should be aligned with and support social issues in a way that is consistent with the unique culture and character of the business.

- The social purpose of a business should be genuine, ongoing, and unassailable.

In this chapter, we've seen that businesses have always had a social purpose and that there are many reasons why companies contribute to social change and many ways that they do this. Some use philanthropy to improve their reputation or to help justify behaviour that would otherwise be seen as unethical. Some businesses are motivated to change for good by external events or pressure from employees and consumers. Others have a deep-seated, genuine commitment to making the world a better place. Still others are participating in the making of social change by simply being in business and doing what they do.

I think every business needs to be clear about why contributing to social change is a priority. Those that are using philanthropy as a smoke-screen for inappropriate business practices should stop doing both. Companies that are motivated by genuine altruism should continue to contribute in whatever way is most core to their culture. Businesses that practise CSR Lite have an opportunity to change for good by shifting from an approach that prioritizes investing the least amount possible to one that contributes to positive social change outcomes as well as improved business results. Those that are motivated primarily by external pressures have an opportunity to change for good by proactively deter-mining what social issues they can contribute to solving.

Regardless, I believe the social purpose of a business starts with sup-porting the needs of employees and creating the opportunity for them to co-create the company's approach to Change for Good.

CHAPTER 3

Change for Good Employees

There's a remarkable organization in British Columbia called Power To Be that helps people with cognitive, physical, and other barriers access nature. impakt was asked to help them understand and express their social purpose, and I helped lead a two-day session with their staff at Prospect Lake, Power to Be's incredible wilderness site located on Vancouver Island. We had developed a full two-day agenda of workshop-based discussions that would be done in their building overlooking the lake and surrounded by nature.

The first day was spent following the agenda, but it wasn't really working. Nothing was wrong, but nothing was very remarkable either. That evening, I realized that we were with a group of people whose work and passion was all about nature. The following day, we changed it up. We got them outside, divided them up into groups and had them build sculptures that represented the organization's social purpose from what-ever they could find on the site. Not surprisingly, what these teams built was incredible. We recorded each team describing the sculpture they built and how it represented Power To Be, and then together they all created a manifesto called "Everyone Belongs in Nature." It was a com-pelling narrative of who the organization was and why it mattered — in their own words.

Contributing to the well-being of employees, their families, and their communities has never been as important as it is today. The COVID-19 crisis has created a new imperative for businesses to contribute to communities in ways that are meaningful. Doing this starts with listening to what matters to employees and involving them in helping to solve social problems. In this chapter, I'll be sharing some examples of how businesses are partnering with their employees in meaningful ways, alongside some of my own experiences in building programs that were based on listening to employees. I'll also share an approach I use to understand what social issues are important to employees that is rewarding to participants because it is based on co-creation.

THE ROLE OF EMPATHY: A CONVERSATION WITH DR. ERIC SOLOMON

I'd like to share a conversation I had with Dr. Eric Solomon about empathy, a critical component when considering making Change for Good. Dr. Solomon has held leadership positions with some of the world's top technology brands, including YouTube, Spotify, and Instagram, and he is a pioneer in building what he calls human operating systems for organizations. The first time I spoke to Dr. Solomon, I knew that his belief in the importance of empathy in a business context was complementary to my views on why and how businesses should contribute to social change. Dr. Solomon believes corporations that are empathetic towards their employees are also better positioned to solve social problems. I think corporations that want to Change for Good need to be more empathetic. He and I have had some inspired conversations, and I think you'll appreciate Dr. Solomon's take on why empathy is so important to business today.

[Paul Klein] *How did you discover that empathy should be important to businesses?*

   [Dr. Eric Solomon] I was Director of Global Brand Strategy at Spotify, and one of the things they had put up on the wall that was part of the company's value statements was the word empathy.

   During the time I was at Spotify, my father was murdered, and even though they knew that I had a tragedy in the family, nobody had even bothered to ask me about what I was going through or how

I was feeling. Four months after I lost my father, I had one of those
meetings with your boss when you walk in and there's somebody
from HR sitting in the room. I was asked to give them my computer,
and I was escorted out of the building. And I began to start to
think of how it's so easy for corporations to say the word [empathy]
without ever defining what it means and then behaving in a way that
I view as anathema to being empathetic. This is another example of
corporations that say one thing, as more or less a PR exercise, and
simultaneously behave in ways that are the opposite.

What does it mean to be empathetic?
Empathy is one of those words that everybody thinks they
understand, but there's actually a lot of variation in what it means.
The most common definition that people point to is putting yourself
in somebody else's shoes, something that's called perspective taking.
But empathy can also be much more functional, like showing up on
time for a meeting or treating somebody kindly. Sometimes "kind"
and "empathy" can be used interchangeably. The business world has
led us to be curious about what people can do and what their skills
are, but not who they are as people. I think that being empathetic
involves trying to understand somebody else's experience, and that
starts with being curious. I also think companies have gotten really
good at using the word empathy precisely because it's slippery and
you don't actually have to define what it means.

Why is it important for corporations to be empathetic?
I believe that there's an expectation that businesses, as part of our
cultural fabric, have a responsibility to stand up and have a point of
view on divisive issues. More and more people, especially younger
people, are looking for employment opportunities that align with
their personal values. I think the risk is more people not joining
the workforce at companies that don't do what they say they're
going to do and more employees leaving their jobs because of the
same thing. During COVID-19, we saw people like Elon Musk

who were being the least empathetic, getting richer and richer. I
think COVID-19 has taken us to a crossroads, where people are
really willing to walk away from companies that don't listen to what
matters to their employees.

What are some companies that embody empathy?

Find me a good, good-hearted leader who has started a company
and built a company with the right values and purpose in mind, and
those are the companies that are most empathetic. Patagonia would
be on my list because it has a founder who is so driven by a purpose
and has made profit because of that purpose, not in spite of it. To
some extent, Ben & Jerry's, but I think it's more driven by what their
culture was before they were acquired by Unilever. Today, they are
the crown jewel of social responsibility at Unilever and have done a
pretty good job this year of putting money where their mouth is and
making their employees feel valued.

On the other hand, Mark Zuckerberg and the leadership team
at Facebook have a lot of good qualities, but in a culture of "moving
fast and breaking things," their impact on other people isn't one of
them. That approach is absolutely opposite to thinking about other
people. A lot of tech companies are not thinking about who they're
impacting and what it would be like to be on the other end of it.
When you look at the financial industry that is 100 percent focused
on ROI, why would it benefit them to ever care about anybody?

How does a company become more empathetic?

I think it starts with companies writing a letter to themselves about
who they are and what they believe in, and then describing the
ideal state of what they would want the world to look like if they
went out of business. Then you have a vision that gives employees a
reason to get up and go to work there in the morning (as opposed
to doing something else) because their company's mission is to
make the world a better place. I call this having a "human operating
system," where work is done with purpose and employees are

evaluated based on how they are helping other people as opposed to just completing tasks. Then you have a business system where what's being said and what's being done are completely aligned because everything is built on human values.

Speaking with Dr. Solomon helped me understand why empathy is such an important quality for businesses that aspire to solve social problems. The conversation reminded me that, like him, many of the people who are working to help corporations solve social problem have gone through a Change for Good shift themselves. Almost every day, I speak with people who are looking for more meaning from their lives and their work. This was the case before COVID-19 and is even more apparent today.

HUMAN OPERATING SYSTEMS IN ACTION

I think businesses that have human operating systems based on empathy and built on human values are Change for Good organizations that listen to and involve their employees in social change. Unfortunately, this is a far cry from how most corporations operate and approach what they do in the social change arena.

Typically, I've found that corporations usually involve employees in ways that are largely transactional and ineffective. Encouraging employees to volunteer to sort food at a food drive or to help clean local parks and beaches in the community has become a proxy for meaningful engagement. I'd call this a "check the box" approach that gives businesses the ability to say they've accomplished something without really doing anything that's meaningful to employees or valuable to their communities. Some companies have even used these activities as replacements for higher-cost team-building workshops and training normally provided by consultants and specialized agencies.

Change for Good involves listening to what matters to employees, creating opportunities to co-create social change programs, and participating in these initiatives in ways that allow employees to tap into what they are good at and passionate about. Before discussing how to involve employees in a more empathetic and meaningful way, I think it's helpful to consider a few examples. Ally Financial, Pfizer, and PepsiCo are all companies that listen to what matters to their employees and involve them in social change in ways that are substantive.

Ally Financial is one of the largest automotive finance businesses in the United States offering automotive dealerships and consumers financial services and insurance products. In an industry where products and services are virtually identical from one company to the next, Ally has embedded social change throughout its business and made its highest priority the needs of its employees. "This pandemic has shown how critical it is to embrace our humanity, be understanding and caring — and that holds true for companies, too," said Kathie Patterson, chief human resources officer of Ally Financial. "Make sure 'human' is prioritized in Human Resources."[1]

Prior to the pandemic, Ally was already supporting its eighty-seven thousand employees through what Patterson called a "lens of care and support," which included providing employees with generous financial, medical, and mental health benefits. When the crisis hit, Ally went above and beyond what was already in place: it sent employees home, including older adults, people with serious underlying medical conditions, and others who self-identified as high-risk according to CDC guidelines.

Beyond the immediate response, Ally's commitment to the health and welfare of its employees went much further. The company ensured that employees making less than $100,000 received $1,200 in tax-free financial assistance payment to help cover unexpected costs related to working from home, provided immediate paid medical leave for any employee diagnosed with COVID-19, expanded childcare and elder care support, provided paid caregiver leave for employees caring for an ill family member, and delivered well-being modules to help employees stay physically and mentally healthy at home. Related to its core financial services business, Ally provided employees with free access to certified financial planners to help them navigate the uncertainties of the crisis.

Pfizer's Global Health Fellows and Global Health Teams programs are helping to strengthen healthcare systems and increase access to care for the most vulnerable people in the world.[2] This is done by creating opportunities for employees with diverse professional backgrounds including research, supply chain, medical, and market analytics to apply what they know best in partnership with local health organizations. Pfizer participants help these organizations to streamline and strengthen administrative systems, write grant applications, develop systems for managing clinical trials, increase efficiency to pharmacy management systems, and reduce waiting times for care.

By connecting the expertise of its colleagues with the specific needs of its partners, Pfizer is developing breakthrough approaches to help people in need. Since 2003, more than 650 Pfizer personnel have volunteered approximately 400,000 hours in 51 countries. The Global Health Fellows and Global Health Teams programs are helping to address the SDGs, contributing to the professional and personal growth of participants, and delivering business value to the company. For example, an independent evaluation of Global Health Fellows and Global Health Teams revealed that 100 percent of participating employees gained professional, technical, and leadership skills. A participating NGO partner experienced a 217 percent improvement in service delivery, and Pfizer's brand was strengthened through communications of the program by partner organizations.[3]

In 2011, PepsiCo launched a similar program called PepsiCorps, a one-month skill-based volunteer program that involves employees from around the world using their business skills to address societal challenges. PepsiCorps' teams offer pro bono consulting services to local governments, social enterprises, and non-profit organizations with an aim to encourage healthy lifestyles, improve availability of affordable nutrition, provide access to clean water, and enhance sustainable agriculture — all areas that are aligned with PepsiCo's Global Citizenship vision and Performance with Purpose goal of "achieving long-term, sustainable success by aligning what is good for business with what is good for society and the planet."[4] According to the company, employees who participate in PepsiCorps' assignments become more creative, adaptable, and flexible leaders, returning home with deeper understanding of the connections between business and social needs, combined with a renewed commitment to the organization's social purpose of Performance with Purpose.

I think Pfizer and PepsiCorps are involving their employees in ways that are substantive. However, it's important to consider how corporate programs like these are actually impacting the lives of vulnerable people. Is it appropriate for PepsiCorps' teams to improve the lives of people in need in ways that also deliver benefit to PepsiCo? Are these programs contributing to social change, or are they an exercise in social responsibility optics? To what degree are people with lived experience involved in planning, executing, and evaluating these programs? Who is benefiting the most: global companies, their employees, local organizations, or local people in need? Can short-term efforts result in long-term change? What happens during times when delivering programs such as PepsiCorps isn't possible? Have the lives of people in need become dependent on decisions of global businesses?

I think the answers to these questions depend on the ways in which a company's core business is contributing to the social good. Pfizer is a pharmaceutical powerhouse that has been targeted for unethical practices such as conducting high-risk clinical trials in developing countries.[5] (The practices of companies such as Pfizer that are in the business of health will always be viewed with a high degree of scrutiny — and should be.) However, at its core, Pfizer is a company with a social purpose: to change patients' lives for the better.

On the other hand, in 1965, in what was called a "marriage made in heaven," Pepsi-Cola and Frito-Lay became a single company that delivered "perfectly-salty snacks alongside the best cola on earth." Today, PepsiCo is a $67 billion business with a mission to "create more smiles with every sip and every bite." Its vision is "to be the global leader in convenient foods and beverages by winning with purpose."[6]

While it may appear that social purpose is missing in action at PepsiCo, the company has many important social and environmental initiatives, including partnering with Catalyst, a non-profit organization that supports diversity, inclusion, and gender equity at work. PepsiCo also pledged to achieve net-zero emissions by 2040 by powering Tropicana production with windmills, delivering Cheetos with electric trucks, and fertilizing crops with Walkers potato peels. However, I think these positive actions will always be seen with a high degree of skepticism because, ultimately, PepsiCo's measure of success is making a profit from producing products that many people would consider to be unhealthy.

The tension between profit and purpose works both ways. Sometimes there are reasons to be skeptical of companies that are imbued with purpose and seem genuinely committed to social change. Ben & Jerry's has a legendary commitment to social activism that is reflected in issue-oriented ice cream flavours such as Pecan Resist (in support of Black Lives Matter) and Change the Whirled (aligned with NFL quarterback and racial justice advocate Colin Kaepernick). It also makes ice cream that is high in saturated fat, which can contribute to heart disease. The company's "super premium" products that are beacons of social change are also priced out of reach for many consumers. (In response to increasing awareness of the importance of healthier choices, the company introduced Moo-phoria, a line of lower-calorie versions of popular flavours such as Cherry Garcia.)

In the 19th century, Cadbury was a company that, like Ben & Jerry's, was steeped in social purpose. At the time, as a result of industrialization, chocolate had shifted from being a luxury to being a commonplace snack that was also used for wellness and to treat illness.[7] Much has changed since then. Concerns that are commonplace today, such as the importance of healthy eating and ethical sourcing of commodities like cocoa, were not considered in the 1800s. Today, virtually no one would associate Cadbury with Quakerism, and eating too much chocolate is known to lead to diabetes, obesity, heart disease, and other chronic conditions.[8] It would be interesting to know how Cadbury's employees balance the company's ethical origins with what it stands for today.

A few years ago, I was speaking with Nick Saul, Canadian food and social justice activist and the president and CEO of Community Food Centres Canada, about a social purpose project impakt was doing with one of the world's largest food and beverage companies. I asked him what he thought about their opportunity to solve social problems related to nutrition and food insecurity. Nick responded that they should start by making food that's healthy.

THE ORIGIN STORY

In my experience, there's no off-the-shelf template for engaging employees in a way that is meaningful and avoids the pitfalls and skepticism that we see in how most corporations involve employees in social change programs. My approach has always been to start with getting to the core of why companies should be helping to solve social problems and then consider how employees can become co-creators and active participants. This usually means understanding what matters most to a company's founders. I've found that, even if founders are no longer directly involved, their influence on the company's culture, business, and relationship with society is still present, particularly in the minds of employees.

For example, as noted earlier, Cadbury was founded based on the principles of Quaker capitalism. Because of that, it responded to the needs of its employees and their community in ways that genuinely reflected the principles of the Quaker movement: integrity, equality, simplicity, community, stewardship of the earth, and peace. Most companies don't have a legacy as profound as Cadbury's. Regardless, it's important to begin by understanding what social concerns mattered most to the founders of the company. Businesses that don't begin their Change for Good journey with understanding the genesis and essence of their social purpose end up with check-the-box approaches to involving employees in social change — which will be seen by people inside and out of a company as inauthentic or meaningless.

Virtually every company was started by an entrepreneur who had an idea for a business that would solve a problem. From Andrew Carnegie's role in establishing public libraries to the commitment Bill Gates has made to reducing poverty and increasing access to health care, most entrepreneurs are people who are also committed to helping their communities by supporting issues that matter to them or their families.

For example, Lilly is a global pharmaceutical company that was founded by Eli Lilly, a pharmacist and businessman who opened a drug manufacturing business in 1876. By 1890, Lilly had turned over the management of the company to his son to allow himself more time to focus on work with charitable organizations and civic advancement.[9] The elder Lilly became the primary patron of Indiana's branch of the Charity Organization Society and personally funded a children's hospital in Indianapolis. Today, the company's purpose is to "unite caring with discovery to create medicines that make life better for people around the world."[10]

Tobias Lütke is the co-founder of Shopify, the global e-commerce platform launched in 2004. Lütke and wife Fiona McKean are also committed to addressing Sustainable Development Goal 13, climate action. "We passionately believe that finding novel approaches to decarbonization is critical to addressing climate change,"[11] McKean and Lütke said in a letter posted on the website for the Thistledown Foundation, the organization they established to fund promising technologies that reduce the use of fossil fuels, a process known as decarbonization. (During the pandemic, the foundation focused on getting money more quickly into the hands of COVID-19 researchers and on finding new sources of the protective equipment needed by front-line medical workers.)[12]

Jenn Harper is the founder and CEO of Cheekbone Beauty, an Indigenous-owned Canadian cosmetics company based out of St. Catharines, Ontario. Cheekbone Beauty creates high-quality, cruelty-free beauty products, such as liquid lipsticks and complexion products including contour and highlight palettes.

In 2020, Harper shared her origin story with me on impakt's Change for Good leadership platform.

> The story was this dream I had in 2015 after I got sober from a six-year battle with alcoholism. In this dream, I woke up and there were these little native little girls. I woke up and said, "Okay, I'm going to make lip gloss and then start a foundation in my grandmother's name,

Emily Paul, who was a residential school survivor. I literally started writing this out that night at two in the morning, and this became the beginning of what is now our business plan. 2015 was my "aha year" and also a year of reckoning because I read the final report of the Truth and Reconciliation Commission. [The Truth and Reconciliation Commission provided those directly or indirectly affected by the legacy of the Indian residential school system with an opportunity to share their stories and experiences and was the largest class-action settlement in Canadian history.] The final report gathered information about what happened because of residential schools and what Canada, together with Indigenous people, could do to make the situation better. I am a 38-year-old woman that looks clearly Indigenous, clearly looks like an Ojibwe woman. My grandmother suffered the way she did because our families didn't talk about it. When one event impacts a family or a generation, that in turn impacts the next generations. Even with that concept, having this reckoning and realizing that, "Okay, that was the trauma, let's now have this generational healing." Cheekbone Beauty is ultimately about showing Indigenous youth that anything is absolutely possible and mountains can be overcome with the support of the right community. We are creating a new narrative for all Indigenous people: to show them that everything is possible regardless of past traumas.

Cheekbone Beauty's origin story is reflected in its commitment to create a space in the beauty industry where Indigenous youth feel recognized, represented, and feel their value in the world. Harper's business is solving a social problem. True to its roots, Cheekbone's definition of success is not based on what you attain for yourself, but instead on what you give back to your community.

Lilly, Shopify, and Cheekbone Beauty are completely different kinds of businesses that have one thing in common: each company has social change built into their DNA.

EMPLOYEES MAKE ALL THE DIFFERENCE

Over my many years of helping corporations assess and improve their impact on society, one of my most consistent initial discoveries is that very few employees are actually involved in helping to develop the organization's social change programs or participate in them. Beyond that, often employees of large corporations aren't even aware of what their employers are doing in this area. This is despite corporate social responsibility programs that are developed with the best of intentions and communicated in ways that seem like they should be very effective, and also despite the vast amount of credible research suggesting that involving employees in social impact initiatives is often the most valuable aspect of business and social change.

A 2019 blog by Matt Gavin in Harvard Business School Online suggests that purpose-driven firms create opportunities for their employees by sharing the company's vision for change and by making sure that their contributions are seen as meaningful. For example, Gavin writes that encouraging employees to volunteer is a practical way to involve staff in social impact initiatives and boost morale. This is backed up by a recent survey by Deloitte that found that 74 percent of workers said they believe volunteerism provides an improved sense of purpose.[13] Gavin also offers the example of organic food producer Clif Bar & Company, where volunteering is core to the company's business model. "By fostering a culture that inspires employees to give back, companies can empower their workforce to engage with issues that matter to them and instill a sense of shared purpose," says Gavin.[14]

Dirk Matten, professor of strategy at York University's Schulich School of Business in Toronto, believes that being socially responsible is a key recruitment tool. "We are in a stage where employees want to do well for themselves," said Matten. "They want to have a great job; they want to have money. They want to look at their career path . . . certainly the millennials — the current generation entering adult life — want to be part of a meaningful story."[15] A 2018 study of one thousand workers by the Upside Foundation found that almost three quarters (72 percent) of North American employees believe it's important that employers have strong corporate social responsibility practices.[16]

A study by the Kenexa High Performance Institute of 30,000 employees in 21 countries revealed just how much employees care about CSR. "Our study shows a statistically significant relationship between corporate responsibility and organizational success. Employees who work in organizations that have a greater sense of responsibility towards their communities and environment, both ecological and social, have an engagement level that is four times higher than it is for employees who work in a low CSR culture," said Dr. Brenda Kowske, research manager at the Kenexa High Performance Institute.[17]

Again, there's every reason to believe that employees could be participating in what their employers are doing to change the world; however, in my experience, this is rarely the case. In my work with large corporations, I've found that even the most basic corporate volunteer programs have very low levels of engagement (between 5 percent and 10 percent employee participation). More in-depth involvement, such as creating opportunities for employees to use their professional skills and experience to help non-profit and other organizations better understand how to solve social problems, is less common. One of the best examples of this kind of initiative is the IBM Corporate Service Corps, which provides IBMers with opportunities to use their professional skills to help people and communities tackle complex issues. The program entails small groups of IBM staff partnering for several weeks with non-profit, government, educational, and civic leaders to address high-priority issues in education, sustainability, health, and economic development.[18]

THE CHANGE FOR GOOD ORIGIN STORY PROCESS: HOW TO TAKE ACTION

Change for Good depends on understanding what social issues are important to employees and co-creating a space for participation that will be rewarding for them and for the business. There are two key steps in this process:

1. **Start with your company's social purpose DNA.**
    Making the shift to Change for Good needs to begin with ensuring that employees understand the company's origin story. This goes for companies that have been in business for many years, such as Lilly, as well as for newer start-ups, such as Cheekbone Beauty. Whenever possible, the most effective way to do this is for the founder or CEO to share their personal story with small groups of employees at a lunch or other social occasion. As I mentioned earlier in the book, the word "company" is derived from *compagnia*, which refers to the sharing of bread, after all. I believe the sense of community that happens when people in a company get together for a shared experience contributes immensely to the organization's culture and values and, ultimately, to the role it plays in society. It's important that this isn't a "one-off" activity. Companies should ensure that their founders or CEOs are breaking bread with a group of employees at least once a month.

    It's also possible to do this remotely or to feature founders at an event such as a company town hall meeting. In addition, I'd recommend recording a video of the founder's story to include as "required watching" for new recruits and employees. The closer employees are to the founder's origin story, the more likely it is that employees will be inspired to reflect this in designing programs that address social priorities today. For example, it isn't possible to listen to Jenn Harper from Cheekbone Beauty without considering the circumstances of Indigenous youth and what can be done to help. It goes without saying that this type of sharing isn't just of value to employees. Founders will be just as inspired and learn just as much from listening to employees' own stories as the other way around.

2. **Listen to your employees.**

   Finding common ground for mutual benefit is a foundation of Change for Good. Doing that is only possible when businesses are genuinely curious about the social concerns of their employees, when they take the time to listen to them, and when they create spaces where they can listen to each other. Here's where Dr. Eric Solomon's ideas about why businesses need what he calls human operating systems that are built on empathy become so important.

   Here's how your business can begin to listen better:

   - **Write letters to yourself as a company.** I love Eric Solomon's idea of having companies write a letter to themselves about who they are and what they believe in and then describing the ideal state of what they would want the world to look like if the company went out of business. This can also be a great way for employees to express what they believe their employers could be doing to change the world in ways that align with their origin story. Have employees write anonymous letters like this and then compile them into a collective narrative that can be shared with leaders and used to help guide the company's journey to Change for Good.

   - **Bring it back to the origin story.** Many companies already begin meetings by sharing something that has been designated as a priority. For example, Petro-Canada begins every meeting with a "safety moment," and meetings at Starbucks often begin with a coffee or tea tasting. Change for Good takes this a step further and involves beginning every meeting with giving employees an opportunity to share a personal story that relates to the company's origin story and social purpose today.

   - **Start the process during recruitment and onboarding.** The recruitment and onboarding process is a great opportunity to communicate why and how the employer contributes to social change. It's also a time to listen to what social issues are important to new employees and to begin to consider how their talents can be best applied to social change in ways that are rewarding for them, for the business, and for the community.

- **Tie social responsibility to employee job performance to get valuable feedback.** I think the gauging of job performance for anyone who is leading or managing others in a business should be, in part, based on the degree to which they are listening and empathetic to the people who report to them. This can be operationalized by embedding specific questions into formal and informal discussions about job performance. When is the last time your manager asked you questions such as how are you feeling about what our company is doing to be socially responsible? In what ways do you think we could be better in this area, and how do you think you could play a role in helping us to solve social problems?

It's very common for employees to have difficulty in expressing what matters to them and their families in a business context. That's why it's also important to create opportunities for employees to express themselves in ways that are creative, fun, and consistent with who the organization is and what it does.

Painting a picture of the future state of an organization can be a very powerful way to create a pathway to Change for Good. It's also an opportunity to involve employees in the creation of this future state or "preferred reality." In addition to having corporations write a letter to themselves, as Dr. Eric Solomon recommends, I've also found that writing a press release set for a date in the future can be very compelling. Here's an example of one that I co-wrote with Milinda Martin that was published by *Forbes* in 2014[19]:

January 1, 2025, Irving, Texas: ExxonMobil is proud to announce that its exit from the extraction and production of non-renewable resources is now complete. Back in 2015, the company began its 10-year journey out of fossil fuels by committing itself to a bold set of changes that have transformed the company and indeed the world. Key actions over the past decade include:

- hiring a new chief executive, formerly the president of the Environmental Defense Fund, an organization that believes economic prosperity and environmental stewardship go hand in hand;

- being certified as a B Corporation, a designation stipulating a material positive impact on society and the environment;

- introducing a new class of shares whose value reflects both financial and environmental performance; and

- transforming more than 10,000 Exxon and Mobil stations into local centers of sustainable transportation where customers can recharge their electric vehicles, buy or rent bicycles, and purchase discounted passes for local transit systems.

What seemed far-fetched in 2014 is sounding very realistic today. Perhaps ExxonMobil read what Milinda Martin and I had to say!

GOING BEYOND EMPLOYEE ENGAGEMENT

"Employee engagement" is one of the most ubiquitous phrases used by corporations to describe their relationship with employees. In my discussions about CSR and social change with businesses, there's virtually never been a time when employee engagement isn't referenced as a reason for doing this work and also as a benefit. The problem is that employees are often "engaged" in such a superficial way that there's very little in the way of benefit — to them or to their employers. I hope some of the ideas I've shared in this chapter will help your organization shift from a place of "engagement" to a Change for Good that really captures the hearts and minds of employees, because they're the ones who've been the architects of the approach.

CHAPTER 4

Change for Good Risk

"There is a fifth dimension, beyond that which is known to man. It is a dimension as vast as space and as timeless as infinity. It is the middle ground between light and shadow, between science and superstition, and it lies between the pit of man's fears and the summit of his knowledge. This is the dimension of imagination. It is an area which we call the Twilight Zone."

— Introduction to the first episode of
The Twilight Zone by Rod Serling[i]

In my work over the last 20 years, the "business case" for social change has been validated over and over again. Businesses that commit to solving social problems are more successful at recruiting and retaining great people, are more clearly differentiated from their competitors, are more attractive to investors, are more likely to preserve their reputations in times of crisis or scandal, and are more profitable. One of the most difficult aspects of doing the research for this book has been combing through countless studies that underscore the business value of social change. I realized that there is so much evidence to support the proposition that business is good for social change and social change is good for business that it is now such a foregone conclusion, it shouldn't need to be re-substantiated in this book.

However, despite how ubiquitous corporate social responsibility has become, there are only a handful of companies that are repeatedly cited as leaders. Grow Ensemble's list of 10 of the most socially responsible companies and brands to model in 2021 includes Patagonia, Dr. Bronner's, Toms, Ben & Jerry's, and Warby Parker.[2] And Classy, a social enterprise that creates online software for non-profits, points to Google, Ben & Jerry's, The LEGO Group, Levi Strauss, and Warby Parker as socially responsible companies to applaud.[3]

There are also companies that are routinely outed for contributing to social problems. For example, *Slate*'s "Evil List" of tech companies that are doing the most harm put Amazon in the pole position for initiatives such as its shipping operation, which has allegedly "led to burnout, injuries, and deaths, and warehouse operations that, while paying a decent minimum wage, are efficient in part because it treats its human workers like robots who sometimes get bathroom breaks." Amazon is followed by Facebook and Alphabet in the number two and three positions.[4]

Between the world's best and the worst companies lie the vast majority of other businesses that do some things that are contributing to the world in positive ways and other things that may be irresponsible or harmful. This is a space where companies aren't about to make any best-of or worst-of lists, and also where businesses may have the biggest opportunity to Change for Good.

Much of what I see in this space are companies that practise what I referred to earlier to as CSR Lite. They have a check-the-box approach that involves paying taxes, complying with laws and environmental regulations, supporting their communities through philanthropic contributions, and producing an annual corporate social responsibility report. By checking these boxes, they have enough proof points to claim that they are socially responsible without really doing very much. I've often thought that the primary objective for the majority of these companies is to try to establish a small business advantage over their competitors, and to "engage" their employees by doing and spending the minimum amount possible.

I think many companies stick with the CSR Lite approach because they believe that doing too much will be too risky. Being a social purpose leader means taking bold action that will generate increased attention and profile (a goal that most businesses would generally see as a positive brand-building accomplishment). However, more often than not, decision-makers in corporations see leadership in this area as a potential reputational risk. Will taking action to make change cause advocates and other critics to uncover practices that are unethical or irresponsible? Will putting more attention and resources into a social change program detract from "core business" priorities? Will the company be seen as not knowing enough or doing enough to be credible?

In some ways, businesses that practise CSR Lite are right to be cautious because there are so many examples of companies that have tried to position themselves as leaders but ended up with reputational damage because what they do isn't substantive enough or is at odds with other business practices that are harmful or unethical. This is known as "social washing" and is the social change equivalent of "green washing," which refers to corporations that misrepresent their efforts to reduce environmental impact in order to mislead their customers. Today, companies that claim to be more socially responsible than they actually are run a considerable risk of being found out. Earlier I shared the crisis that Gerber created when it appointed its first "spokesbaby" with Down syndrome while denying life insurance to children with Down syndrome.

Related to social washing is a new term know as "SDG washing," which involves companies that claim to be contributing to the UN Sustainable Development Goals but, in reality, aren't as committed to these goals as they let on. For example, Vedanta, an Anglo-Indian mining company, claimed that it adhered to the highest industry safety standards and was committed towards the Sustainable Development Goals. At the same time, it was in the news for contributing to mining deaths, environmental destruction, and spreading carcinogens in the local communities for almost a decade.

The potential risks go beyond consumer backlash. ESG (environmental, social and governance) performance has become a key consideration for institutional investors. Companies that misrepresent their value to society run the risk of losing investment capital. During the COVID-19 crisis, institutional investors paid attention to the degree to which companies were adhering to social principles. Investors wanted to know how companies were treating customers affected by the pandemic-induced economic shutdown, how companies handled pay reduction, and if these reductions were equitable between executives and workers.

In this chapter, I'll be exploring how businesses can move past the risks they associate with doing too little or too much to help solve social problems, and I'll suggest ways that can help corporations find their way out of the Twilight Zone and Change for Good.

DOES SOCIAL CHANGE REALLY HAVE A RISK?

In 2015, Hudson's Bay asked impakt to help the company and its foundation contribute to social change in a way that supported its business objectives. We developed a number of options, including one we thought was particularly compelling: a commitment to helping end domestic violence, the incidence of which remains unacceptably high and disproportionately impacts women (who are the majority of Hudson's Bay employees and shoppers). When we shared our thoughts with Hudson's Bay, it was immediately clear that helping to solve this social problem was seen as too risky for the department store. This was despite the clear societal need to reduce domestic violence, the relevance this problem had to their business, and the fact that the issue had been identified as an SDG priority by the United Nations (UN SDG 5, Achieve Gender Equality and Empower All Women and Girls, includes eliminating all forms of violence against all women and girls in the public and private spheres[5]).

Ultimately, Hudson's Bay developed their own program, which involved inviting customers to participate in Giving Day, an all-day shopping event where, "for just $5, ticket holders will gain access to special in-store events and can enter to win a $5,000 shopping spree. Proceeds from ticket sales will help fund Boys and Girls Clubs of Canada's new national initiative — the HBC Summer Brain Gain program."[6] Today, there is no reference to

Giving Day, the Boys and Girls Clubs, or the HBC Summer Brain Gain program on the company's website. And, as a result of the COVID-19 pandemic, violence against women and girls has intensified.[7] In the end, what I realize is that Hudson's Bay only really wanted to generate more sales by creating what was essentially a social change promotion. When they saw our ideas about how they could contribute to solving an issue that was highly relevant to their employees and customers, they felt this was too risky.

In May 2021, the Hudson's Bay Foundation announced the launch of the Hudson's Bay Charter for Change program. A promise to accelerate racial equity by changing how the company invests in communities. The new program involves a commitment of $30 million over 10 years to organizations working to advance racial equity and inclusion, through three key areas of focus: education, employment, and empowerment. "Racial equity is one of the most urgent issues facing society, and through Hudson's Bay Charter for Change our goal is to create tangible and measurable change that makes a difference in the lives of Canadians," said Iain Nairn, president and CEO of Hudson's Bay. "With our own 350-year company history that in the past included discrimination and inequity, we have a responsibility to take action and drive progress in creating a fair and equitable Canada for all." Perhaps this new program will address not just responsibility but also the need to mitigate the risk of being seen to be tone deaf in the context of Indigenous reconciliation and Black Lives Matter.[8]

Reducing risk is one of the most commonly cited reasons why corporations align themselves with social change. Regardless of the label (corporate citizenship, community investment, corporate social responsibility, shared value, etc.), much of the business case for socially minded initiatives is based on mitigating reputational risk. I think the more convincing way to make a case for investing in social change is actually to frame it as an opportunity rather than a risk. This approach is central to Change for Good and is a theme throughout this book.

The results of a study published by Deloitte Risk Advisory in 2016 in a report called *Reputation Matters: Developing Reputational Resilience Ahead of Your Crisis* indicated the importance of building what they describe as reputational resilience in advance of a crisis.[9] The study revealed that 73 percent of business people who participated in a *Forbes* survey conducted on behalf of the Deloitte Center for Crisis Management believe that corporate reputation was the area that made them feel most vulnerable. Further, the same study suggests that there are three dimensions to how a company's reputation is judged, and this includes corporate social responsibility:

- How it creates goodwill by demonstrating care and consideration for others' interests ahead of its own.

- How it builds trust through openness and integrity and by demonstrating corporate values and ethical behaviour.

- How it instills confidence through sound financial performance, quality, safety and security, its ability to respond to a crisis, and corporate social responsibility.

It inherently makes sense that companies that do these three things successfully will build a positive reputation. It's also logical to conclude that companies with a positive reputation would endear a company to employees, consumers, investors, and other stakeholders and that a commitment to corporate social responsibility is a key component to bolstering reputation.

A BANK OF GOODWILL

In the context of reducing risk, corporate social responsibility is often seen to be valuable because it contributes to a "bank" of goodwill that can be drawn on during times when a company's reputation is threatened due to a harmful incident or activity or a negative behaviour. Corporate leaders believe that if their company experiences a reputational crisis and financial losses as a result of actions it is responsible for (such as a toxic spill, violation of labour laws, or failure to pay taxes), its history of doing the right thing will lessen the impact to its reputation and bottom line.

I don't think there's any credible reason to believe that having been socially responsible in the past will help shore up the reputation of a company that has acted irresponsibly. More than that, Margaret Ormiston, an assistant professor of organizational behaviour at London Business School, believes that there is evidence to suggest that corporate social responsibility can actually cause corporations to be irresponsible.[10] According to a principle of social psychology called moral licensing, people who engage in moral behaviour, such as supporting charitable organizations, believe they obtain "credits" to subsequently engage in morally questionable behaviour.[11]

Ormiston gives the example of Kenneth Lay, the former CEO of Enron who was also well known as a generous philanthropist. Under Lay's leadership, Enron became notorious for an accounting fraud that contributed to the company's collapse in 2001. Ormiston suggests that Lay's philanthropic efforts may have earned him moral credit that made him feel he could endorse irresponsible actions inside Enron. "Top leaders may feel that when they have acquired moral credits through a CSR strategy that balances the needs of multiple stakeholders, they can then put forth a strategy that cuts corners or is potentially harmful to stakeholders," said Ormiston in an article co-written with Elaine Wong titled "License to Ill: The Effects of Corporate Social Responsibility and CEO Moral Identity on Corporate Social Irresponsibility."[12] Ormiston and Wong's 2013 study of moral licensing in 49 Fortune 500 firms revealed that prior corporate responsibility of CEOs was connected to increased corporate social irresponsibility afterwards.[13]

BP is a company that had built a strong reputation as a corporate social responsibility leader. The company was named number one on *Fortune* and AccountAbility's annual rankings of the world's most responsible companies in 2007, and it was the runner-up for the Openness & Honesty reporting category at the Corporate Register's 2010 CR Reporting Awards.[14] After the 2010 explosion of BP's Deepwater Horizon oil rig in the Gulf of Mexico, BP's track record of being socially responsible didn't mitigate anything. In addition to the obvious environmental devastation, by 2013 BP had dropped from the second to the fourth largest of the world's four major oil companies, and its gas stations in the United States reported a sales drop of between 10 and 40 percent due to backlash against the company.[15]

Ironically, the company's years of leadership and extensive reporting of its CSR performance actually *contributed* to its reputational crisis and financial losses. After the spill, BP's stakeholders examined the company's environmental track record and discovered a chronic lack of attention to risk management and regulatory compliance that likely contributed to 104 oil spills in the arctic between 1997 and 1998 alone. It also came to light that the company had received the largest fine in the history of the US Chemical Safety and Hazard Investigation Board: $87 million for failing to correct safety hazards revealed in the 2005 Texas City explosion.[16]

Today, BP's purpose is "to reimagine energy for people and our planet" and to "help the world reach net zero and improve people's lives, and do this by being a safe, focused, responsible, well-governed and transparent organization." This commitment is backed up by an approach that delivered impressive results in 2019, including: launching the BP labour rights and modern slavery principles, producing zero net growth in operational emissions, concluding a five-year ethics monitorship to build and embed best-in-class ethics programs across the company, being recognized as one of the *Financial Times'* Leaders in Diversity, and being included in The Times Top 50 Employers for Women list.[17] Despite what I would say is a world-class commitment to sustainability that should be emulated by others in the oil and gas sector, BP remains a lightning rod for people opposed to the industry.

MORAL LICENSING AND MORAL CLEANSING

It's not just corporations that use responsible behaviour as a way of justifying unethical business practices. This phenomenon can also contribute to poor behaviour on the part of employees who work in companies that have made social responsibility a high priority. This is contrary to the very compelling business case for corporate responsibility that, over many years, has repeatedly pointed to the positive impact of CSR on employees.

Research by John List, the Kenneth C. Griffin Distinguished Service Professor in Economics at the University of Chicago, suggests that company-sponsored social initiatives can result in poor employee performance because doing good deeds can contribute to employees behaving unethically.[18] List and University of Chicago postdoctoral scholar Fatemeh Momeni hired more than three thousand gig workers through Amazon Mechanical Turk, a crowdsourcing marketplace, to complete transcription tasks. They paid workers part of their wages up front, a decision made intentionally to encourage misbehaviour. The researchers figured that some participants (not knowing they were part of a study), with payment in hand, would simply not do any work — or might cheat by reporting images for transcription as unreadable.

For half of the workers, the idea of corporate responsibility was incorporated through messaging, some of which said that the consultancy would donate cash to UNICEF for educational purposes. To trigger feelings of moral licensing, the researchers framed this group's contribution as a donation "on behalf of the workers." As a result, some workers more strongly identified with the company's larger mission and felt their role was part of the firm's social purpose. The participants who read about this CSR effort were 20 percent more likely to act detrimentally towards the employer by either taking the upfront payment and not finishing the job or by reporting images for transcription as unreadable. The average intensity of cheating per worker also increased by 11 percent among participants who knew about the UNICEF program. When participants knew their employer was donating to UNICEF and that their work was having a larger social impact, they engaged in behaviour that they would have otherwise considered unethical. When workers feel their good behaviour benefits a charity, "CSR can improve workers' self-image and license less ethical subsequent acts," the researchers concluded.[19]

The opposite to moral licensing can also be true. Psychology research suggests that when people recall their recent bad behaviour, they are likely to compensate for it by doing something morally responsible. This is known as moral cleansing — behaviours aimed at restoring moral self-worth in response to past transgressions.[20] Moral cleansing is also present in corporations, and sometimes entire industries, that have acted irresponsibly or unethically and are then motivated to become socially responsible.

On April 24, 2013, the Rana Plaza factory building in Bangladesh collapsed, killing 1,134 people and injuring thousands more. It was the worst industrial incident in the garment industry. After the catastrophe, it was revealed that some of the Western world's largest retailers sold clothes that were sourced from the factory. It also brought worldwide attention to the long-standing practice of major brands purchasing clothes with the sole objective of reducing cost and turnaround time and with little or no oversight of where products were sourced or how they were made.

After the disaster, murder charges were brought against 38 people connected to the incident, and more than two hundred apparel companies from 20 countries signed the Accord on Fire and Building Safety in Bangladesh to prevent similar tragedies from happening again. The signatories included American Eagle Outfitters, Abercrombie & Fitch, Zara, and H&M, which was the first and largest brand to sign on.[21] Another agreement is the non-binding Alliance for Bangladesh Worker Safety, which was signed by Walmart, Gap, and Target.

Both agreements have contributed to improved working conditions in some of the country's most dangerous factories, created awareness for other countries to adopt similar standards, encouraged Western retailers to cut ties with factories that are not compliant, and motivated brands to introduce ethical supply chains that ensure responsible treatment of workers, minimize impact on the environment, and share these practices with consumers. For example, H&M introduced a "consumer-facing transparency layer" that allows shoppers to find out the country where clothing was manufactured, details on materials and recycling, the name of the supplier or authorized subcontractor where a garment was made, as well as the factory address and the number of workers employed there. Despite new best practices, a 2019 *Wall Street Journal* investigation revealed that Amazon continued to sell clothes from factories in Bangladesh that other retailers had blacklisted because they hadn't complied to safety requirements.[22]

Examples like BP and the fashion industry's response to the Rana Plaza collapse show that doing good doesn't make up for or cancel out doing something wrong. However, I also think that doing something that is irresponsible doesn't negate what a company is doing to create positive change. Bad practices need to be prevented and good practices should be enhanced.

CORPORATE SOCIAL RESPONSIBILITY-CREATED RISK

In another interesting twist, many corporations routinely question the degree to which doing good will result in *more* risk, and often they decide not to pursue programs that have the potential to contribute to society and to their own success. There have been decades of research on the positive effects of CSR, along with a growing industry of consultants, conferences, and organizations that exist to champion the benefits of social responsibility for the business sector. However, there is evidence of how contributing to social change — something one would think is a very positive thing to do — can also create a risk for business.

Recently I discovered a CSR-related acronym I hadn't heard of before: CSRCR (Corporate Social Responsibility Created Risk), coined by a group called AntiCSR.[23] This group is an excellent resource for a more balanced perspective on the benefits of CSR, which I've outlined above and in previous chapters.

CSR Created Risk is the probability that corporate social responsibility creates negative consequences for a corporation in areas including: governance, reputation, financial performance, employee relations, regulatory compliance, and opportunity cost. AntiCSR points out that those with a vested interest in the upside of CSR don't acknowledge the possibility that there are also many risks for businesses that are doing good things for society. In all the years I've worked in this area, there aren't enough times that we've looked at how social change programs can be harmful.

CHANGE FOR GOOD RISK CHECKLIST: HOW TO TAKE ACTION

Asking the right questions will help organizations determine the benefits and risks for their CSR efforts. Here's a Change for Good Risk Checklist that I use when we're helping corporations create social change programs:

1. **Is the company committed to meaningful social change, or is it practising CSR Lite that is focused only on donations to charities?** This is perhaps the most common pitfall of corporate actions in this area, and there are countless examples of corporations who claim to be socially responsible but whose only contribution to social change is making large donations to charitable organizations. This is a transactional approach that rarely delivers business value or social change.

2. **Are corporate leaders making decisions based on their personal interests at the expense of decisions that could instead reflect the priorities of employees, customers, and communities?** For many years, it was common for companies to adopt the personal cause or community interests of their executives. Often this led to huge philanthropic donations being made to causes that had no alignment whatsoever with the company's core business. While I don't see as much of this today, it's still something to avoid wherever possible because shareholders can push back, and employees can be resentful.

3. **Is there an expectation that CSR will contribute to new or revised regulations that will be more favourable to the business?** Corporations in the resource extraction industry commonly provide support for local communities to buoy up their own

efforts to secure project approvals from government agencies. This is called securing a "social license to operate," and is viewed as a risk mitigation tool by companies in this industry. Having a social license to operate is seen as a way to create a "bank" of goodwill that will contribute to reduced fines, legal fees, and other costs that will be incurred in the event of an environmental mishap (which are common in this industry). One reason that companies produce annual corporate social responsibility reports is to proactively communicate positive actions in the areas of governance, social change, and environmental performance so that they will be seen more favourably by investors and regulators during a crisis. As we've seen, this is a strategy that really doesn't work — at best, it provides a false sense of reduced risk.

4. **Will investment of time and money in CSR divert resources from other priorities, such as fair and equitable treatment of employees?**
   Socially responsible business starts with fair and equitable treatment of employees, a commitment to diversity and inclusivity, and a safe work environment. Corporations that engage in social programs without these foundations run a strong risk of being targeted for irresponsible behaviour and "social washing": misrepresenting themselves as being more socially responsible than is actually the case.

5. **Is there an opportunity cost to CSR, such as inadequate resources to invest in employees, research, or technology?**
   It's possible that excessive spending in the area of social change could limit a company in other ways (such as in its ability to provide support for employee training or to provide technology that helps employees access internal resources), some of which could be counter to the priorities of being socially responsible. In practice, this isn't likely to happen because the social spend is generally very small in comparison to costs in these other areas.

6. **Are social programs being deployed as a way of creating a false image of the company or its brands in the minds of employees, consumers, or advocacy groups?**
Unfortunately, this is a very common scenario and a real risk. A few years ago, Coca-Cola, launched Coca-Cola Life in a number of countries and was accused of "health washing," or tricking the consumer into believing they were purchasing a healthy product. The company's new product was sold in a green can but still contained 22 grams of sugar, the equivalent of six teaspoons and 89 calories. University of Sydney nutritionist Dr. Kieron Rooney told *Daily Mail Australia* that "Coke Life should not be considered a healthy option . . . it should not even have a seat at the table."[24]

7. **Are we supporting social change because we believe it will reduce the impact of negative consequences in the future?**
Irresponsible behaviour is what it is. No extent of previously good behaviour will cancel out the consequences of doing something wrong. Companies that believe social change is a priority need to commit to doing it and to take effective action regardless of what may happen in the future. Companies that don't take this approach tend to be in the CSR Lite camp of doing the minimum amount possible to be seen as being responsible.

8. **Is there the possibility that supporting a social issue or cause could be seen as offensive or inappropriate?**
Being a social change leader means there is a risk of losing customers, employees, and investors. As Howard Schultz did when he supported gay marriage despite blowback from some shareholders. [25]

9. **Is the company partnering with charitable or non-profit organizations that could be targeted for ineffective or unethical behaviour?**

Being a charitable or non-profit organization doesn't guarantee ethical behaviour. In Canada, the WE Charity almost collapsed after it was awarded $912 million in government funding for the Canada Student Service Grant program. It was revealed that WE had paid Prime Minister Justin Trudeau's mother, Margaret; brother Alexandre; and wife, Sophie Gregoire Trudeau, for speaking appearances at WE-related events. Corporations, including the Royal Bank of Canada, ended their partnerships with the charity.

10. **Is the business helping to solve a social problem, or creating a program/promotion that will contribute to a short-term business objective or mitigate a current risk?**
Millennials and Gen Xers are paying particular attention to how corporations contribute to issues that matter to them. They are likely to be loyal to brands that align with their values and to boycott brands they believe are social washing or "woke washing" (when brands co-opt the language of social justice movements and activism to appeal to socially conscious shoppers while still operating business models that rely on inequality and exploitation). If a company isn't committed to helping solve a social problem in an authentic, transparent way, it is creating a reputational risk that can result in losing the loyalty of employees and customers.

THE BUSINESS CASE FOR SOCIAL CHANGE

Another related issue, which isn't exactly a risk but is kind of a black hole of decision-making in corporations, is how decisions are made with respect to investing in social change. Companies allocate hundreds of millions of dollars each year to new brand and product marketing and then question a much more modest investment in a new social change program. To Change for Good, it's important to understand how business decisions are made and to have a solid approach or "case" for investing in social change.

According to Harvard's ManageMentor, creating a business case involves defining the business value of the opportunity, exploring options, analyzing alternatives, assessing risks, and creating an implementation plan.[26] In other words, it is a rationale that managers develop to demonstrate how a new initiative will have a positive impact on the company's bottom line. It's a way for managers to justify the allocation of resources to a new initiative that they will be accountable for developing and delivering. Simply put, the business case makes the argument for why the finite amount of time and money in a business should be spent on one thing rather than another.

And, in my experience, commitments of time and money towards social change are almost never the priority for new investment. That's because managers of corporate social responsibility or social change don't actually have a solid business case for social change. Unlike managers in IT, marketing, HR, operations, logistics, or other functional areas of a company, people in CSR don't have a comprehensive way to justify investments in social change. As a result, it's no surprise that executives view social change as a risky investment and programs in this area are almost always under-resourced.

There are, however, statistics that support the business case for corporate social responsibility. Some of the most credible reports that support the business case include *Corporate Responsibility: Burden or opportunity? Grant Thornton's 15th Survey of U.S. Business Leaders*,[27] the 2010 *Cone Cause Evolution Study*,[28] and the 2006 *Cone Millennial Cause Study*.[29]

Executives

- 77 percent of executives believe that CR programs will have a major impact on business strategies over the next few years.

- 73 percent of executives say corporate citizenship needs to be a priority for companies. However, only 60 percent report that corporate citizenship is part of their business strategy,

39 percent report that corporate citizenship is part of their business planning process, and only 28 percent of companies have written corporate citizenship policies or statements.

- 40 percent of executives cite CR programs as being very important in achieving strategic goals.

Investors

- 82 percent of investors consider CR criteria when evaluating investments.

- 73 percent of shareholders and 59 percent of investor relations officers believe CR impacts share price.

- 66 percent of Americans consider a company's commitment to social change when deciding which stocks/mutual funds to invest in (up from 40 percent in 2001).

Employee Recruitment

- 79 percent of people aged 18–25 want to work for a company that cares about how it impacts/contributes to society.

- 77 percent of Americans consider a company's commitment to social change when determining where to work (up from 48 percent in 2001).

Employee Retention

- Employees whose companies support social issues are 40 percent more likely to say they are proud of the company's values and nearly 25 percent more likely to be loyal to their employers.

- 72 percent of employees wish employers would do more to support a cause or social issue (up from 52 percent in 2004).

- 69 percent of employees feel that a company's social/ environmental activities make them proud to work there.

- Nearly 90 percent of companies said that corporate volunteer programs improve employee retention and morale, aid in recruitment, and build better teams.

- Half of the respondents reported that they believe there is a direct correlation between volunteerism and profitability.

Consumers

- 92 percent of consumers acknowledge they have a more positive image of a company that supports a cause they care about.

- 91 percent of consumers have a more positive image of a company that is environmentally responsible.

- 90 percent of consumers say companies should support causes that are consistent with their responsible business practices.

- 87 percent of consumers want a company to support issues based on where the business can have the most social/environmental impact.

- 83 percent of consumers say companies have a responsibility to help support causes.

- 80 percent of consumers choose health as the leading issue that companies should address, with education, environment, and economic development tied for second at 77 percent.

If you were reading these numbers carefully, you may have already noted that some of the statistics included in this business case are from as far back as 2001. I used this business case in a presentation to 3M in 2007 that helped convince the company's leadership to invest in a new approach to social change. The problem is that many years later, the business case for social change is essentially the same. I can assure you that virtually everyone in the CSR space today would be very familiar with the positive story that is illustrated by these statistics and would have used some version of this business case to demonstrate why investing in social change is justified. The problem is that, despite what seems like very clear evidence of business value, this case isn't convincing enough and very little new investment in social change is being made by corporations.

I think it is because the most compelling case isn't only based on statistics. To Change for Good, managers need a new business case for social change that includes the perspectives and impressions of people with lived experience in the areas they wish to impact, presents a realistic picture of the opportunities, and doesn't only rely on numbers that have been around for years.

THE REAL CASE FOR SOCIAL CHANGE: HOW TO TAKE ACTION

If your organization has identified an aspect of social change that aligns with the company's origin story and business purpose or you think there's an opportunity to increase the impact of an existing social strategy, here's how to approach developing a Change for Good business case to help secure support and investment.

1. **Learn from people with lived experience.**
    What do people with lived experience of the issue believe needs to be done? From their point of view, can the problem be solved or ameliorated? What community, government, or other types of organizations do people with lived experience see as accomplishing most on their behalf? Is there an opportunity

for people with lived experience to participate further in developing how the corporation could help? If so, what will this look like?

The Home Depot Canada Foundation's commitment to helping end youth homelessness came from a visit to an organization in Toronto called Eva's Initiatives that "provides shelter, transitional housing, and programming to help young people build brighter futures free of homelessness." When our impakt team was there, the organization's staff and the youth involved in the programs told us that it was possible to end youth homelessness. After the meeting, it was so clear that the focus of Home Depot's new program should be to help end youth homelessness. If we hadn't gone to Eva's, this "aha" moment never would have happened. You can't build a business case for social change without learning about the issue first-hand.

2. **Conduct a social issue audit.**
Who does the issue impact most? How has this changed over time, and what is expected to happen in the future? In what ways are non-profit organizations, governments, and other businesses involved in providing advocacy, research, funding, and direct services? Are there examples of the issue being effectively addressed in other jurisdictions or other countries? Is this issue a priority for your competitors? Is it relevant to business partners in the value chain? Who are the subject matter experts on the issue, and what is their perspective on how to best solve the problem?

This audit can be done in a few ways, including by conducting a review of available research on the issue that your company is considering and speaking with one or two subject matter experts (academics who do research in the area or executives at related charitable organizations). In our work at impakt, we have found that six to ten conversations with the right people are usually enough to get an initial understanding of the social problem. This is also a great way to begin to build relationships with experts and demonstrate that you have a credible understanding of the issue when you share the case with internal leaders.

3. **Assess interest and relevance to employees.**
   Is the issue relevant to employees and their families? Does the company have a history of supporting this issue (even in small ways)? Is the social problem relevant to employees in different locations? Have employees been involved as volunteers or shown interest in other ways? Are there ways that employees' knowledge and/or skills can be applied (for example, a logistics company with internal expertise might be able to help improve the operations and efficiency of charitable organizations such as food banks).

   At this stage, it's usually premature and often not possible to conduct a survey of employees. Without knowing more about what the potential social program could look like, survey questions are hypothetical and there's a high likelihood of getting a response bias (people answering questions based on what they think will be seen as the most acceptable answers). I've found that having a few informal conversations with groups of employees in each functional area of a company is usually enough to get an initial understanding of whether or not an issue will gain internal support and traction. (COVID-19 has accelerated the use of Zoom and other platforms, so it's easier than ever to listen to and connect with groups of employees.) Wherever possible, it's best to encourage people to share personal stories of their experiences. When impakt helped to develop Petro-Canada's approach to caregiving, it started with employees sharing their experience of being caregivers or being cared for by someone else.

4. **Complete the Change for Good Risk Checklist.**
   You'll find it earlier in this chapter.

5. **Engage your leaders.**

What are your company's strategic priorities in the current year and in the foreseeable future (taking into consideration that the pandemic has shortened planning cycles for many businesses)? In what way does the company's current or proposed investment in social change align with these priorities? What do executives need to make an investment decision? Who else do leaders recommend that you engage in the process of developing the Change for Good business case?

A number of years ago, I was helping to develop Pfizer Canada's corporate social responsibility strategy, and I travelled to Montreal to present our plan. It wasn't particularly well-received because we hadn't taken the time to understand the CEO's priorities for the company and learn how he viewed CSR as contributing to the business. He told me something I've never forgotten: "I don't want to see something that I haven't already seen." It may sound obvious, but it was a great lesson in the importance of involving people along the way and making sure that people see their perspectives and ideas reflected in what you are ultimately sharing for their approval.

6. **Co-create the business case.**

What is the collective view of colleagues and external stakeholders? In what ways will what you've learned so far be validated, disputed, or enhanced? How can you begin to build a community that will support the development or further growth of social change at your company?

This is where the work done in advance really comes together: by creating a space where what you've heard and learned can be shared, workshopped, and further refined. When we were helping to develop Petro-Canada's CareMakers Foundation, we convened an incredible group of people from different levels, functional areas, and parts of Canada, along with

community stakeholders and experts in caregiving. During a full
day at the YMCA of Greater Toronto (a place where caregiving
actually takes place), participants shared stories and experiences
and workshopped different ideas about what the company could
to do make a difference for caregivers in Canada. The ideas
that came from this session formed the essence of a business
case for change that was approved by the company's executive
leadership — some of whom participated in the co-creation.
We also videotaped this session and created an edited version
of inspirational highlights that I think made a significant
contribution to this program being approved.

7. **Assess your return on integrity.**
   What is doing the right thing really worth? I think integrity
   has become a common denominator that is redefining what
   successful businesses look like and is central to everything
   that Change for Good stands for. In an article I wrote for
   Forbes titled "What's Your Return on Integrity?" I mapped out
   four areas that I think add up in ways that may be difficult to
   measure but are highly valuable nonetheless[30]:

   - **Honesty:** Corporations that are honest with their
     customers, business partners, investors, and regulators are
     seen to operate with integrity.

   - **Respect:** To work together, corporations, their employees,
     and their stakeholders need to respect and leverage their
     differences. Integrity depends on building a culture of
     empathy and respect both internally and externally.

   - **Accountability:** Business integrity only happens when
     people are passionate about being accountable to each
     other — within companies and between companies, cus-
     tomers, and communities.

- **Trust:** There's really only one way to establish trust: set the right expectation by saying what you're going to do, meet the expectation by doing what you said you would do, and then remind people what you did. Over time, your employees and people outside your company will trust you. Unfortunately, this simple approach is rarely done, and most companies continue to struggle with low trust scores from the people who matter most.

YOU CAN'T ELIMINATE ALL OF THE RISK

As the sign in Albert Einstein's office is reputed to have said, "Not everything that counts can be counted and not everything that can be counted counts." Or, as Sydney Biddle Barrows, also known at the Mayflower Madam, famously said, "I ran the wrong kind of business, but I did it with integrity."

As you consider how to develop a business case for social change in your organization, it's important to remember that this isn't a generic exercise or process. You'll need to adapt your approach to reflect the context of your business and the social issue you're interested in addressing. As an example, if your company is an international retailer, you'll need an efficient way of really understanding the relevance of social change to employees that live in very different locations. It's also a good idea to bring leaders to meetings with community organizations and, where possible, hold meetings at community organizations that are addressing the issue being considered by your company.

In my experience, this is great way to create a convincing, evidence-informed rationale for investing in social change that will also build relationships and trust and will help establish credibility inside and outside the company. However, I can't promise that it will always be successful. In my experience, the overall business case for investing in social change is becoming more accepted, but there are still more losses than wins in this area.

Eliminating all risk isn't possible, and moving your company out of the Twilight Zone of CSR Lite to a place of Change for Good will ultimately depend on leaders believing that doing it is the right thing to do. In 2012, when impakt was collaborating with the Home Depot Canada Foundation to develop the Orange Door Project to end youth homelessness, we developed a business case by going through a process very similar to what I described above and we presented it to the board of the Foundation, which included the president of the company and the senior leadership team. I remember thinking that what we were recommending was the right thing from a social change perspective, but it didn't seem that convincing in terms of its value to the business. At the end of our presentation to the board, the president said, "This is going to be really hard, and that's exactly why we have to do it." That's social purpose leadership, and Change for Good can't happen without it.

CHAPTER 5

Change for Good Action

Once when my kids were younger, I took them down to my office. There was a flip chart there and they made a list of adjectives that described me. "Impatient" was the first word on the list. (I think "Bossy" might have been the second word. I still have a *Bizarro* cartoon on our fridge called "At Home with the Springsteens" that has a picture of Bruce's daughter looking up at him with the caption, "Yeah, well, you're not the Boss of me!")

Being impatient hasn't lent itself particularly well to helping corporations solve social problems. The pace of change inside corporations is often glacial, and moving the needle on social problems happens over a very long time. In my experience, in the very fastest cases, getting to the point where a new program is implemented in a large corporation takes one or more years. (Action taken by corporations during the pandemic has demonstrated that it *is* possible for businesses to move more quickly. It remains to be seen whether this sense of urgency will be maintained post-COVID-19.)

Social change is even slower. A mistake I've made repeatedly is being overly optimistic in terms of what's possible and unrealistic in terms of how long it will take. One example is when we developed HireUp — a national social enterprise platform that connected youth who'd experienced homelessness with entry-level employment at large corporations, including Home Depot Canada, TD, and Walmart. Initially, we partnered with Workopolis, who helped us launch a pilot platform that was essentially a re-branding and customized version of what they already had. Later, we secured funding from the federal government of Canada to develop our own proprietary platform. In our application for funding, we had to indicate how many youth would gain employment over a three-year period. We were pretty confident that we could create employment for five thousand youth — which works out to an average of 10 jobs each month for each of Canada's 13 provinces and territories over three years. In the first year of HireUp's operation, there were two youth hired, and one of them was someone we hired ourselves.

What seemed like a real failure was a lesson in how difficult social change is and how long it takes. People who knew a lot more than we did about the barriers that face youth in securing employment weren't surprised at all by our results. The second year, almost two hundred youth got jobs through our platform. This was still far less than we'd predicted, but it was seen as real success by people in the homelessness sector.

One of the first in-depth social responsibility programs we developed at impakt was the Healthy Communities program for 3M Canada. We began by facilitating a discovery session in March 2008, and the program was launched a year later. I didn't know it at the time, but now I realize that in the context of change within a large corporation, this was extremely fast. In reminding myself of what we did with 3M, I discovered these questions that guided our discovery session with them in 2008:

- Are stakeholders (employees, customers, and communities where the company operates) aware of 3M's investments in education, health and human services, the arts, and diversity?

- What impact do the company's social initiatives have on its reputation in the minds of these stakeholders?

- How do stakeholders find out about the company's initiatives in this area?

- To what degree do these investments contribute to the company's three-part growth strategy (differentiating the business, prioritizing and focusing sales, and increasing competitive advantage) in terms of improved reputation, better recruitment and retention, and relationships with key customers?

- What could 3M do differently to reach more stakeholders and have more impact on their impressions of and relationships with the company?

- What aspects of the company's current community program can be most easily leveraged (such as commitment to education or commitment to volunteerism), and how will they inform the development of a new national community program?

- In the context of an increasingly crowded marketplace of corporate community programs and sponsorships, what can 3M do that will be differentiated from other corporate programs?

- What internal and external communications will have the highest ROI and be seen as authentic/genuine by stakeholders?

It's very interesting that, similar to the business case I shared in Chapter 4, 12 years later, very little has changed. These questions could easily be the basis for a discovery session today, and that's not a good thing. The world, and the world of social change, is considerably different than it was in 2008, and therefore the questions corporations should be asking themselves about their social purpose should also be different. This is a good illustration of the power of inertia and the slow pace of change.

It's clear that COVID-19 exacerbated problems for vulnerable people around the world and set back much of the progress that was being made towards achieving the Sustainable Development Goals. It also accelerated change and innovation within corporations and created a context for many businesses to move much faster in responding to the social needs of their employees, customers, and communities. This chapter will share what the most innovative corporations are doing to increase the speed of social change. I will reflect on how some large corporations have been able to pick up the pace of change as well as on my own experiences in encouraging businesses to take action. I will also share a new blueprint I developed to help companies Change for Good — faster.

WHAT IS THE PACE OF CHANGE?

"Obviously acting fast is the critical thing right now. I'm part of a membership called The Philanthropic Workshop. They're an incredible group of philanthropists from around the world. I was on a call yesterday and someone asked, 'Do you want to be in a position where you look back and say, I wish I could have done this?' I personally don't want to be in that position. I think you have to take risks," said Tim Cormode, executive director and founder of Power To Be and an expert on how to harness philanthropy for social good.[1]

This is what Cormode said in the first Change for Good conversation we had on April 2, 2020, shortly after the first lockdown. In the week of March 13, 2020, at impakt we started to wonder what we could do to help people in the social change space have a sense of community, learn from each other, and be inspired to look for new opportunities as COVID-19 was unfolding. Two weeks later, we launched Change for Good, a series of weekly conversations with me and social change leaders from around the world, and Tim Cormode was our first guest. We kept going and shared weekly conversations with social change leaders from around the world throughout the first year of the pandemic.

Even in the early days of COVID, it was clear that people who were vulnerable before had quickly become even more vulnerable and that some privileged people found themselves struggling too. Bruce MacDonald, the president and CEO of Imagine Canada, an organization that works to bolster the impact of charities, non-profits, and social entrepreneurs, put the extent of the social damage very clearly when he told me that people who had been donors to food banks were now in line to receive food for their families.

As the Change for Good conversations continued, there were three consistent themes related to corporate social change: the need to undo overly bureaucratic processes inside businesses, the need for more tolerance for risk, and the need for a drastic increase in the pace of change and action.

In another Change for Good conversation, Andrea Barrack, the global head of sustainability and corporate citizenship for TD, told me that the big change she had seen during the early days of the pandemic was that the company was willing to accept risks in a way that it hadn't before. Financial institutions such as TD are built to generate the most profit at the lowest level of risk, so this must have been a significant change for the organization. For a large corporation such as TD to acknowledge that it's better to do something imperfectly than to do nothing and let people fall through the cracks is what I would call a Change for Good.[2]

Here's an excerpt from an article I wrote for the *LSE Business Review* that summed up what we were starting to learn from leaders like Cormode, MacDonald, and Barrack about the need to pick up the pace of change:

> Funders need to address the urgent needs of front-line organizations by increasing philanthropic giving and ensuring that these funds get out the door as quickly as possible. One good example is GIVE5.ca, an initiative of Canadian foundations that have pledged to donate at least 5 percent of their assets in the current year. In another example, by the end of April the TD Community Resilience Initiative was launched to allocate $25 million to organizations engaged in COVID-19 response and community recovery. More corporate funders are finding new ways to increase and accelerate their giving and ensure it's getting into the best possible hands.[3]

I've always felt that the most important social change question for any organization — corporation, non-profit, or government — is:

What is the least expensive way to make the biggest difference in the shortest period of time? For me, this is the essence of social innovation. It's also the inspiration behind an article titled "The Other Innovation: Unleashing Canada's Capacity for Good," which I co-wrote for *Policy Magazine* with Tim Draimin, senior advisor to The J.W. McConnell Family Foundation. Tim and I shared ideas that we believed were necessary to improve more lives.[4]

We proposed the following 10 recommendations:

1. **Innovate innovation: Technology, business, and social innovation.**
   A comprehensive strategy that integrates technology, business, and social innovation and supports incubation, market access, procurement, talent development, social financing, and partnership building. This will require new policy and funding to link economic and social goals and accelerate the integration of mainstream and social innovation.

2. **Make Canada's brand inclusive innovation.**
   Establish inclusive innovation as Canada's global brand, identified as all sectors combining strengths to develop new value capable of deploying solutions to Canada's biggest challenges in lockstep with economic objectives.

3. **Update policy to unlock Canada's powerhouse of social assets.**
   Overhaul the regulatory environment in which social good operates. Enact a set of reforms to unlock critical social assets among charities and non-profits across Canada.

4. **Accelerate "Social R&D."**
   Dramatically improving Canada's social performance will require the acceleration of research and development capabilities across the social sector.

5. **Shift government from silos to cross-sector co-creation.**
   Break down silos and improve cross-sector collaboration by
   shifting from focusing innovation exclusively on building assets
   in-house (i.e., each department hosts an innovation lab) to
   brokering partnerships with outside non-profits and businesses
   for new collaborative hybrid platform supports.

6. **Set 10 audacious goals for 2030.**
   Establish 10 grand challenges for Canadian institutions and
   citizens to collectively solve by 2030. Align federal departments
   to champion and collaborate cross-departmentally and across
   sectors around their particular challenge.

7. **Establish a multi-sector solutions finance agency.**
   Provide financing vehicles for each stage of the social innovation
   life cycle from ideation to scale, including: catalytic first-loss
   capital, demonstration funding, social R&D, matching dollars
   for intermediary platforms financing performance and outcomes
   vehicles, and scale capital, especially aligned with the 10 grand
   challenges. Capital sources would include philanthropy, private
   equity, and public partners. Business Development Bank of
   Canada could be the host.

8. **Create a National Inclusive Innovation Agency.**
   Build on the experience of other national platforms like Nesta,
   the UK government's endowed foundation for innovation,
   establishing an endowment for an arm's-length agency to
   mainstream social innovation.

9. **Create a National Social Innovation Council.**
   A government-appointed advisory council tapping social
   innovation expertise and networks from the community and
   business sectors, to guide the deployment and evolution of

integrating social innovation into the federal government's innovation agenda.

10. **Support a national social innovation network.**
To successfully support the integration of social innovation into a next-generation innovation agenda, co-create a multi-city Social Impact Network to fast-track development of new collaborative hubs and partnerships for tackling complex challenges.

AGILITY AND SOCIAL CHANGE

Many of these ideas are consistent with agility, which has been identified as one of the most important priorities in business today and has been flagged by McKinsey as the "dominant organizational paradigm for the next 100 years."[5] Agility in business has been defined as the qualities that allow organizations to respond rapidly to changes in the internal and external environment without losing momentum or vision.[6] And innovation is seen as the key to maintaining business agility.

Agility is more important than ever as businesses try to respond to the impact of the pandemic and the ongoing disruption resulting from new technology and rapid innovation that has eroded competitive advantage for many corporations. Today, organizations in all sectors can't afford to rely on bureaucratic organizational structures in which new ideas are seen as risky and decision-making is slow.

The United Way of Greater Toronto is the largest United Way organization in the world and, next to the government, is the largest funder of social services in the Greater Toronto Area. It's also a large organization that needed to quickly become agile at the outset of the pandemic. President and CEO Daniele Zanotti described how his organization took action in a Change for Good conversation we had in April 2020:

We became, in a very quick and overnight way, this local systems solution provider. We are partnering, for example, with the City of Toronto. We are linked with their emergency response. We are co-chairing nine place-based community tables across Toronto, and one table for the Indigenous community, and one for city-wide. Every day, those community tables convene. They talk about what's happening on the ground, who's closed and who's open, how they might pivot and allocate dollars in new ways. There are amazing things that are bubbling from that in real time. We started to hear there were no hand washing [facilities] or bathrooms for the homeless, and we quickly went back to the city's emergency response and got them to activate that across the city. We heard that there were shortages for food supply, partnered with the Toronto Public Library, got a couple of our United Way agencies together, and now libraries are being used for food distribution mechanisms.[7]

In the same conversation, Zanotti also told me: "Everything is possible. It would have taken us years at United Way to move to having 250 people at work, and we did it over a weekend. I will never take, 'No, that's not possible,' as an answer anymore. Everything is possible."

EXAMPLES OF ACCELERATING CHANGE: HOW TO TAKE ACTION

The novel coronavirus has accelerated change that was long overdue in many areas of society, including social change. The shift from a business model that is exclusively focused on the interests of shareholders to one that encompasses the interests of all stakeholders was already underway and created a context for action that I think contributed to the responses we saw in 2020 and has set the stage for even more change in the future.

The turning point for this shift was the 2019 message from the Business Roundtable that established a new standard for corporate responsibility and emphasized the primacy of stakeholders.[8] (See Chapter 2, page XX.)

The Business Roundtable's new statement of purpose was, in effect, a commitment to Change for Good. It recognized that all stakeholders are equally important and that the future success of companies, communities, and the country depends on delivering value to all of them.

Today, social innovation and accelerated change is needed more than ever and is already underway. Here are some remarkable examples of how attitudes and actions changed quickly in very quick response to the pandemic, and which I think are the building blocks of a new approach to social change for businesses that's here to stay.

Leadership

The 2021 Edelman Trust Barometer revealed that the public is now expecting business leaders to focus on societal engagement with the same rigour, thoughtfulness, and energy used to deliver on profits. People today expect business to fill the void left by governments and they have high expectations of businesses to address and solve today's challenges. Edelman's research showed that 86 percent of people believe that CEOs must publicly speak out on issues including pandemic impact, job automation, societal issues, and local community issues. And 68 percent believe that CEOs should step in when governments do not fix social problems.[9] To that end, one of KPMG Australia's COVID-19 golden rules is: "Responding rapidly to customer and employee needs, government requests and finding solutions to new customer problems."[10]

Health and Safety of Employees

Corporations had no choice but to operationalize corporate social responsibility by taking immediate action to ensure the health, safety, and welfare of their employees. In addition to supplying essential personal protective equipment, many companies increased wages for employees working on the front lines of health care and in retail, food, and other essential services — many of whom were risking their lives. (As mentioned earlier, some including Amazon and Cargill have been targeted for negligent actions on the part of their employees, but I think they are in the minority.)

In the first few months of the pandemic, Walmart announced $365 million in bonuses for full-time and part-time hourly employees and Target announced $300 million in special payment to its employees. Lululemon continued to pay its employees and provided a pay relief fund even after it temporarily shut down all its stores in North America.[11] And companies including Walmart, Apple, and the Olive Garden updated their sick leave policies to provide additional coverage and support for their most vulnerable workers.[12]

According to KPMG Australia, "The virus will be a big accelerant for remote working and online education. It is likely that this shift will impact morale, productivity and mental health of workers throughout the globe and businesses need to prepare for it."[13]

The Public

The speed at which companies took action on behalf of the public during the early days of COVID-19 was unprecedented. Response included offering consumers free access to products or services, changing operations and systems as needed to produce or procure essential products, and donating millions of dollars to causes related to COVID-19 relief. *USA Today* shared these examples of social change actions that took place in the six weeks between the day of the first stay-at-home order in the United States and the end of April in the same year[14]:

- **Audible,** an audio book streaming company, began giving away its core product for free. As children across the country were locked out of schools, the company responded by providing a free collection of educational and entertaining children's literature.

- **Beyond Meat,** the plant-based food company, pledged to donate and distribute over one million of the company's vegetarian

Beyond Meat burgers to hospitals and food banks. The company's pledge came at a time when many Americans were struggling to afford or access healthy meals.

- **Nike** converted portions of its factories to make face shields and air-purifying respirators. The company worked with Oregon Health & Science University to repurpose padding, cords, and shoe soles into personal protective equipment that was donated to the university beginning in April.

- **Uber** provided ten million free rides and food deliveries to health care workers, seniors, and people in need across the world. It also used its Uber Eats delivery service to provide free meals to first responders and health care workers.

- **Wells Fargo** paused all evictions and auto repossessions and offered fee waivers and deferred payments to customers. The bank's foundation also donated $175 million to help public health, housing, and food efforts. (Perhaps the reputational crisis that hit Wells Fargo after its role in the subprime mortgage crisis of 2008 and its fake account scandal from 2016 contributed to its offering of one the most expansive COVID-19 relief packages among banks in the United States.)

THE POSSIBILITY OF SPEED

Throughout 2020, companies continued to take action and demonstrated that helping to solve social problems was possible at a higher speed. Following are some more notable examples.

In July, Verizon announced Citizen Verizon: a plan for economic, environmental, and social advancement with the goals of providing ten million young people with digital skills training by 2030, being 100 percent carbon neutral company-wide by 2035, and preparing half a million people for "jobs of the future" by 2030. "With Citizen Verizon, our team is making a significant commitment to move the world forward through the power of action and technology," said Hans Vestberg, chairman and CEO of Verizon. "There has never been a more critical moment to demonstrate the power of purpose. To continue being one of the world's technology leaders, we must address the economic, environmental and societal issues that are most pressing."[15]

In response to COVID-19, beauty company Mary Kay made an early $10 million commitment to support organizations and target those populations disproportionately affected by COVID-19. In the United States, the Native American population had been particularly hard hit, especially the Navajo Nation in the Southwest. Mary Kay provided seventy-five thousand units of hand sanitizer to the Indian Health Service (IHS), the operating division within the U.S. Department of Health and Human Services that provides medical and public health services to federally recognized Native American tribes and Alaska Native people. The contribution from Mary Kay was able to help supply 26 hospitals, 59 health centres, and 32 health stations within the nationwide IHS network. "The countless stories of families affected in our country's great Native American population are devastating," said David Holl, chairman and CEO of Mary Kay. "It's our hope that organizations continue to support the Indian Health Service so frontline workers can safely stop the spread and provide care for those already affected by the virus."[16]

According to the World Bank, small and medium-sized enterprises (SMEs) represent about 90% of businesses and more than 50% of employment worldwide.[17]

In recognition of the importance of these businesses to the national economies and local communities, some large corporations were quick to step in to support SMEs during this difficult time: Amazon announced a $5 million relief fund for small businesses in the vicinity of its headquarters.[18] Google pledged $1 million to organizations affected by the pandemic in Mountain View, California. Billionaire Mark Cuban reimbursed employees who purchased lunch and coffee from local restaurants.[19] And Target created a SAFE Retail Toolkit, to help other retailers open safely.[20] Corporations that moved quickly to address the needs of their SME suppliers and local businesses contributed to social change by helping to ensure job stability.

A BLUEPRINT FOR CHANGE FOR GOOD: HOW TO TAKE ACTION

The COVID-19 crisis showed that it was necessary and possible to accelerate social change in large organizations. I think it also paved the way for businesses to address social change in ways that prioritize innovation and co-creation. Here's a blueprint for how to make that happen in your business.

1. **Revamp governance.**
   According to Edelman's research, 86 percent of people believe that CEOs must be social change leaders, but this isn't likely unless there is change on the corporate boards they report to. According to a 2021 paper called *Where Are the Directors in a World in Crisis?* that was co-authored by University of Toronto professor Sarah Kaplan and business veteran Peter Dey, corporate boards in Canada are trapped in the past.[21] Kaplan and Dey believe boards must be revamped for a world where institutional shareholders are also demanding stronger environmental, social, and governance performance from the companies they invest in. This starts with diversity. Directors are still predominately white, older, and male. Among the top five banks in Canada, there isn't one female CEO, none of their boards are 50-50 male-female, and "the representation of people of colour, people with disabilities, Indigenous people, is very poor."[22] In public companies, Change for Good needs to start at the level of governance. Without that, even the most progressive CEOs are likely to have an uphill battle and change will be slow or non-existent.

2. **Recruit agents of change.**
   The degree and speed of change we saw during COVID-19, and which we need today, won't happen with the usual suspects in your corporation. These people are well-meaning, but they're not likely to have what I call "a bias for change." That's what is needed to shift a company from the low-risk CSR Lite approach to new territory that improves results — for society and for business. I recommend identifying one person from each functional area of your company (this will likely include marketing, IT, HR, operations, supply chain, communications, and investor relations) to be seconded to a Change for Good sprint — a six-week ideation and jam session with one objective: develop a blueprint for change focused on an SDG that aligns with your company's purpose by 2030. (Refer to the Change for Good process in Chapter 3.)

   Participants in the sprint should be selected based on these three criteria:

   I. **Full spectrum and cognitive diversity.** Along with inclusion based on demographics, ensure participants reflect diverse backgrounds, experiences, strengths, and perspectives. The goal is to ensure that participants bring different ways of thinking, different viewpoints, and different skill sets.

   II. **Lived experience.** Some of the participants must have direct experience with the social issue that is being considered. In addition, wherever possible, this group should meet in community locations where social change takes place or is needed. Local community centres, charitable organizations, and social enterprise cafés located in vulnerable communities are all good options.

III. **Creativity.** There is a direct connection between creativity and social change. Artists and creative thinkers use songs, paintings, and other visual arts to raise awareness of oppression, inequalities, and injustice. Today, technology has added to how creativity can contribute to social change. Participants in the sprint don't need to be professional artists but do need to bring their own creativity to the process and be open to collaboration that involves creativity and play. I've seen groups of executives have so much fun cutting pictures out of magazines to create incredible collages that represent their company's current commitment to social change today and their vision for what Change for Good will be like for them in the future.

3. **Reframe the opportunity.**
The questions I used to help create change at 3M in 2008 were useful and appropriate at that time but are now outdated. Companies that use the same considerations today will end up with approaches that are ineffectual for society and for their businesses. Here are the questions I think are most important for companies shifting from corporate social responsibility to Change for Good:

- Has the issue under consideration been identified as a United Nations SDG priority? What are the specific objectives that the UN has targeted for 2030? What must happen in order for us to have helped solve the problem and end our program by 2030?

- What would life be like for our employees, customers, communities, and our business if this problem isn't solved?

- Where are we causing harm? Wherever we choose to focus, how do we go beyond reach and create impact?

- What gives us a strong reason to believe that we can contribute to solving this problem?

- How can we involve more people with lived experience in developing our approach, implementing the program, and monitoring and evaluating progress?

- How will we resource our investment in change? (e.g., leaders, time, skills and capacity, partners, capital, reputation, technology, physical and digital presence.)

- What is the riskiest thing we could possibly do to help solve this problem? And what would be the most controversial non-profit organization to partner with?

- How can we promote and communicate what we're doing in a way that's humble and transparent?

- If our plans didn't work out, would we still believe it was worth the effort?

- What would it take to feel genuinely proud of what we've accomplished?

The blueprint at the end of your sprint can be in the form of a video, written manifesto, or collection of reflections, stories, and experiences of participants. It can be anything except a written report or PowerPoint presentation and, wherever possible, should not be presented in your company's office. The most convincing way to communicate your plan and motivate people to take action is through something experiential, like a visit to a community service organization where you can share your ideas alongside people with lived experience.

Your blueprint for change should provide a clear vision of the change you're after. Include a model for how this will happen (including the people, processes, and technology required) and describe how it can be implemented and tested quickly in the form of a pilot project.

4. **Pilot for change.**
   Almost all the social change programs I've been a part of that didn't work were because we started too big. I've learned that transformational ideas for social change need to be put into action quickly and also at a scale that can be evaluated and adapted as needed before growing. That's why your blueprint should contain a plan for a pilot program that can be implemented quickly. Features of a social change pilot include:

   - A focus on one social change objective, relative to one population in one location. For example, targeting social isolation among older people in a specific city or neighbourhood.

   - Embedding people with lived experience in the design, implementation, and evaluation of the pilot. Using the example above, this could involve establishing an advisory council of older people who live in the neighbourhood.

   - Collaborating with an expert on social change monitoring and evaluation to help design the program and assess its performance. Ultimately, this will lead to the creation of a "theory of change" for your program. (A theory of change explains how the activities undertaken by your social change program will contribute to the outputs and outcomes you've identified as priorities.[23])

When impakt was collaborating with Nestlé Canada, we developed a new community-informed approach to promoting healthy dietary habits for families based on specific community needs. We piloted this approach in Toronto's Sterling Road neighbourhood because it is an area affected by a combination of socio-economic conditions (visible minority groups, gentrification, rent increases, community in transition) that had an impact on families' ability to provide healthy food. Developing the pilot involved visiting local schools, community centres, and social service organizations to gain a first-hand understanding of the situation from the point of view of people with lived experience. Change for Good programs can't be designed in your office.

IMPATIENCE IS A VIRTUE

When I was working at the Toronto Symphony, one of my colleagues used to always describe my approach as "I want it now!" At the time, I suppose my level of self-awareness must have been particularly low because I didn't understand why she kept saying this. In retrospect, I think she was absolutely right. I think change should happen faster, and so should you. Not for its own sake but because social change is urgently needed.

Helping to solve social problems in ways that prioritize innovation, co-creation and involving people with lived experience are important because they will result in responsible solutions that are based on real-life situations — not on flip charts in boardrooms. This approach will also accelerate change because there's nothing more motivating than getting first-hand experience of why change is needed, understanding what people involved believe needs to happen, and seeing how taking action in a responsible way changes people's lives for the better.

CHAPTER 6

Change for Good Responsibility

Earlier in the book I wrote about how, in 1948, leaders in Canada's garment industry, along with union leaders from the industry, devised a way to bring Holocaust survivors from displaced persons camps to Canada to work in the garment industry. Our team at impakt had the opportunity to uncover the stories of these tailors for the Tailor Project book.

During our conversations with survivors and their families, I began wondering what the situation was like for refugees today. We started to learn about the experience of Syrian people who had come to Canada more recently as refugees, and we found there were many similarities with Holocaust survivors who had come decades earlier. They were coming to Canada without being able to speak English or French, most had very low levels of education, and many had post-traumatic stress disorder or other mental health conditions. Similar to the Holocaust survivors after the war, we found that many newcomers had experience as tailors. In developing countries, tailoring is a trade that can be taught at home, is a way to generate an income for people with lower levels of formal education, and can create earnings for women who are also balancing running households and raising children. However, very few refugees who are tailors have employment and even fewer have employment in the apparel industry.

We thought we could help by starting a social enterprise that employed tailors who were refugees, and we named it after the original Tailor Project from decades ago. Over the next year, we learned more about this industry and got to know a number of tailors who had come to Canada as refugees to escape the conflict in Syria. Mohamad was one of these people. He had come to Canada, along with his wife and daughter, and had experience as a tailor and an apparel entrepreneur. In collaboration with Mohamad, we decided to focus the Tailor Project social enterprise on manufacturing made-to-measure shirts; he volunteered to design and produce the first prototypes. In May of 2019, Mohamad presented one of his handmade shirts to Prime Minister Justin Trudeau at a special cere- mony for members of the Tailor Project and their families.

One day, Mohamad came to see me and my colleague Leah at the office and asked for help. His wife had become ill, he wasn't employed, and he thought we could help him start a clothing import business. We weren't in a position to do this or to help his family in the other ways they needed, but we did manage to help him get a job at an apparel business in Toronto.

In the end, we couldn't find a way to get the social enterprise off the ground and had to abandon the idea. Along the way, we learned a lot about how difficult it is to be successful in the apparel industry and, more importantly, we got to know Mohamad. Prior to the civil war, he had been a successful entrepreneur. During the conflict, he was the victim of violence.

Another thing that our collaboration with Mohamad made clear was that we weren't just sitting in our office developing a social change idea or program for a client. We were having a direct impact on someone's life — and we weren't remotely prepared or trained to have this level of responsibility. I've thought a lot about this experience and what it means for businesses that want to adopt a Change for Good approach. Like us at impakt, corporations don't have the expertise to provide direct social support in a responsible way. Change for Good doesn't mean that businesses need to become social service organizations, but it does mean getting much closer to social issues than is possible sitting in your office.

In this chapter, I'll share why taking more responsibility for the social welfare of employees and for communities is foundational to the Change for Good approach. Doing this will involve a return to many of the ways that this was done prior to today's "outsourced" method, which involves looking after employees though external services such as employee assistance programs and relying solely on charitable organizations to address the social needs of communities. I will also provide a practical step-by-step approach to help companies take action.

TAKING RESPONSIBILITY FOR EMPLOYEES

My long-time mentor and advisor, Larry Enkin, who was the CEO of the Coppley Apparel Group, went back to school after his retirement and earned a degree in social work. Years earlier, Larry had the innovative idea to provide employees at Coppley with access to social services. Some of Coppley's employees had come to Canada with the Tailor Project, and others had arrived more recently, some of whom I imagine had experienced challenges similar to Mohamad.

The history of businesses taking direct responsibility for the well-being of their employees can be traced to the 19th century temperance movement in the United States. During that time, the consumption of alcohol went from being commonplace at work to being an activity that was linked to industrial accidents. Companies felt they had a moral responsibility to address the diminished health and productivity of their employees.[1] One of the earliest "inebriate homes," the Chicago Washington Home, was launched in 1863 and based on an experiment by employer Robert Law, who rehabilitated one of his alcoholic employees by moving him into his own home. In *The Evolution of Employee Assistance: A Brief History and Trend Analysis*, William White and David Sharar wrote that efforts like this were seen as "rescue work" by business leaders, who saw themselves as the head of the company "family."[2] This reflects the etymology of the word "company," noted earlier, as referring to the sharing of common bread and the importance of family in life and in business. (The authors also suggested that by the 20th century, companies became more "depersonalized" and therefore more likely to simply fire employees who were alcoholics.)

The more structured practice of employers providing counselling at no cost to their employees began shortly after the end of World War II. After the war, many soldiers returning home who had experienced the horrors of the battlefield and struggled to reclaim a place in society often found comfort by turning to alcohol. Some large companies that were looking for ways to help employees who were troubled by alcohol dependency developed their own in-house alcohol abuse programs, which later became known as employee assistance programs.[3]

Today, over 97 percent of employers in the United States with more than five thousand employees have employee assistance programs (EAPs) that provide confidential, short-term counselling services for employees with personal difficulties that affect their work performance.[4] Modern EAPs are run by private vendors and help employees deal with a wide variety of issues, including emotional, family, marital, substance use, legal, financial, nutritional, and work-related concerns.

Despite the wide adoption of EAP programs by businesses, the financial value of helping employees in areas that fall outside the direct scope of work has been challenging. EAP providers have struggled to define the business case for employers who invest in looking after the well-being of their employees. According to research psychologist Marc Milot, the challenge lies in attempting to convert important but intangible outcomes (e.g., improvements in employee mental health, well-being, life satisfaction, and work engagement) into financial values. Milot argues in favour of a return on value (ROV) approach that links credible evidence of intangible outcomes with cost savings for employers. For example, better mental health is consistently associated with higher work productivity, and improving psychological health can be expected with reductions in disability claims related to mental health problems.[5]

Similar to the space of business and social change, many experts are skeptical about why corporations invest in this area. In a 2019 article for The Balance Careers, HR and management consultant Susan M. Heathfield suggests that EAP programs are making employers feel better than employees. "EAPs do give the employer an option when dealing with troubled staff members whom they feel are ill-equipped, and not in the business, to serve," writes Heathfield.[6]

Taking responsibility for employees has shifted from being something that companies once believed was a part of looking after the well-being of their "family," to being an outsourced service that is intended to deliver financial value. While some companies are genuinely committed to supporting the needs of their employees (as mentioned in Chapter 1, Ally Financial prioritizes "human" in human resources and exemplifies what it means to support the health and welfare of employees), many others view supporting the well-being of their employees as simply a cost of doing business that they would eliminate if the optics of doing so wouldn't be so damaging. I don't think this is taking responsibility for employees; it's self-interest in the disguise of social responsibility.

The things that are of value to people and their families don't necessarily make "business sense" but do make "people sense" and make sense for the planet. Family-run businesses can be more effective at maintaining their values and bringing this ethos to decision-making. Recently, I had a Change for Good conversation with Gilad Lang, who is the vice president of The Madison Collection, a family-run business that was started over 20 years ago by Gilad's mother, Charmaine, an undocumented immigrant in the United States.

As a way of supporting herself and her son, Charmaine sold point-of-sale cash terminals to stores and restaurants. This often meant being away from home for days at a time and staying in hotels and motels. After years of experiencing itchy, scratchy, heavy towels and robes, she had an idea for how to bring a touch of warmth, like the touch of being hugged by a family member, to the experience of being in a hotel or motel. Since then, The Madison Collection has become a global company that sources, designs, and manufactures sustainable cotton towels, robes, and bath accessories, and takes responsibility for the well-being of its employees and their families.

Key to The Madison Collection's approach is a partnership built on shared values and trust, with a fifth-generation, family-run factory in the south of Brazil, where the processing of the cotton, the sewing, the dyeing, and the shipping happens under one roof. "Where you have a family business partnership, like ours with this factory, we have the privilege to ask, 'How is this going to benefit our children?'" said Gilad. This ethos is entrenched in the company's mission statement: "To protect and improve the environment, promote workplace wellness and support clean water rights." The company's mission statement does not reference making a profit and sets the stage for a remarkable set of innovative initiatives that are making a meaningful difference to the environment and to the lives of employees.

Here's how this family-run business is making Change for Good, with ways that are innovative and sustainable, that involve people with lived experience, and that are also inspiring:

- **Less water:** The Madison Collection's water purification plant in Brazil uses a costly, lengthy, live-bacteria process to purify and clean the water used to make its products. After the bacteria has eliminated the dye pigments and all of the impurities, the liquid is put in barrels for up to 10 years. After the toxicity has dissipated, the remaining bacteria is given to local farmers for use as fertilizer. Through this process, the company is able to return water to the Amazon and other local rivers cleaner than it was when originally captured.

- **Women in leadership:** Managers at The Madison Collection are elected by their peers, and women now comprise 82 percent of shift management. (Prior to introducing the election process, more than 95 percent of the shift management were men.) Over four hundred worker suggestions for workplace safety, efficiency, and happiness have been implemented. Management elections are an employee-generated suggestion that has consciously crafted and evolved a culture of respect, fairness, equality, and happiness.

- **No microfibres:** Most other towels and robes have a synthetic blend of cotton and petroleum-based polyester. When washed, thousands of microparticles wash into the waterways and compromise aquatic ecosystems. It's cheaper to create microfibre towels that last longer, but the company has made a commitment to only use 100 percent cotton in its products.

- **Regenerative energy:** At its factory in Brazil, The Madison Collection makes fuel briquettes from combining twigs and seeds scooped up during the spinning process with wood chips from local furniture factories that use only replanted trees. These briquettes fuel a fire that creates hydro energy, which is converted into jet air and used to power 100 percent of the production machinery.

- **Profit sharing:** 25 percent of The Madison Collection's net profit is shared equally among everyone, from the people in the fields, to the janitors, to the marketing directors. This has impacted families in many ways, including having more disposable income and an increased sense of well-being. Since implementing this program, The Madison Collection has also been more profitable because of the high quality of its products, which results in fewer items being rejected.

- **Buy one, gift one:** For every purchase of a robe, The Madison Collection gifts a locally made organic ceramic water filter that provides seven to 10 years of safe, clean drinking water to one family (seven to 15 people per family) living in the Dominican Republic, Haiti, and Cuba. In partnership with Wine to Water,[7] an international NGO, each family that receives a water filter must co-invest, even if it's a few dollars or time volunteered in the community.

  Wine to Water has conducted research, monitoring, and evaluation, and they estimate that providing these water filters has resulted in school attendance increasing by 24 percent because there are fewer sick days, work attendance increasing by 31 percent because parents don't have to stay home and look after sick children or they aren't sick themselves, and family income has increased by 17 percent because purchasing bottled water isn't required and medicines that treat waterborne illnesses are no longer needed. In addition, because women and girls and children usually bear the responsibility of daily water collection and it's often a three- to five- kilometre walk to the local well, more time is available for other activities, such as starting a business or helping the kids with their homework. Finally, reported sexual, verbal, and physical abuse of women and girls on their way to collect water has gone down by 19 percent.

The Madison Collection doesn't have a contract with its factory because they have a family-to-family relationship that's all based on trust. I don't think this degree of impact would have happened if its leaders had not directly experienced the need for social change. The Madison Collection is a family-run business started by a single immigrant woman who had little or no opportunity for success and was taken advantage of in the workplace.

Her son, who is the architect of the company's approach to social change and sustainability, was a Peace Corps Volunteer who had the experience of marketing and selling condoms in a program where 100 percent of the profits were reinvested into behaviour-change communications among the most vulnerable populations in Romania. "I always felt really uncomfortable in my privilege later on in life, my education, the things that I had, the opportunities that I had," says Lang. "I felt really compelled to find positive ways to leverage and use this privilege knowing there were so many other people out there that might not have gotten some of the things that I just happened to get."

Despite many positive social, environmental, and business outcomes, Lang acknowledges that there are many questions that are key to improving the company's impact but remain difficult to answer. These include: Where are we causing harm? Wherever we choose to focus, how do we delve beyond reach and go into impact? How can we promote and communicate what we're doing in a way that's humble and transparent and helps us to make money to survive so we can continue doing this? (I love these questions and, as you may have noticed, I included some of them in my recommendations for how to reframe the opportunity for change in Chapter 5.)

TAKING RESPONSIBILITY FOR THE COMMUNITY

Long before the concept of corporate social responsibility was developed, there were many examples of companies, such as Cadbury, that had a social purpose and made it a priority to support the needs of their communities in a very substantive way that included providing housing, schools, and health care. There were also many examples of company towns that were the antithesis of Bournville, the model village in England that was founded by the Quaker Cadbury family for its employees. The town of Lynch, Kentucky, was built in 1917 by U.S. Coal and Coke and had a commissary, theatre hotel, and hospital; however, similar to other coal mining towns in Kentucky and West Virginia, it was also a bare-bones settlement where residents lived in poverty.[8]

Today, we see companies such as Facebook creating modern versions of 21st-century company towns. For Facebook's Menlo Park headquarters, the company hired the same consultants who helped design Disneyland to build a main street lined with employee benefits and services and small businesses. This approach may work well to keep its high-paid tech employees fuelled up at Philz Coffee, but it's a far cry from addressing the more fundamental needs of people in many communities.

The way many corporations contribute to social change has shifted from doing this important work directly to outsourcing social responsibility to other businesses and to charitable organizations. This has led to the development of whole industries to support internal social programs in the areas of employee assistance, corporate wellness, and work-life balance. Externally, many corporations partner with charitable organizations that deliver programs on their behalf. "Corporations outsource everything from accounting and manufacturing to human resource functions," said Carol Sanford, author of *The Responsible Business* and *The Responsible Entrepreneur.* "For the most part, charity and Corporate Social Responsibility (CSR) are methods of outsourcing responsibility, handing off the heavy lifting to someone outside the company who will make strategic decisions to bring about transformations and decide when success has been achieved."[9]

Sometimes outsourcing social responsibility can lead to very positive outcomes and is an appropriate approach for companies that want to make change but don't have the internal resources. In other cases, however, it is done by companies that believe outsourcing it will be more cost-effective, lower-risk, and consistent with a broader business trend to outsource functions as needed to reduce the head count of full-time employees.

As I mentioned in Chapter 4, despite the need to be seen as socially responsible, most corporations don't believe there is a solid enough business case for building internal capacity in this area or are simply trying to get the highest possible return from the lowest possible investment. That's why it's not unusual for corporations that employ tens of thousands of people to have only one or two people responsible for social purpose activities that are positioned as central to who the company is and what it stands for. Because they lack internal capacity, they are essentially paying charitable organizations to do this work by making large donations that don't detract from marketing resources or other areas that are seen to be more valuable. Finally, corporations believe that their work in the area of social change will be seen as more authentic and less a source of potential reputational risk if done by a charitable organization.

Despite the ubiquitous nature of outsourcing social responsibility, there are many examples of businesses that have developed and operate proprietary social change programs. There are also a growing number of newer businesses, such as The Madison Collection, where social change has been embedded in their purpose from the outset.

The first time I went to a Ronald McDonald House, I was shown a beautiful box filled with pictures, handwritten stories, and hospital identification bracelets. These are called "memory boxes" and are made by children with terminal illnesses to leave for their parents after they've passed. I don't find it possible to remember this experience without wanting to cry. After leaving the House that day, it occurred to me that without the commitment of a fast-food corporation, these boxes would never have been created and the parents of these children would be without these special memories.

The first Ronald McDonald House began in Philadelphia in 1974 when three-year-old Kim Hill, the daughter of Philadelphia Eagles football player Fred Hill and his wife, Fran, was being treated for leukemia at St. Christopher's Hospital for Children. Noticing that other families of hospitalized children were spending each night in waiting rooms or on their child's hospital room floor, eating out of vending machines and having nowhere to rest or reflect, the Hills knew there had to be a better way for families in times of crisis. After collaborating with leaders from the community, the first Ronald McDonald House opened in Philadelphia.

Today, there are 368 Ronald McDonald Houses worldwide and the organization's approach to supporting families and children is based on "family centred care," an approach that is rooted in the belief that optimal health outcomes are achieved when patients' family members play an active role in providing emotional, social, and developmental support.[10] Research by impakt in 2015 revealed that Ronald McDonald Houses improve access to Canada's paediatric health science centres for seriously ill children and their families. By doing so, they ease the financial burden for out-of-pocket expenses, provide families with emotional and physical comfort and a community of support, improve the family's coping and cohesion, enable parents to be involved in the child's care, and enhance the child and family's hospital experience as well as quality of care.

"The number one thing a sick child wants is to be with their mother and father and their siblings," said Cathy Loblaw, president and CEO of Ronald McDonald House Charities (RMHC). "This is what we provide."[11] Although RMHC Canada is a separate entity from McDonald's, the organization's head office is located in the McDonald's Canada headquarters, the fast-food giant remains an important source of funding, and executives and employees of McDonald's are regular volunteers.

WALKING THE WALK

In 2017, Starbucks invited me and my colleague Preston Aitken to participate in its Dallas Opportunity Fair, an event where more than 30 companies conducted interviews and hired Opportunity Youth — young people between the ages of 16 and 24 who face systemic barriers to meaningful jobs and education. Throughout the day, representatives from Starbucks and the other participating companies helped youth with their résumés, provided interview tips, created online job candidate profiles, and interviewed them for jobs. We were invited to do mock job interviews to help participants get ready for the real thing. While I was interviewing one of the youth, I looked over and noticed Starbucks Executive Chairman Howard Schultz conducting a mock interview at the next table over.

Earlier the same day, Schultz highlighted the role and responsibility of businesses to contribute to social change. "The only way that we can succeed as a society, as businesses, as citizens, is to be more compassionate and understanding," he said. "We can't succeed as a society if we leave millions of people behind because of their station in life."[12]

In 2015, Starbucks launched a program to open stores in 15 diverse, low- to medium- income urban communities in the US to operationalize its commitment to support youth. The company's 100,000 Opportunities Initiative set a target of hiring 100,000 Opportunity Youth by 2020 and had hired more than seventy-five thousand youth by 2019.

To determine the best locations, Starbucks reviewed available data on the socio-economic health of America's cities to understand which communities had the biggest opportunity gaps, which had the biggest need for business investment and leadership, and where there was local movement already underway to build a better future for residents. After the optimal locations were identified, Starbucks collaborated with local women and minority-owned contractors and businesses in the design and development of these stores, and worked with women and minority-owned suppliers to bring locally made food products to the stores. Each of the locations featured an on-site training space for young people to learn customer service and retail skills, based on the same training other Starbucks employees receive. Starbucks also partnered with local youth services organizations and government to leverage existing programs that helped connect young people with internships, apprenticeships, and jobs in the community. In 2020, the company announced plans to open 85 more community stores to provide economic opportunity in underserved rural and urban communities across the United States.

I believe Starbucks genuinely committed to making social change and taking responsibility for its actions. Its response to the racist incident in Philadelphia is a good example. In 2018, video footage captured the arrest of two African American men in a Philadelphia Starbucks location for failing to make a purchase as they waited for a friend to arrive. In the seven days that followed, Starbucks issued a public apology to the two men, their customers, and their employees. CEO Kevin Johnson personally took responsibility for the crisis and met with the two men. Senior management got the advice of community leaders to help assess the situation and develop a plan of action, and the company announced it would close eight thousand stores for half a day to conduct unconscious bias training with staff.

When I was in South Korea in 2016 participating in the SK Foundation's 10th Anniversary Celebration, I learned about Hyundai's Energizing Project for Taxi Drivers.[13] This innovative program helps improve nervous system and spinal cord health among aging taxi drivers, which keeps them healthy and reduces the incidence of car accidents — some of which are caused by these health issues. There are two parts to this program: the "Energizing Station," where taxi drivers can get a health check-up and use exercise machines, and the "Energizing Bus," which has similar features and circulates to locations where taxi drivers can be found.

When I heard about this from Hyundai's CSR team at the company's headquarters in Seoul, I thought it was just a very cool idea but didn't think it had actually been implemented. I've never forgotten this as an incredible example of how it's possible for a company to leverage their assets to change lives. This isn't outsourcing social change; it's taking direct action and responsibility.

Warby Parker was founded with the objective to "offer designer eyewear at a revolutionary price, while leading the way for socially conscious businesses." The company has disrupted the eyewear industry by creating an alternative model that provides beautifully designed and high-quality prescription eyewear at a fraction of the going price. Warby Parker also believes that everyone has the right to see. The company puts this belief into action by ensuring that for every pair of glasses sold, a pair is distributed to someone in need.[14]

Here's what Warby Parker says about how its business started: "Every idea starts with a problem. Ours was simple: glasses are too expensive. We were students when one of us lost his glasses on a backpacking trip. The cost of replacing them was so high that he spent the first semester of grad school without them, squinting and complaining. (We don't recommend this.) The rest of us had similar experiences, and we were amazed at how hard it was to find a pair of great frames that didn't leave our wallets bare. Where were the options?"[15]

It turns out there was a simple explanation. The eyewear industry has been dominated by a single company that has been able to keep prices artificially high while reaping huge profits from consumers who have no other options. This means that essential eyewear is out of reach for many people in the United States and for many more in developing countries. Almost one billion people worldwide lack access to glasses, which means that 15 percent of the world's population cannot effectively learn or work. Warby Parker can't solve this problem on its own, but it is contributing in a meaningful way and raising awareness about the importance of this issue.

During the pandemic, glasses weren't the highest priority for the communities that were the beneficiaries of its Buy a Pair, Give a Pair program, and eye examinations posed a social-distancing danger. In response, Warby Parker, donated personal protective equipment to communities in need with its long-time partner, VisionSpring — in the US and abroad. "There's nothing like a global pandemic to make us realize we have bigger goals here," said David Gilboa, co-CEO of Warby Parker.[16]

NOT TAKING RESPONSIBILITY

Before we look at how to apply the practices and principles from these examples into an approach to Change for Good, I think it's also important to understand what not taking responsibility looks like.

At impakt in 2011, we were helping one of Canada's biggest mass retailers to improve their corporate responsibility program — which was essentially a very large donations program focused on supporting a number of high-profile charitable organizations in the health sector. During the course of working together, it occurred to our clients that perhaps it could be possible to pass on the cost of their donations (which was approximately $10 million a year) to their suppliers. Essentially, the idea was to outsource the program delivery (through the charities) *and* save money by increasing the amount that suppliers had to pay this company for marketing and promoting their products, thereby offsetting the cost of their donations. These discussions culminated in a meeting I facilitated with a number of the company's category managers who were responsible for buying in various categories like confection and clothing.

I went into this discussion very reluctantly, and it played out in an even more surreal way than I'd expected. When presented with the opportunity to pass on the cost of the donations programs to vendors, the category managers were completely in support of the idea. Why? Because part of their compensation was based on how much costs could be reduced, and this was an opportunity to do that.

OWNING YOUR RESPONSIBILITY

In terms of taking responsibility for the impact of business on people's lives, I think there's much to be learned from the mining industry. In this industry, businesses have a direct environmental and social impact on the lives of people in local communities. Social programs from businesses in more consumer-facing industries tend to be done in partnership with charitable organizations, whereas social programs in the mining sector tend to be done directly with the communities themselves, and this means that companies in this space need to take responsibility for actions in ways that are much more material than in many other cases.

In 2012, I wrote an article for *Forbes* titled "Ten Ways for Mining Companies to Work Better with Indigenous People."[17] While these recommendations have a particular relevance to companies in the mining sector, the essential approach can be used for any business that wants to take more responsibility for its impact on the lives of communities.

Here's what I recommended the companies do:

1. Spend time learning the history and culture of local Indigenous people with the goal of building relationships and trust.

2. Acknowledge the right of Indigenous people to informed consent. Engage third-party experts, chosen in consultation with affected communities, to assess and verify local conditions.

3. Ensure communities have timely access to all relevant information about any proposal affecting Indigenous territories, and offer resources in formats that are culturally appropriate, available in Indigenous languages, and easy to understand.

4. Recognize that Indigenous people are seeking the same community goals as corporations: better education, more employment, and improved economic opportunities.

5. Understand that Indigenous people look at time horizons and development differently and that actions taken must benefit future generations.

6. Remember that there are unique rights that are protected and advanced by Indigenous people. Indigenous people have a stewardship relationship with the land; they support development, but they must also care for the land.

7. Be realistic. It takes time for communities to respond to employment and business opportunities that are presented by extraction projects. Mining companies need to spend time working with communities to understand and act on those opportunities well in advance of the approval stages.

8. Establish co-management and co-responsibility. Accountability begins with shared responsibility for targets and outcomes.

9. Support local economic development. During the course of a mine's operations, Indigenous communities need to diversify and develop their own economies so that once the mine leaves, there are sustainable gains.

10. Ensure that the community has a consent process in place prior to initiating environmental and social impact assessments.

A few years ago, our team at impakt was asked to help an oil and gas company mediate a dispute it was having with the community in Peace River, Alberta. Members of the local community were accusing this company of causing odours and emissions from its operations that were making residents ill.

We went to Peace River to assess the situation and meet with members of the community. We were taken to remote sites where production from heavy oil wells came out of the ground and was stored in holding tanks. Trucks came along to take the heavy oil from these tanks to a railway line for transportation. We found that this company's operations had no perceptible odours or emissions and that the nearest neighbours to these sites lived very far away. Our observations were backed up by evidence from instruments that had been placed to detect and measure odours and emissions. In discussions with representatives from this company, we found people who were genuinely committed to doing whatever they could to minimize their environmental impact.

During a meeting with members of the community, it became clear that most people were actually grateful for the company's presence because it was a source of jobs for residents and of new business for local companies that were suppliers. They pointed out that the complaint for odours and health impacts was coming from only a few residents. We realized that the most inclusive approach to involving this community was to give them the responsibility of assessing this company's social and environmental impact. This "community-informed" approach was used to establish an annual "Good Neighbour" report card that was a transparent approach to tracking the company's performance against what the community expected. It also diffused the conflict and helped the local community to take more responsibility.

I share this story not to endorse the fossil fuel industry, but rather as an example of a situation where taking responsibility was harder than it looked and where, ultimately, empowering the local community to assess this company's impact was the best approach.

MAKING RESPONSIBILITY A REALITY: HOW TO TAKE ACTION

In *Radical Everyone*, a study by Wolff Olins in partnership with CitizenMe, seven thousand people in five markets indicated that they want fundamental change in the world and want businesses to drive change. The study also revealed a significant gap between expectations and action. While 41 percent of respondents believed that businesses should be bringing about positive change, only 13 percent feel businesses have been the primary driver of positive change in the past decade. When asked why this is the case, 42 percent suggested that focus on profit was a barrier. When asked how businesses should be creating positive change in the world, the most popular suggestions were: focusing on sustainability, doing good in the local community, and fostering innovation and research to tackle problems. "People want business to take an active role and aren't looking for delegation or distance," the study reported.[18]

Today, I think businesses that continue to outsource responsibility for social change are at risk. Harvard Business School historian Nancy Koehn put it this way: "The CEOs of big public companies don't walk out onto the plank of social and political leadership by default. But today, to keep silent is to jeopardize the reputation of the company."[19] In 2020, the Black Lives Matter movement, together with the US election crisis, combined to propel some of the world's most prominent businesses to become advocates for change. Speaking up is important, but taking effective action is even more important.

Here's how to take responsibility and make Change for Good happen in your business:

1. **Start with leadership for change.**
   In all honesty, if the most senior leaders in your company aren't prepared to see beyond profit as the exclusive purpose of business, then I'd suggest you stop reading and start looking for work at another company. As the old joke goes, "How many psychiatrists does is take to change a lightbulb? One, but the light bulb has to want to change." If you believe your leaders are prepared to take responsibility for the well-being of communities and the families of employees, or if you're a leader yourself, then keep reading.

2. **Save money by "insourcing."**
   Corporations view outsourcing as a way to tap into expertise and/or to save money, and sometimes this works very well. In the area of social change, companies that don't internalize

their efforts run the risk of reputational damage and spending more than is needed. Here's the case for insourcing social change:

- **Employees:** There's nothing more meaningful and valuable than creating opportunities for your "family" to take responsibility for each other. It's also cost-effective. At FirstService, one of North America's largest providers of essential property services, caring for each other is part of their DNA and is embodied in the #FirstServeOthers program. In 2020, #FirstServeOthers focused on the physical and mental health and wellness of people throughout the company and provided financial assistance to people in need through the FirstService Relief Fund.

- **Customers:** Examples like Hyundai's Energizing Project for Taxi Drivers and Starbucks' Community Store program show that companies can take responsibility for the social needs of customers in ways that don't just save money but that can also be a source of new or repeat business. In the case of Hyundai, taxi drivers are important customers who become more loyal to the company as a result of their experience with the company's Energizing Project.

- **Investors:** Taking responsibility to make real change doesn't create more risk, it reduces risk. Taking genuine, authentic action will close the gap between what people expect from companies and what is actually taking place. This will add value to your brand and reputation and make your company more attractive to investors who, increasingly, are influenced by a company's performance in the ESG (environmental, social, and governance) areas.

- **Media:** Taking direct action to make meaningful social change will attract attention without the need to pay for external public relations support. At impakt, we've experienced this many times with programs we created ourselves to help solve social problems, which made headlines across the county — at no cost. These included programs such as HireUp, the Tailor Project, and Change for Good Health, an initiative we developed to take action on improving the physical, mental, and emotional health for all Canadians during and after the pandemic.

3. **Reward social "intrapreneurs."**
   Identify an internal team of innovators in different functional areas and give them the mandate to address a social problem with a business solution. Reward them with a share of the profits based on achieving clearly defined targets. In 2010, Hyundai launched Easy Move Inc., the first social enterprise in Korea to produce and sell vehicles and walking assistance equipment for the disabled and elderly.

4. **Partner with social enterprises.**
   When it isn't possible to create your own programs, consider partnering with social enterprises or small businesses, including your own suppliers. Yuhan-Kimberly, South Korea's leading sanitary product manufacturer, is addressing the needs of the country's aging population and accelerating the growth of its company's senior care business. The Active Senior Program is delivered in partnership with small businesses that produce products such as fashionable walking sticks, reading glasses, and shoe inserts. The aim is to get senior citizens to become more active in society, and the program also involves the company playing a role in helping seniors to secure jobs. (The company also operates Golden Friends, a specialty retail outlet for the elderly located in downtown Seoul.)[20]

5. **Create "lived experience" communications.**
   Rather than hire an expensive agency to design communications for your social program, consider making direct social change by working with designers who have lived experience of the issue you want to communicate. For example, to advocate for more availability of repetitive transcranial magnetic stimulation (rTMS), a therapy for people with treatment-resistant depression, impakt collaborated with Lisa Tarasca. Tarasca is the owner of creative solutions company VividLi EFX, and she's also someone who has a history of anxiety and depression. Tarasca shared her journey in impakt's *rTMS: From the Margin to the Mainstream,* a report we did for Hathaway Research International.[21]

A few years ago, we partnered with the Indian Business Corporation (IBC) and the Business Development Bank (BDC) to explore an important question: What would it take to ensure that every Indigenous woman in Canada had the opportunity to become an entrepreneur? By listening to Indigenous women entrepreneurs share their experiences, we learned that these women faced one primary barrier: lack of access to loans. This discovery led IBC to launch the first loan fund for Indigenous women entrepreneurs in Canada. When it came to communicating this initiative, I felt it was important to involve an Indigenous woman entrepreneur who was also a graphic artist. We collaborated with Megan Currie and her firm X-ing Design, which is First Nations, female-owned, and operated on Treaty 4 land in Saskatchewan.

MOBILIZING CAPITAL AND INCREASING RESPONSIBILITY

Taking responsibility for social change in the ways that I've suggested will have more impact and can also be profitable. It also turns "responsibility" from being an important, but passive, moral imperative to being a source of action and positive change. Approached in this way, companies will position themselves as attractive to future talent, create more loyalty among employers, engage consumers and customers, and be seen as a high-value investment opportunity by institutional investors who are making decisions based on ESG performance.

In the next chapter, I'll be sharing how the Change for Good approach can mobilize capital to deliver even more impact and create new opportunities to generate a return on investment that can contribute to your bottom line or be reinvested in new social change programs.

CHAPTER 7

Change for Good Investing

"It's a lot harder than opening a shoe factory." That's how Cameron Voyame — our first employee and someone who was experiencing homelessness — described the challenges we had building and financing HireUp, the social change platform we developed to connect vulnerable people to meaningful and stable employment. As difficult as I imagine it is to open a shoe factory, Voyame's comment made me laugh because our experience felt more challenging than I could have ever imagined.

impakt developed HireUp with the objective of helping to end homelessness by giving youth economic stability and enabling businesses to improve recruitment by tapping into a pool of talented and motivated young people. Our approach to solving these problems was to create a national social change system to connect employers to youth-serving organizations across Canada that prepare youth to enter the workforce. We wanted to operate HireUp as a social enterprise because it provided a valuable recruiting service to businesses who needed entry-level employees and who would pay an annual fee to use our service. By using HireUp, employers would have access to job-ready candidates and also contribute to our social mission.

The problems with securing financing for HireUp started almost immediately. Even though our platform was contributing to social change, it wasn't a charitable organization and businesses couldn't provide support from their philanthropy budgets. (We also couldn't qualify for funding from private foundations or many government programs that would only support registered charities.) When we presented HireUp as a business solution for recruiting entry-level workers, this was also a problem because it was too early to demonstrate the return on investment, and we were seen as a risky bet compared to other services and platforms. Finally, we tried to get investors, but that wasn't successful either because they wanted to know when they could exit from their investment and what their return would be. Needless to say, we couldn't answer these questions.

To keep HireUp going, impakt itself has had to provide financing, and this nearly bankrupted the company. I remember thinking how absurd it was that our small company was paying for a social innovation that was aligned with the business priorities of many organizations and the social priorities of many funders — yet we couldn't get funding from either. In the end, we received a grant from the federal government and ended up giving HireUp to Raising the Roof, a national charitable organization with a mission of providing long-term solutions to end homelessness, which would be able to secure philanthropic support for the platform and program we'd developed.

Combining private and public approaches to finance promising solutions to social problems is starting to shift, but there's a long way to go and social entrepreneurs I speak with can relate to the problems we experienced in developing HireUp all too well. Despite an immense growth in the number of innovative social enterprises such as B Corporations that exist to make a profit and contribute to solving social or environmental problems at the same time, securing financing for social change remains a barrier. That is the case even though, parallel to the growth in the number of social enterprises, there has been exponential growth in impact investing — which refers to investments made to social enterprises or other companies that will generate a measurable social or environmental impact and a measurable financial return.

Today, however, the vast majority of corporations "invest" in social change by making philanthropic donations to charitable organizations. And most foundations are only able to fund charitable organizations that can issue tax receipts. Both situations reinforce a bias that social change should only be undertaken (or is best done) by charities. That leaves early-stage social entrepreneurs in a precarious position where, in addition to the risks associated with starting any new business, the route to securing financing is even more uncertain.

I think the relationship between business and social change is at a crossroads. On the one hand, the COVID-19 crisis revealed and contributed to social inequities, and the importance of businesses helping to solve the Sustainable Development Goals has never been more of a priority. On the other hand, despite some positive change, businesses still rely on an archaic approach to funding social programs. Without a shift in how capital is used for the purpose of social change, there's a very real risk that the most important social problems won't be solved.

Why haven't more corporations adopted impact investing as a tool for social change? What would it take for large business to shift from a philanthropic approach to one that includes a component of impact investing? What are the conditions for success for corporations to Change for Good in this area? How will corporations assess social and financial performance in a space where results are most often seen over many years?

I have no doubt that opening a shoe factory is far more difficult than I could ever imagine. I've learned that finding the right way to ensure that solutions for social change get off the ground is equally challenging and, without change, our ability to solve the most pressing problems we face today is unlikely. In this chapter, I'll be looking at how small businesses and large corporations can Change for Good by shifting from philanthropic contributions to social investments that can contribute to solving UN SDGs and generate returns that can be redeployed to create even more value.

INVESTMENT AS A TOOL FOR SOCIAL GOOD: A CONVERSATION WITH ESTHER PAN SLOANE

To learn more about how investment capital can help solve the UN SDGs, I spoke with Esther Pan Sloane, who is head of partnerships for the United Nations Capital Development Fund (UNCDF) and part of the team that negotiated the 2030 agenda and the Sustainable Development Goals. Here's an edited version of a conversation I had with her at the Annual Corporate Partnership Conference in 2020 about the role of small business in social change, the challenges that smaller businesses have in accessing capital, and how blending philanthropy with investment capital can be an effective tool for social change.[1]

[Paul Klein] What's UNCDF's role?

[Esther Pan Sloane] UNCDF is an agency that focuses on the poorest 47 countries, which are known as the least developed countries (LDCs) in the UN. These countries face a range of challenges including limited government finances, high dependency on overseas development assistance from developed countries, and the inability to access sources of capital that are available to more developed countries, particularly for small businesses and enterprises.

What was the impact of COVID-19 on small businesses in LCDs?

When COVID-19 hit, we saw that there was a devastating impact across these countries because their traditional sources of revenue, like tourism or overseas development assistance, declined significantly. As did the economic activity that was supporting them in terms of small business and job growth and activity within the informal sector. You can't be a market vendor who accepts cash for your tomatoes, virtually.

What's an example of how access to capital helped mobilize social change during COVID-19?

The major stimulus packages for LDCs did not address the needs of small businesses where there was a tremendous demand for finance in the right forms. For example, in Uganda, the government asked UNCDF to help a business called SafeBoda, which is essentially Uber on motorcycles, where people would pick up passengers and drop them off somewhere else. They have eighteen thousand drivers, and suddenly, Kampala was locked down and no one could go anywhere, so all these drivers were going to lose their jobs. We helped the company repurpose their online presence to add grocery delivery. By doing this, the drivers could pick up groceries from the market, pay the market vendors, and then bring them to people who were social distancing at home. In this case, access to capital saved the jobs of all those drivers and allowed people to comply with social distancing. It also kept people who are informal vendors linked to the market, and it helped them reach more customers than they would have otherwise.

What is the role of business in social change?

A charity needs donations every year, but a business that's successful can sustain itself. So, if you build a business that has a social impact, or an SDG impact or development impact, that sustains itself and grows as a business, then you as a funder no longer have to support that business, and then the impact continues indefinitely into the future. For example, we have found that at the local level, small businesses are the most effective poverty eradication tool. If you get credit and savings in the hands of enterprising entrepreneurs, they'll pull themselves out of poverty, they'll move their families out of poverty, and they also usually support a long chain of relatives, nieces, and nephews in their home village. So, it's the same kind of entrepreneurial spirit that you see in Silicon Valley and all around the world. It's just a smaller scale. And these entrepreneurs face bigger challenges.

What are the main barriers facing these smaller businesses?

The most important barrier we found is access to capital, because entrepreneurs in poor countries, like everywhere else, need to borrow money to grow their businesses. And we've found that there's a stone wall that entrepreneurs hit, where you can be a successful, profitable business, but no bank will lend you money. One of the things we found is that UNCDF can play a critical role as the guarantor or the first mover by providing access to a concessional loan that is matched with a loan from a local bank within an LDC at a commercial rate. By doing this, businesses that have a sustainable development impact can access capital that otherwise they would not. What usually happens after that is that the entrepreneurs pay us back and the next time they go back to the bank, they get a loan without us. So, we've helped the company become a viable entity and we know that their SDG impact will continue without us.

In what ways are people with lived experience involved in UNCDF's approach to mobilizing capital for the purpose of social change?
Our ultimate beneficiaries are always the citizens and governments of least developed countries, and we never go anywhere unless a local government has come to us and said, "We need your help." When we support small and medium enterprises, it's the entrepreneurs who have the ideas. We find these entrepreneurs through an open-challenge call. For instance, we might say, "We would like to have micro insurance for farmers and rural areas of Papua New Guinea. Who can help us solve this problem?" So, the ideas are always coming from the ultimate beneficiary or recipient. We are just there to support and be essentially their guidance counsellor to help them access financial resources that are supposed to be there to help them but that they can't access.

What is the opportunity to blend loan capital with philanthropic or other types of investment in social change?
Blended finance is a way to kind of take different colours of money — money that needs to do different things — and combine them so that everyone gets what they want. There's the money you would donate, and there's money that you would invest but accept a lower return on. Within that spectrum, you can do a lot of different things with the money, and also consider combining them in new ways to achieve greater impact with the whole portion in a way that you maybe hadn't thought of before. With a blended

finance approach, the commercial investor can meet their rate of return; the government that's looking to create jobs can see that their money is attracting other money; and foundations, charitable donors, or family offices can contribute to social change in a way that preserves their capital and earns a small return.

How could businesses use capital differently to help solve SDGs?
Corporations are increasingly facing scrutiny from investors about the diversity of their boards and management teams, the transparency of decision-making processes, and equitable human resource practices. These social pressures are going to impact your business because the new generation of investors, employees, and consumers really care about what kind of businesses are getting their money. If you are publicly traded, or are scrutinized by any public entity, soon enough someone is going to come to ask questions like, "What is your plan to diversify your workforce, or ensure that transgender people are protected, or all sorts of these issues?" And the data is now coming out to show that businesses can invest in ways that contribute to supporting diversity and solving other social problems in ways that also generate a return. For businesses, taking action to mobilize capital for the purpose of social change starts with asking questions like "Are we using our money in a way that is consistent with our values?" and "Is what we're doing currently helping to achieve the SDGs in a measurable way?" and "Can we track our impact in ways that people will see as being legitimate?"

DEVELOPMENT LENDING

impakt's experience working with the Indian Business Corporation (IBC), an Alberta-based Aboriginal Finance Institution, reinforces Pan Sloane's insights about the ways in which investing in small business can contribute to social change. IBC is increasing access to loan capital for Aboriginal entrepreneurs in Alberta. The organization's approach is known as development lending — an approach to financial inclusion that creates opportunities for impoverished households to raise their living standards, provides countries with the resources to expand access to basic services, and — most important of all — enables citizens to chart their own prosperous futures.

"I was aboriginal, I was a woman. I remember one banker saying, 'Only men do this,' although not in so many words," said Lou Ann Solway, who was trying to start a ranching business on Alberta's Siksika Nation reserve.[2] Solway had inherited 10 head of cattle and needed financing to purchase 20 more. Despite an ability to use her existing herd as collateral, and having lifelong experience ranching, she wasn't able to secure a bank loan. Solway eventually secured a loan from IBC and is now a successful rancher with a herd of 120 calving cows on the reserve about a hundred kilometres east of Calgary.

IBC has a mission to ensure that every First Nations business has access to capital, and it has been providing financing to Indigenous people in Alberta since 1987. Since then, it has lent over $90 million to twenty-five hundred businesses and created nearly seven thousand jobs. Our team at impakt helped IBC learn more about unique challenges faced by women such as Lou Ann Solway in pursuing entrepreneurship and helped the organization launch the first loan fund in Canada specifically focused on the needs of Indigenous women.

Conversations with Indigenous women across Alberta revealed a number of barriers, including lack of property to use for collateral, lack of access to capital for equity, lack of education, lack of credit, and an inability to qualify for a loan from mainstream financial institutions. In response, IBC launched its fund in Alberta, where it had a track record of lending to Indigenous people and the opportunity to assess the needs of women in the province. In launching this fund, IBC also recognized that Indigenous women need to be central to the operations of the fund, and the organization committed to hiring an Indigenous woman as a loans officer and establishing an advisory council of Indigenous women entrepreneurs to provide an ongoing perspective on the needs of First Nations, Métis, and Inuit women in Alberta. Input from Indigenous women in 2019 revealed that the loan fund had made positive contributions to the women who received loans, their families, and their communities.[3]

IBC had already been using loan capital to help change the lives of Indigenous people in Alberta, but it took an already effective approach one step further. By getting a first-hand understanding of the unique barriers that Indigenous women face and engaging these women in the evaluation of the impact of loans, it improved results considerably.

Esther Pan Sloane said it's important for organizations to ask themselves if they are using their money in a way that is consistent with their values. In my experience of working closely with IBC, meeting its Indigenous board of directors, and visiting some of its clients on reserves in Alberta, I found that the organization is genuinely committed to lending in a way that improves the lives of Indigenous people. IBC's approach illustrates the opportunity for other community-level financial service businesses to leverage their expertise and knowledge of local communities in order to contribute to social change by increasing access to loan capital. However, I don't believe this can be done for purely business reasons. Impact investing is more than a technical financial transaction; it's a belief that money should be used to make change for good.

PHILANTHROPY VS. IMPACT INVESTING

Larger corporations have even more opportunity to invest in social impact by harnessing their core business activities, partnering with smaller businesses in their supply chains, and blending philanthropic contributions with loans and other forms of investments. To understand the opportunity for large businesses to solve SDGs through new ways of mobilizing capital, I had a closer look at the extent to which corporations are contributing to social causes through philanthropy and how this compares to impact investing, where money is used to generate specific social or environmental benefits in addition to financial gains.

Giving USA estimated the total donations to charities in the US from individuals, bequests, foundations, and corporations to be $449.64 billion in 2020.[4] According to Chief Executives for Corporate Purpose (CECP), 250 multibillion-dollar companies contributed $24.8 billion, which is approximately 5 percent of total giving as reported by Giving USA.[5]

The newer marketplace of impact investing is already much larger than the charitable giving space. The Global Impact Investing Network (GIIN) has estimated that there is a $715 billion marketplace of impact investing around the world.[6] The organization's research has found that large corporations have invested approximately $2.4 billion in "initiatives and ventures designed to achieve financial returns as well as a positive economic, social, or environmental impact."[7] This represents a tiny proportion of the $715 billion invested for the purpose of social change. Using the 5 percent ratio of corporate donations to total donations as a benchmark, the target for corporate impact investments should be approximately $35 billion, about 15 times what it is today.

One indication of how important impact investing has become to other investors is that, despite uncertainties caused by the COVID-19 crisis, impact investors report that they are unlikely to reduce how much capital they will commit to impact investments this year. "Despite challenges or perhaps because of them, many investors have, and will continue to turn to impact investing to contribute to social and environmental solutions," said Amit Bouri, co-founder and CEO of GIIN. "Investment capital has an important role to play in driving positive impact for our communities and planet, and I believe we'll see even greater possibilities for what impact investing can achieve, in this moment, as well as in the years ahead."[8]

THE RELATIONSHIP BETWEEN FINANCIAL PERFORMANCE AND SOCIAL IMPACT: A CONVERSATION WITH UPKAR ARORA

Upkar Arora is chief executive officer and chief compliance officer of Rally Assets, an impact investment management and advisory firm based in Toronto. He has unique expertise in helping organizations use capital to create positive impact and believes that impact investing can achieve market rates of return or better over the long term. His firm's approach is backed up by more than two thousand studies that have consistently reinforced the positive relationship between financial performance and social impact.[9] I had a chance to ask Upkar about what impact investing looks like for businesses today and what businesses could do differently to change for good.

[Paul Klein] What is the difference between the environmental, social, and governance (ESG) performance of a company and corporate impact investing?

[Upkar Arora] ESG is a risk assessment process that involves the inclusion of material non-financial factors that could have a financial impact on the performance of a company. The goal is still to maximize returns. In the case of Volkswagen, a poor governance structure created the context for fraudulent behaviour happening with respect to the disclosure of emissions. Today, the problem is that many companies are doing the minimum amount possible to show that they're actually thinking about ESG. For example, companies get marks for having a diversity and inclusion policy, but many do that reluctantly without any belief that it actually benefits them or their employees and other stakeholders. That's not that much better than the traditional CSR, where if you've got a policy, you get a checkmark, you're rated really well.

Impact investing is looking in all the aspects of ESG and then going further by asking questions like: What is that company doing to actually have a positive impact in its communities, in society, and on the environment? Are you benefiting stakeholders in some way? Are you making a positive contribution and contributing to solutions? The companies that are doing it well are more open to disclosing what they're doing and showing the world that they're doing it well.

Why have corporations been slow to take action in this area?

We're starting to see a change in thinking about the role of corporations in society. However, the structures around capitalism, profitability, and the measurement of impact are lagging behind the desire to demonstrate change in a meaningful way. The focus is still on maximization of value to shareholders, and very little attention is being paid to multiple stakeholders, employee engagement, and consciousness about the environment and the community.

Another barrier is the increasingly short-term thinking that's become the norm for most businesses. The average tenure of CEOs is decreasing. We've gone from long-term buy-and-hold investment strategies to high-frequency arbitrage that happens within seconds. If we move that time horizon to a little bit longer than short term, then we should be tying incentive structures to social and environmental outcomes. This is starting to happen on a very small scale with some CEO bonuses tied to achieving sustainability targets.

Individual corporations like Patagonia or Ben and Jerry's have been demonstrating a different form of capitalism for years, but now what's happening is that companies like this are starting to become mainstream.

Why should corporations shift from CSR to impact investing?
I think there are three reasons why impact investing is a really good tool for corporations to actually demonstrate that they're committed to purpose and profit.

The first reason is social license. Legitimacy to exist depends on having a social license to operate from stakeholders in society, especially for businesses such as financial institutions or mining. At the end of the day, a corporation's sustainability and future growth is really dependent on how well companies can engage a number of people, create a great deal of cooperation, and generate great ideas by establishing trust, demonstrating their purpose, and living their values in an authentic way.

The second is the attraction, engagement, and retention of employees. All people, but especially those who are younger, want to work in places that are aligned with their values and have a connection with the company's mission and purpose. When

J.P. Morgan created a financial solutions lab that's effectively a corporate impact fund, they had eight hundred people respond immediately to ask, "How do I get involved?"

The third is innovation and opportunities for growth. Comcast launched a corporate impact fund that invests in venture capital funds led by Black, Latinx, and female founders. What they found was that by investing in those funds, they were identifying really cool technology and innovation opportunities related to new products, customers, markets, and niches that had not been served well and which they would not have seen but for these founders. When Thomson Reuters created Thomson Reuters Labs in 2015 and partnered with Communitech, a tech hub that helps start-ups create jobs and prosperity for Canada, they felt they could never unleash that kind of innovation within their own organization because of the legacy structure, compliance, regulatory constraints, and bureaucracy. I think impact investing like this is the lowest cost innovation strategy for corporations.

Why aren't we hearing more from corporations about what they're doing in this area?

In the last few years, there has been an erosion of trust in corporations. When corporations amplify stories about what they're doing to change the world, I think there's an inherent cynicism about those stories. There's a general belief that people are doing it to serve a certain purpose, and not doing it to actually make a difference. Also, the potential for instantaneous exposure of a company's actions with its words through social media is creating a greater risk. Because the gap between what you say and what you do is very easy to point out, and the lack of consistency across all your corporate actions is also more visible and on display and can go viral in a heartbeat. If companies are doing this just for the optics, they run the risk of being exposed by the lack of consistency across their organization as to how they are taking care of people and the planet.

What's your advice to CEOs?

Businesses need to take an active role and use the heft of their resources and their influence. They cannot wait for governments or other actors to lead. Uncertainty, social unrest, or greater income inequality where fewer people can afford to buy goods and services is not good for business. I think it's very short-sighted for business leaders not to be thinking that the world they can help create is one that raises all boats. That means having a longer-term horizon and creating the conditions for people to live a safe and secure life [which] allows those individuals to have the money and willingness to spend it on the products businesses create. I don't think it has to be a soft and fuzzy moral imperative, i.e., do the right thing. I think, ultimately, even if your sole objective was to generate higher profits over the long term, you are more likely to achieve that if you invest in people and planet than if you don't. It's not only the right thing to do, it's good for business.

WAYS TO INVEST WITH PURPOSE: HOW TO TAKE ACTION

For me, Upkar Aurora's comments reinforce themes that are central to the current relationship between business and social change. Deploying capital for the purpose of social change depends on leaders who understand the importance of a long-term commitment to creating value and creating change. It is also essential to believe that innovation is important and have a culture in which it can flourish. One of the best ways for businesses to improve their reputations is to invest in areas that aren't seen as core to the business itself, such as social change. Much of what's currently done is an exercise in optics and checkboxes rather than a genuine belief that investing in change is the right thing to do and that doing this will contribute to long-term value — for business and for society.

For corporations that have the right mix of values, belief, innovation, and money, there are a number of ways to consider mobilizing capital that creates Change for Good. *Investing with Purpose,*[10] a 2016 report by

CECP, includes six approaches of how companies are involved in impact investing, along with examples of each:

1. **Direct Investments**: when a company provides funds from its own balance sheet for a social enterprise, such as the acquisition of Plum Organics by the Campbell Soup Company.[11]

2. **Self-Managed Funds**: when a company creates a captive fund or investment company, such as Cisco Ventures' investment in Husk Power Systems, a company that turns rice husks into energy.[12]

3. **Third-Party Funds**: when a company makes investments through a syndicate or a fund as a limited partner, such as how Johnson & Johnson Consumer Health, Keurig Dr. Pepper, PepsiCo, Procter & Gamble, Unilever, and the Walmart Foundation contributed $54 million to the Closed Loop Fund to fund recycling technology.[13]

4. **Strategic Alliances**: when two companies join together for strategic non-financial partnerships and/or joint ventures with social enterprises. One example includes Vodafone and Roshan, Afghanistan's largest telecommunications provider, an alliance that involved a profit-share model to use the mobile payment platform M-PAiSA.[14]

5. **Accelerators and Incubators**: when a company provides support (such as mentorship, office space, technical support, or access to funding networks) for a specific project or a new venture. AT&T's investment in technology business accelerator Aspire is a good example.[15]

6. **Corporate Foundations**: when the charitable foundation of a company provides program-related investments including loans, loan guarantees, or equity investments to an organization.

A 2016 report from Corporate Citizenship found that one
in five corporate foundations are using impact investing.[16]
In 2017, the IKEA Foundation launched a partnership with
Reach for Change to entrepreneurs in Ethiopia to develop
social enterprises that will improve the health, education, and
protection of children.[17]

TAKING A BLENDED APPROACH

One recent example of a self-managed fund is from TELUS, a Canadian
communications and information technology company with a social
purpose to connect all Canadians for good. Its philosophy to "give where
we live" has inspired its team members and retirees to contribute $736
million and 1.4 million days of service since 2000. According to the company, this unprecedented generosity and unparalleled volunteerism have
made TELUS the most giving company in the world.[18] In November
2020, the company launched the TELUS Pollinator Fund for Good,
a $100 million self-managed social impact investment fund to help
entrepreneurs build solutions to improve healthcare, foster social and
economic inclusion, increase responsible agriculture, and reduce climate
change — all Sustainable Development Goals.

In March 2021, the Pollinator Fund announced a partnership with
Vancouver-based Raven Indigenous Capital Partners, an Indigenous-led
and -owned social finance intermediary. Raven's objective is to create
a positive, lasting impact on the Indigenous and Canadian economies
by accelerating the success of Indigenous enterprises and social purpose
organizations. They do this by providing access to capital and technical assistance within an Indigenous cultural framework. Together, the
TELUS Pollinator Fund for Good and Raven are addressing one of
the most pressing issues facing Indigenous communities across Canada,
and one that IBC is addressing through developmental lending in
Alberta — lack of access to capital.

The $25 million Raven Impact Investment Fund was launched in
response to the resource gap faced by many Indigenous entrepreneurs.

The fund is designed to provide capital to seed and/or early-stage Indigenous enterprises that are innovative, scalable, and purpose-driven. These enterprises are screened through a unique Indigenous-impact lens and receive investments ranging from $250,000 to $2 million. Through these investments, the Raven fund aims to contribute to the development of an Indigenous middle class by reducing poverty and strengthening community resilience. For investors, the fund targets a net annualized rate of return of 6–8% over a 10-year fund life.

"At Raven, we are actively transforming the relationship many of us have with money. Instead of symbolizing power, we want the role of money to be similar to love or medicine," said Jeffrey Cyr, managing partner of Raven Indigenous Capital Partners. "When we treat money differently, it sets us on a path of healing and provides an opportunity to tap the emerging Indigenous entrepreneurial market."[19]

By creating the Pollinator Fund and partnering with organizations such as Raven, TELUS is leveraging its social purpose in a way that is mobilizing more change and creating an opportunity to generate a profit. The telecommunications company is also maintaining its existing commitment to corporate philanthropy and volunteerism and living up to its promise to "build a better future for all Canadians by using our technology for good and giving back to our communities."[20]

I think more large corporations will begin to emulate the blended approach that TELUS has developed, combining internal expertise, philanthropy, and impact investing. There's also a largely untapped opportunity for corporations to partner with the small and medium-sized businesses in their supply chains. By providing suppliers with capital for growth in the form of loans or equity investments, along with business and social change expertise, corporations can amplify their social purpose by improving diversity hiring and fostering innovation. I also suggest that corporations engage their suppliers in helping to inform and distribute philanthropic donations at a local level. By doing this, corporations will help their suppliers build a social license in their communities and improve hiring and retention. That adds up to better relationships with suppliers and more Change for Good.

CHAPTER 8

Change for Good Experience

I've never been without a home, never been in poverty, and never experienced hunger. And during more than 20 years spent in boardrooms with people who want their companies to make a bigger difference in the world, there has never been a time that a person who is experiencing these issues was involved. I think this is why corporations, and the experts who help them, have been largely ineffective in solving social problems.

This shouldn't be surprising. After all, why would a privileged, educated person be qualified to develop a solution to something they've never actually experienced? What is most surprising is that the people best able to solve these social problems are people who have been left out. "History illuminates the power of individuals and communities who have worked to solve the social problems they have directly experienced," says Baljeet Sandhu, a human rights lawyer and founding director of the Migrant and Refugee Children's Legal Unit.[1]

Why should corporations include people with lived experience in developing programs that impact their lives? What examples from other sectors can we learn from? How can companies help people with lived experience become social change leaders? How can corporations take action in a way that's effective *and* practical? I'll be exploring these questions in this chapter and sharing an approach to help businesses involve people with lived experience in the design, implementation, and evaluation of all social change programs.

NOTHING ABOUT US WITHOUT US

The *Oxford Dictionary* defines "lived experience" as any "personal knowledge about the world gained through direct, first-hand involvement in everyday events rather than through representations constructed by other people." The women's rights movement, the civil rights movement, Alcoholics Anonymous, and the world's first safe house for women and children (Refuge) are all examples of effective social change that was led by people with lived experience of these issues.

The expression "Nothing about us without us" conveys the essence of the "principle of participation," which advocates for the active participation of people with a lived experience of a health or social condition in the development of research, policy, and programs and services that impact their lives.[2] Sherry Arnstein's 1969 paper "A Ladder of Citizen Participation" is an important reference point for the rationale and methods of encouraging participation of people with lived experience. The ladder is a guide to seeing who has power when important decisions are being made, and it continues to be relevant because too many decisions are made in ways that don't reflect the input of people with lived experience.

Below are Arnstein's eight levels, starting with non-participation (where the power holders maintain all control) and ending with active participation (in which citizens have control). Her model remains the basis for many current approaches to engaging people with lived experience in the development of programs that are intended to help them.[3]

1. **Manipulation and 2. Therapy**: Both are non-participative. The aim is to cure or educate the participants. The proposed plan is best, and the job of participation is to achieve public support by public relations.

3. **Informing**: A most important first step to legitimate participation. But too frequently, the emphasis is on a one-way flow of information without a channel for feedback.

4. **Consultation:** A legitimate step towards inclusion that involves surveys, neighbourhood meetings, and public enquiries.

5. **Placation:** For example, co-option of hand-picked "worthies" onto committees. It allows citizens to advise or plan, but retains for power holders the right to judge the legitimacy or feasibility of the advice.

6. **Partnership:** Power is redistributed through negotiation between citizens and power holders. Planning and decision-making responsibilities are shared, such as through joint committees.

7. **Delegated power:** Citizens holding a clear majority of seats on committees with delegated powers to make decisions. Public now has the power to assure accountability of the program to them.

8. **Citizen Control:** Have-nots handle the entire job of planning, policy-making, and managing a program, such as a neighbourhood corporation with no intermediaries between it and the source of funds.

Until recently, involving people with lived experience in the development of social change programs has been almost exclusively limited to civil society organizations. The ways in which this has been done include participation on advisory committees, co-design of programs, inclusion in focus groups and surveys, involvement in peer-to-peer programs, and the development of tools to help guide personal treatment or life choice decisions.

The Canadian Association of People Who Use Drugs is an organization that aims to raise the voice of people who use drugs throughout the policy-making process and at every level of government. "Nothing about us without us" is their guiding principle, and their board of directors is composed entirely of people with lived experience of drug use.

The organization's 2014 report, *Collective Voices, Effecting Change*, highlights key issues for people who use drugs in Canada, current actions by peer-run organizations of people who use drugs, and what the organization's plans are to address these issues.[4] Along the same lines, the British Columbia Centre for Disease Control's Peer Engagement and Evaluation Project[5] creates opportunities for people with lived experience of substance use to engage as experts and use their lived experience to inform effective health service programming and delivery.

In the private sector, the model has been what I describe as "about us, without us." In doing research for this book, I couldn't find a single example of a business that has adopted the approach of involving people with lived experience, and it's safe to assume that virtually no businesses are actively involving people with lived experience — or the few that are, do not believe it's important enough to communicate. However, the lack of "first voices" limits the effectiveness of these corporations' social change initiatives and deprives them of other benefits, including increased legitimacy and authenticity, improved program efficacy, and innovation and enhanced ability to build social change partnerships.[6]

The closest that businesses have gotten to this level of involvement is establishing advisory groups to help inform decision-making with respect to corporate social responsibility programs and community investments. For example, a number of years ago, there was the Barrick Gold Corporation's Corporate Social Responsibility Advisory Board — this was first time I can remember a business engaging external experts in this area. This impressive group included Aron Cramer, president and CEO of Business for Social Responsibility; Elizabeth Dowdeswell, president and CEO of the Council of Canadian Academies; Robert Fowler, diplomat and Canada's longest-serving ambassador to the United Nations; Ed Liebow, director of the Battelle Memorial Institute's Center for Public Health Research and Evaluation; and Gare Smith, senior partner at Foley Hoag LLP.

More recently, Mitsubishi Corporation established a Sustainability Advisory Committee composed of external experts representing diverse stakeholder groups including non-governmental organizations, international agencies, ESG (environment, social, and governance) investors, and academia. The corporation's objective with this group is to improve stakeholder engagement and receive advice and recommendations related to a variety of topics including supply chain management and climate change. Mitsubishi also conducts tours of business sites for committee members to deepen their understanding of the company's businesses.

In 2019, Prada established a Diversity and Inclusion Advisory Council for the purpose of elevating voices of colour within the company and the fashion industry and to provide advice as it invests in diverse talent development and expands opportunities for students in the fashion industry. Prada's Diversity and Inclusion Advisory Council members include artist and activist Theaster Gates; director and producer Ava DuVernay; Fashion Institute of Technology president Joyce F. Brown; humanitarian and chief of strategic partnerships at the United Nations Population Fund Mariarosa Cutillo; and associate professor of history of art and architecture and African and African American Studies at Harvard University Sarah Lewis.

And Tata Steel has a CSR Advisory Council composed of "eminent personalities from academia and the development sector." Members of Tata's CSR Advisory Council "provide macro policy-level inputs to the apex CSR and Sustainability Committee and guide the Company's approach towards CSR."[7]

It makes good sense to have external input from experts in related fields, and I'm sure that these corporations are benefiting in many positive ways from these advisory groups. Some of these benefits include gaining a "social license to operate," instilling confidence among investors, establishing a degree of credibility with employees, and gaining support in communities where these companies do business.

THE NEED FOR A NEW PERSPECTIVE

My discovery of why lived experience is so important and what the benefits are of involving those with lived experience happened inadvertently.

In 2015, when our team at impakt was helping the Home Depot Canada Foundation to develop its social change focus of helping to end youth homelessness, we learned from experts in the homelessness sector, and from people who had themselves experienced homelessness, that access to employment was key to ensuring people had stable housing. We also learned that most youth-serving organizations in Canada offered "pre-employment" training to youth and that, despite a well-documented shortage of labour for entry-level positions in large corporations, very few of these youth were able to secure employment.

This discovery led us to develop HireUp, what I believe was the world's first platform to connect youth with lived experience of homelessness to entry-level positions in corporations. I remember realizing at the time that I had made a commitment to help change the lives of youth through employment but no one on our team had ever experienced homelessness or unemployment. How could we develop an innovative response to this important problem without any direct experience?

We reached out to the Yonge Street Mission in Toronto for their help in finding a youth with lived experience of homelessness who could help us build HireUp. We had the very good fortune of hiring a young man named Cameron, who was still experiencing homelessness at the time he joined our team. Cameron was instrumental in helping us build HireUp and help to connect youth to entry-level positions at companies including Home Depot Canada, Walmart Canada, and Scotiabank. During the two years he worked for impakt, Cameron was able to secure stable housing and enrol in university.

It was the first time I realized that we had never involved people with lived experience in the development of social impact programs for our corporate clients. Beyond our work, I wasn't aware of any other corporation that had done this. Across the board, corporate investments in social change were being led by people who had never experienced any of the social problems they were trying to address.

It's not hard to see why this was the case. Try to imagine a large corporation inviting a group of people experiencing homelessness into their boardroom to hear about their lives. It's equally unlikely that most corporate executives would visit a settlement organization to speak with refugees about the challenges they face in finding employment and ensuring their families are secure. How about asking young people with alcohol and drug dependencies to decide what youth-serving organizations should receive grants?

A few years ago, we convened a group of youth who'd experienced homelessness to help allocate $400,000 in charitable grants to youth-serving organizations. This involved a remarkable session in a downtown social service organization where these youth reviewed applications for funding from a variety of community organizations. The questions they asked about these groups really showed the importance of their perspective. Their questions included asking if the organizations applying for funding included the youth they were serving in developing the programs. They also asked very specific questions about how the proposed funding would be used, which revealed their experience of seeing funding that was often misdirected to initiatives that didn't deliver enough impact.

More recently, we had a group of executives from Canada's largest oil and gas corporation participate in a series of presentations from potential community partners at a social enterprise restaurant and catering company in downtown Toronto. It was clear that this experience contributed to the executives' understanding of these organizations in a way that would never have happened in one of their boardrooms.

All that being said, there are many reasons why people with lived experience are left with the last voice or no voice at all in business decisions that impact their lives. Here are a few of those reasons:

- **It takes time to involve people with lived experience.** Businesses need to identify community organizations that exist to support vulnerable populations, meet with people who could participate and, over time, establish their trust.

- **There is always an eye on the bottom line.** As some businesses become increasingly focused on what Roger Martin, former dean of the Rotman School of Management at the University of Toronto, has called "quarterly capitalism,"[8] managers in these companies are incentivized to improve the bottom line in the very short term. Because there is no "business case" for engaging people with lived experience, managers do not make this a priority.

- **We are all biased.** Involving people with lived experience also means overcoming the entrenched biases that exist about people with different life experiences: they aren't smart enough, they are dangerous, or their vulnerable situation is a choice rather than a result of circumstances beyond their control.

- **Systemic racism remains an important reason why some people are not included.** Some white business leaders regard many racialized people as recipients of social services and philanthropic support rather than having any material value to their company's bottom line.

- **Vulnerable people face multiple barriers.** There are also practical issues that most corporations haven't had experience with, such as the need to provide transportation for people without cars or money for transit fare and the need for daycare that some parents require.

- **Real, meaningful change isn't always the goal.** In spite of the fact that virtually every large corporation has made a commitment to corporate social responsibility, this remains a largely superficial, check-the-box activity. The number of corporations that want to help solve social problems in a substantive way is few and far between.

- **Most business decisions are made based on some degree of external validation.** In this case, involving people with lived experience has been done so rarely that there's no base of evidence from other businesses that this is worth doing.

• **Including people with lived experience is something that simply never occurs to people in business.** Surprisingly, even people who work in civil society organizations don't understand why this is so important and how doing so would help to accelerate social change.

PRINCIPLES FOR EQUITABLE REPRESENTATION

In 2019, I was invited to be a speaker at the Canadian Partnership Conference in Toronto. For the first time in Canada, a group of corporate social change leaders and charitable sector leaders came together to discuss how to build and improve social change partnerships. I started my presentation by asking the group who was missing in the audience. Some people suggested that perhaps the university sector hadn't been included. Others thought that international development organizations weren't present. No one recognized the irony that there was a complete absence of the people we were there to help. An important event like this could have involved people with lived experience in the development of the program and as participants alongside people from the corporate and charitable sectors in the presentations.

What can we learn from how this is being done in other areas and, most importantly, from people with lived experience themselves? During the 2014 Canadian Alliance to End Homelessness conference in Vancouver, the Lived Experience Advisory Council came together with a common goal: to ensure that people with lived experience received equitable representation from service providers, researchers, policymakers, and others, so that they can better understand and tackle the problem of homelessness.

The group's first action was to articulate principles for the inclusion and leadership of people with lived experience in organizations and initiatives that aim to address homelessness.[9] The principles they developed included:

1. **Bring the perspective of lived experience to the forefront.**
   This principle recognizes that, as found by members of the
   Lived Experience Advisory Council, many years of top-down
   research, service provision, and policy-making have not ended
   homelessness and that this will only be possible if the priorities
   and insights of people who have experienced homelessness are
   recognized.

2. **Include people with lived experience at all levels of the
   organization.** People with lived experience are typically
   the recipients of social services or the subjects of research.
   Transformational change is only possible if people with lived
   experience are included at all levels.

3. **Value participants' time and provide appropriate supports.**
   People with lived experience who are providing valuable
   input to organizations deserve to be compensated for their
   time — like anyone else. In addition, other supports that may
   be needed include training, barrier-free access, childcare, and
   transit fare.

IMPROVE YOUR IMPACT: HOW TO TAKE ACTION

I think the Lived Experience Advisory Council's ideas are the foundation for a new approach that businesses can take to improve the impact of their investments in social change. I've developed a tool that is based on input from people with lived experience and impakt's work in developing social change programs that businesses can use to improve the social impact of their community programs.

	Typical Business Practices	Additional Actions to Involve People with Lived Experience
Selection of social issue focus	1. Leadership decides. 2. Anecdotal understanding of issue by business executives and managers. 3. Modest secondary research: done by corporate social responsibility (CSR) managers.	Business leaders and CSR managers obtain first-hand understanding by visiting community organizations.
Social program planning	1. Initial plans developed by CSR managers with internal business support and/or external consulting support. 2. Plans shared with executives for feedback and approval.	1. Formation of a social change advisory group composed of business managers and issues experts (academic, leaders of community organizations, and people with lived experience) to inform program planning and development of social change objectives and measures of success. 2. Develop theory of change with input of advisory group.
Implementation	1. Internal: CSR department with support from branding/marketing and/or human resources. 2. External: advertising agency, PR agency, social change agency, managers from community partner organizations.	1. Continue involvement of social change advisory group to inform all program implementation. 2. Create opportunities for people with lived experience to participate in selecting community partners and developing materials (e.g., videos, website, local community communications). 3. Involve advisory group or others with lived experience in evaluation of funding requests and selection of grantees.
Evaluation	1. Anecdotal. 2. Reports provided by community partners. 3. Media/social media coverage.	Advisory council and/or others with lived experience assess program results against pre-established social change objectives and measures of success.

Figure 8.1 Ways to improve impact by involving people with lived experience. (Source: impakt)

There are a number of considerations that are necessary throughout the steps outlined above. The following list will help ensure these are in place and that businesses and their partners with lived experience are set up for success.

1. **Build trust with lived experience experts:**

   - Understand each individual's strengths and personalities, and don't push them out of their comfort zone. Some people might be willing to speak openly in a meeting or on camera/video, but others may not.

   - Assign one corporate social responsibility manager to be the principal liaison with participants with lived experience — at and in between meetings.

2. **Ensure adequate briefing and training before your project begins:**

   - Provide communication skills, such as media training, to help them talk to people in their communities and gather feedback, and training to understand business and other language that may be unfamiliar to them.

   - Offer briefings prior to meetings to ensure full participation and to help people become familiar with the agenda, meeting protocol, and documents for review.

   - Provide use of and access to technology. Ensure that experts with lived experience have the necessary resources to participate — like a phone plan with data, a laptop, or a tablet to use for the duration of the process.

   - Be sensitive to dress and attire. It can be difficult for those who've never worn a suit to meet with people in suits.

3. **Offer necessary support to ensure participants can actually be involved in the program:**

   - Ensure meetings take place at accessible locations and provide transportation or transit/taxi fare if required. Provide adequate notice for meetings.

   - Provide funds for childcare for parents who need it so that they can attend program meetings and events without worry.

   - Share agendas or other written documents in advance of meetings to allow experts with lived experience enough time to read them.

   - Pre-pay for hotels and flights if needed, and provide cash or gift cards for meals.

   - Provide compensation equivalent to what would be provided to any external consultant/advisor.

The ideas above will help ensure businesses can meaningfully engage experts with lived experience in tackling issues of social change in a way that will build trust, is sensitive to their priorities and circumstances, and will make corporate leaders and managers feel comfortable.

THE VALUE OF LIVED EXPERIENCE

Involving experts with lived experience isn't necessarily easy. However, the personal, business and societal benefits of doing this are always rewarding. I think involving people with lived experience is core to what it means to Change for Good. I also believe that the reason most corporate social change programs don't work well enough is that these companies aren't involving people with lived experience in developing solutions to problems that affect them.

When I was at the annual conference of the Canadian Alliance to End Homelessness a few years ago, I heard a story I'll never forget. A professor from the University of Calgary was collecting data about homelessness during the worst part of the winter. (For people who haven't been in Calgary during the winter, it sometimes gets so cold that even cars with block heaters won't start.) This involved walking downtown and speaking with people who lived on the street and making notes about their lived experiences. This particular night was cold enough for his pen to freeze, so he kept a number of back-up pens inside his jacket to use when the first pen stopped working. This happened while he was speaking to one of the people on the street. The person asked the professor if he ever tried using a pencil.

Change for Good can only happen when people with lived experience are involved in all aspects of corporate social change programs. Making that happen actually starts on the inside. By creating meaningful employment for vulnerable populations, corporations are creating social change by improving the lives of people who can also contribute to the success of their businesses.

CHAPTER 9

Change for Good Jobs

I founded the Impakt Foundation for Social Change to formalize the work that impakt had already been doing with clients and on our own to develop initiatives that create employment for vulnerable people. Our foundation was established with a mission to create pathways to employment for people in need, and our first priority was to help address the employment needs of refugees and other people new to Canada — specifically by connecting them to good jobs in the apparel industry, a sector that had a shortage of labour and a long history of being a source of employment for newcomers.

When the Impakt Foundation was ready to hire its first executive director, we decided that it would be important to hire someone with lived experience of being a newcomer to Canada. We posted the job description on a platform called CharityVillage, which is an important resource for those looking for jobs in the non-profit sector. We also tapped into the network of an organization called Jumpstart Refugee Talent, which supports the employment needs of refugees. We were overwhelmed with applications, many of which came from people with the experience we were looking for and a few were also newcomers.

In the end, we had two very promising candidates and asked each to prepare and present a plan for their first 90 days as executive director. One of our candidates had deep experience in the social sector, lots of connections with potential funders, and a perfect plan. There was every reason to hire this person. The other candidate was a newcomer who had come to Canada as a refugee. She had work experience in Nigeria, a great education, and an excellent plan for her first three months with us. However, she hadn't had as much experience in the business and charitable sector in Canada as the other candidate. We hired her.

It goes without saying that corporations need to put a much bigger priority on diversity and inclusion in all aspects of business and to do this in a way that reflects the perspectives and needs of racialized people and communities. In my experience working with hundreds of corporations and charitable organizations, I've found a consistent lack of diversity in both groups.

Beyond being the right thing to do in terms of the moral argument for social responsibility, there is so much evidence of the business value of diversity. Yet, like other aspects of business and social change, progress in this area isn't nearly adequate and there is an urgent need for change. I also think the value of having a good job as a driver of social change is rarely considered. For me, some of the most important questions businesses can ask include: In what ways does employing people contribute to social change in terms of better education for their children, in terms of reducing domestic abuse, and in terms of improving health and wellness?

In this chapter, I'll be exploring why we need more diversity in business and why hiring people in need is one of the most important things corporations can do to Change for Good. I'll review why diversity and inclusion is a moral imperative and a civic responsibility as well as a business advantage. (However, similar to many aspects of business and social change, and despite an unprecedented growth in awareness of why diversity and inclusion are so important, even some of the world's biggest brands are far behind where they need to be in this area.) I'll also share how businesses can help solve social problems, and benefit from doing so, by hiring people who face barriers to employment because of vulnerabilities including socio-economic status, level of education, or status as a newcomer or refugee. Based on my experience, I've also developed a new Change for Good road map, to help business take action.

THE CASE FOR DIVERSITY AND INCLUSION

In early 2021, Nike announced a five-year plan to achieve 29 targets in five priority areas: investing in employees, water conservation, reducing its carbon footprint, education, and the Black community. Some of these targets include ensuring 50 percent representation of women in its global corporate workforce, ensuring 35 percent representation of racial and ethnic minorities in its US corporate workforce, ensuring that 100 percent of women in its supply chain have increased access to career opportunities, and investing $125 million to support organizations that are levelling the playing field and addressing racial inequality.[1] Part of Nike's investment in the Black community included a new partnership with National Urban League in support of its Urban Reentry Jobs Program, which helps formerly incarcerated people find sustained employment, and Home Is Where the Wealth Is, a campaign that helps expand first-time home ownership opportunities for Black Americans through financial education and individualized coaching.[2]

The company's 2020 targets are focused on three areas of impact: sustainability, including its environmental footprint and social/labor standards in its supply chain community investments, particularly investments made in getting kids active; and in diversity and inclusion. Nike's target in this area is to "attract and develop an increasingly diverse, engaged, and healthy workforce." Specific metrics of performance include providing visibility to the company's diversity and inclusion progress; investing in employees through growth and development; implementing well-being initiatives; and providing comprehensive, competitive, and equitable pay and benefits.[3]

A closer look at Nike's 2020 *Impact Report* reveals a company that it is far behind where it should be. The report's 2020 Target Summary does not contain any metrics whatsoever about diversity and inclusion. In other areas (manufacturing, product, materials, carbon and energy, water, and chemistry), the report includes specifics for targets met, substantial progress, and targets not met. Beyond these, the metric for community impact is "Annual Investments as % of Pre-Tax Income." In this area, Nike continued to invest 1.9 percent of its pre-tax income in the community.

As I write this, there is only one Black man and one Black woman on Nike's 13-member board of directors. There is not a single Black person among the five people on the company's senior leadership team. An important part of Nike's new plan is that it will be starting to tie executive compensation to achieving diversity targets. Unless they have a very low target, it doesn't look like these executives will be up for any raises for some time.

Why are so many companies so far behind in this area? To what degree does diversity at the most senior level contribute to diversity throughout a business? What will it take for more companies to take action in an area that is so fundamental to what it means to be "responsible" today?

The evidence is clear: consumers expect businesses to take a stand on social issues and make a positive contribution to society. Edelman's *Earned Brand 2018* report showed that 64 percent of consumers would reward firms that they see as engaged in some kind of activism.[4] The firm's *Special Report: Brand Trust in 2020* showed that 80 percent of people believe solving society's problems matters most for brands today and 60 percent believe that brands should invest in addressing the root causes of racial inequality.[5] It's also clear that Nike isn't an outlier: as of 2020, only four out of America's five hundred biggest companies had a Black chief executive.[6]

Too much of what we've seen in this space is "hashtag activism," but making real change involves more than hashtags. Pepper Miller, who is the author of *Black "Still" Matters in Marketing* and co-author of *What's Black About It?*, has doubts about the latest surge in brand activism. "Companies need to draw long-term plans for social inclusion and racial equality that go beyond them saying that they 'stand with black people,'" Miller says. "Experience, however, tells me that's not the case. Most initiatives are one-offs."[7]

Edelman's *Special Report: Brand Trust in 2020* revealed that 47 percent of people's trust in brands depends on how they respond to racial injustice by setting an example within their organizations. It also showed that 63 percent of consumers believe brands and companies that issue a statement in support of racial equality need to follow it up with concrete action to avoid being seen as exploitative or as opportunists.

Ironically, I've also noticed a remarkable lack of diversity in social change organizations themselves. Mide Akerewusi, who is the founder and CEO of AgentsC, a non-profit consulting firm that helps organizations around the world improve how they contribute to solving SDGs, is doing important work to understand the lack of diversity in the social sector and develop new approaches to addressing this gap. In 2020, AgentsC held an Equity Summit to address the non-profit sector's systematic exclusion of Black and Indigenous people and people of colour (BIPOC). Their experience and research contributed to the development of an Equity Charter for this sector that lays out five critical starting points: strengthening the competencies of boards and increasing BIPOC representation, implementing fair and transparent recruitment and retention measures for staff and boards, establishing best practices for culturally appropriate communications and marketing standards, achieving equitable philanthropy for societal priorities and community-based non-profits, and research to gain more knowledge about the experiences and roles of BIPOC in non-profit organizations.[8]

For me, real change in this area for organizations in all sectors, needs to start with the second point of AgentsC's Equity Charter: implementing fair and transparent recruitment and retention measures. A few years ago, the CEO of a global company invited me to participate in a full-day session with its leaders and many of its most important stakeholders. One of the company's stated priorities was to increase the number of women in senior leadership positions to 30 percent over five years. A number of people from outside the company actually started laughing at the notion that the company's target was only 30 percent and that it would take *five* years to achieve this inadequate target.

Similar to every aspect of the relationship between business and social change, there is a clear case for why companies should put a priority on diversity. Here are two key proof points that demonstrate that companies with diverse workplaces are seen as more desirable employers, outperform competitors, and achieve greater profits:

1. **Better outcomes:** A Boston Consulting Group survey found that that increasing the diversity of leadership teams leads to more and better innovation and 19 percent higher revenue. Their research revealed that people with different backgrounds and experiences often see the same problem in different ways and come up with different solutions, increasing the odds that one of those solutions will be successful.[9]

2. **Increased performance:** In *Diversity Wins: How Inclusion Matters*,[10] a McKinsey study of more than one thousand companies in 15 countries, the firm found that companies with gender diversity and ethnic and cultural diversity are now more likely than ever to outperform less-diverse peers on profitability. The firm's 2019 analysis found that companies in the top quartile for gender diversity on executive teams were 25 percent more likely to have above-average profitability than companies in the fourth quartile — up from 21 percent in 2017. The McKinsey study also found that more is better: the higher the percentage of women executives, the more likely they were to outperform their competitors.

In the case of ethnic and cultural diversity, McKinsey found that the likelihood of outperformance is higher for diversity in ethnicity than for gender. Despite this, they report that progress in this area has been slow. Across a global data set that began tracking performance in 2017, gender diversity increased by only one percentage point — to 15 percent, from 14 — in 2019, and more than a third of the companies in McKinsey's data have no women at all on their executive teams. Similarly, the representation of ethnic minorities on UK and US executive teams was 14 percent in 2019, up from 12 percent in 2017. McKinsey reports that lack of material progress is consistent across all industries and in most countries.[11]

Diversity in business involves more than just change in the boardroom and in the head office. It also involves more than gender, race, and ethnicity. To move past the optics and hashtag activism, businesses need to build diverse and inclusive workplaces — at all levels. That means embracing the value and perspectives of employees with diverse religious and political beliefs, education, socio-economic backgrounds, sexual orientation, cultures, and those with disabilities. Again, this is not just a moral imperative, it's also very good for business.

A few years ago, I had the opportunity to visit the Xerox Research Centre of Canada (XRCC). The leader of XRCC was a scientist from the Persian Gulf region who told me that he hired scientists for the centre specifically based on diversity. According to him, it was because of this that XRCC was able to develop approximately 360 new patents every year — one per day. His experience is backed up by the findings of the *2018 Hays Asia Diversity and Inclusion Report*, which identified the top three benefits of diversity to be improved company culture, leadership, and greater innovation.[12] (The report also indicates that a significant proportion of respondents believe that factors including age, disability, ethnicity, gender, family commitments, marital status, race, religion, and sexuality could hamper access to pay, jobs, and career opportunities for those of equal ability.)

It is estimated that by the year 2025, 75 percent of the global workforce will be made up of millennials.[13] As people in this group become leaders, they will bring new perspectives on diversity to all important decisions regarding how businesses impact people's lives — inside and outside the office. "Older generations tend to view diversity through the lenses of race, demographics, equality, and representation; millennials see diversity as a melding of varying experiences, different backgrounds and individual perspectives," said Peter Economy, author of *Wait, I'm the Boss?!?* "They view the ideal workplace as a supportive environment that gives space to varying perspectives on a given issue."[14]

THE SOCIAL VALUE OF HIRING VULNERABLE PEOPLE

It's equally important to look beyond the moral responsibility for businesses to be diverse and the benefits that doing so will bring to companies.

Change for Good also means understanding the impact that having a good job has on improving the lives of employees and their families — especially people who have been vulnerable.

The Tailor Project is one of the most remarkable examples of hiring being a tool for social change. In the years following World War II, people were aware of the Holocaust, yet anti-Semitism prevailed in many countries, including Canada. At the same time, Jews who had survived the Holocaust languished in displaced persons (DP) camps in Europe. In response, leaders of the Jewish community collaborated with executives from the apparel industry and labour unions to present the Canadian government with a proposal to address a labour shortage in the industry. Their proposal was approved by the government, and a team of apparel industry executives and labour leaders was sent to DP camps in Europe to find tailors and their families who could come to Canada with this program. Unlike programs for refugees today, the Tailor Project was successful because the survivors were provided with employment in the garment industry as soon as they arrived in Canada.

The business leaders who developed this program in 1947 believed that their businesses could contribute to social change, and benefit from doing so, by creating employment for these vulnerable people. They were right. In doing research for the Tailor Project book, we had the opportunity to meet many of the tailors and their families. These people came to Canada with no money, no understanding of English, and little to no education. But they had jobs, which helped them begin to overcome the challenge of restarting their lives in Canada and paved the way for their families to become settled and successful in this country.

Also during our research for the Tailor Project book, we had a close look at the situation for refugees and other newcomers to Canada today. We found their circumstances today to be similar to what the tailors and their families would have experienced in the years after they were brought to Canada from the DP camps; however, one of the primary differences is that most newcomers today do not have employment when they come to Canada.

Change for Good hiring puts a priority on increasing and improving diversity in the workforce at all levels. It also means understanding how employment itself contributes to social change for vulnerable people. Despite innovative examples such as the Tailor Project, there are very few businesses that consider the social value of hiring vulnerable people.

One example is Canada Sportswear, a Toronto family-owned apparel firm that was started by Charles Goldfinger, one of the Holocaust survivors who came to Canada with the Tailor Project in 1948. For the last number of years, Canada Sportswear has been run by Ralph's sons, who understand why it's so important to hire newcomers and other vulnerable people and have made this a priority in their business today.

UN Sustainable Development Goal number 1 is to end poverty in all its forms everywhere.[15] Achieving this goal will only be possible if more employers prioritize hiring workers who face more barriers than others. These groups include people living with disabilities, youth, LGBTQ+ people, Indigenous peoples, racialized minorities, immigrants, and those with low socio-economic status. (According to Arif Jetha, assistant professor at the University of Toronto's Dalla Lana School of Public Health, even when employed, these groups are more likely than population averages to earn lower incomes, experience hazardous working conditions, work precariously, have limited access to employment legislation or statutory benefits, and have fewer opportunities for career advancement.[16])

My own experience in developing social change programs designed to create jobs for vulnerable people and anecdotal observation show that this is something that corporations haven't addressed or have been reluctant to address. In researching this aspect of social change for this book, I discovered, not surprisingly, that it is an area that is underserved in terms of research and is lacking in best practices.

One source of data is the Law Commission of Ontario's publication "Quick Facts about Vulnerable Workers and Precarious Work."[17] This report indicates that economic factors, technology, global competition, and changes to the ways businesses are structured have contributed to the end of widespread full-time, secure work, where employees have access to good wages and benefits. (And this was prior to the impact of COVID-19.) In its place, precarious part-time, temporary, and casual forms of work have become increasingly common and "workers at the lower end of the wage and skill spectrum find themselves struggling to make a decent living, with few or no benefits, little job security and minimal control over their work conditions."

The Law Commission of Ontario report includes some of the most significant ways that precarious employment contributes to negative social outcomes.[18]

- Precarious work is more likely to involve health and safety risks, particularly for recent immigrants who are more likely than Canadian-born workers to be engaged in physically demanding work.

- Precarious work can cause significant stress due to job insecurity, the pressure of holding multiple jobs, irregular or long hours, insecure visa status and lack of legal protections.

- Precarious workers may also suffer health consequences as a result of their lower income.

- Low wages also affect workers' access to safe transportation and sufficiently nutritious food.

- Low pay often leads to working more than one job and long hours, which, in turn, increases susceptibility to illness and injury and has negative impacts on family life, affecting children and communities.

- Due to low wages and lack of benefits, precarious workers often have difficulty accessing medicine, particularly prescription drugs.

- Pregnant women engaged in precarious work are often not covered by statutory personal emergency leave provisions and, with insufficient time off, may not obtain necessary medical care.

- Precarious workers have limited opportunities to access training or education allowing them to upgrade their skills. Without training, they are less likely to find more stable and better paid work. This contributes to long-term economic vulnerability and perpetuates the cycle of precarious work.

An Impakt Foundation review of the employment for newcomers to Canada revealed that there are too many people without jobs at a time when there are also too many job vacancies. Despite their having similar or greater levels of educational attainment, the disparity between education and employment outcomes (like unemployment, underemployment, and wage gaps) persists for immigrants, particularly those from racialized backgrounds. And approximately three million immigrant youth and young people between 15 and 35 face employers' prejudice and discrimination. At the same time, up to 39 percent of small and medium-sized enterprises are having difficulty finding new employees[19] and only 11 percent of employers say they are taking full advantage of a diverse workforce, thinking how inclusion could help them to "innovate."[20]

There are a number of reasons that more employers don't hire vulnerable people. Some reasons are more general and related to a lack of awareness and understanding of how to recruit people with different lived experiences. Other employers have preconceptions, concerns, or biases related to specific populations such as people with disabilities, youth who've experienced homelessness, and newcomers.

While we were developing HireUp, we heard some interesting reasons from employers for not hiring youth with lived experience for entry-level jobs:

- Some employers didn't believe that youth who've experienced homelessness, many of whom have low levels of education, would have the right qualifications or the aptitude — even for entry-level employment.

- Employment managers questioned whether youth would even be interested in their job openings. Others were concerned that they would need a new HR process.

- Some had a policy not to hire anyone who had a criminal record and believed that if they hired youth who had experienced homelessness, these youth might be violent in the workplace. Related to this, managers told us that they wouldn't know what to do if the youth had a problem.

- Many HR managers were concerned that hiring youth who've experienced homelessness would have a negative impact on existing employees. There was a common view that youth would be unreliable. Managers weren't clear about what might happen if the employment relationship had to be ended.

- Some businesses actually thought it was illegal to hire people who had been homeless.

Some of what we discovered was validated in a recent YouGov poll of UK employers and employees, which found that 40 percent of employers did not know it was legal to hire someone who was homeless and nearly 17 percent were concerned that hiring someone who was homeless would have a negative impact on other employees.[21]

Needless to say, in our experience none of these concerns materialized and we were able to help youth secure entry-level jobs in large corporations including Scotiabank, Tim Hortons, TD, and Home Depot Canada among many others. I think there were a combination of reasons why we were able to convince these large, risk-averse corporations to hire youth who had been homeless. These include:

- We partnered with companies that had already decided hiring vulnerable people was important but didn't know how to do this or hadn't yet taken action.

- We targeted companies that saw hiring vulnerable youth as a way to demonstrate their broader commitment to corporate social responsibility.

- All our employer partners had human resource leaders who genuinely believed it was the right thing to do — not just checking a box on their list of diversity and inclusion priorities.

- We shared that impakt had already hired a youth who had experienced homelessness.

Beyond our direct experience with corporations who made hiring these vulnerable youth a priority, there is very little research to validate what we at impakt know to be true: there are benefits for companies that hire youth who have experienced homelessness.

I found a UK-based platform called Refreshing a Career that shared four reasons companies should hire people who've experienced homelessness.[22] Here's a summary of what they suggested:

1. **Recognition from the local community:** Businesses displaying a commitment to helping end the cycles of poverty that contribute to homelessness will be positively recognized by their customers.

2. **Loyalty and dedication:** Homeless or ex-homeless workers are significantly more loyal and dedicated than regular staff members. This will help businesses reduce their need to re-hire, which research suggests is one of the biggest unnecessary expenditures.

3. **Building inclusivity:** By hiring people in vulnerable situations, employees will appreciate their employers' commitment to being inclusive and overlooking stigmas. This means they will also become more loyal and dedicated to their jobs. (As described throughout this book, establishing your organization's Change for Good brand has to start from within.)

4. **Untapped talent:** There are thousands of homeless people who could have skills that companies need.

THE MANY BENEFITS OF DIVERSE HIRING

Companies that hire people with disabilities also benefit in many ways — some of which echo the business benefits of other aspects of social change programs. A 2018 University of Toronto study titled "A Systematic Review of the Benefits of Hiring People with Disabilities,"[23] revealed seven of these benefits:

- **Cost effectiveness:** For example, workplace accommodations for people with various types of disabilities helped to increase profits, especially through cost savings of not having to re-hire and re-train new workers.

- **Turnover and retention:** Employers reported that hiring people with disabilities improved retention and reduced turnover. For example, in one study on janitors with intellectual disabilities, employees had a significantly higher retention rate compared to workers without a disability.

- **Employee loyalty:** For example, employees with disabilities working in supermarkets were found to be more loyal than employees without disabilities. In the food service and leisure and hospitality industries, employers rated employees with disabilities most positively in terms of loyalty and punctuality.

- **Company image:** Research revealed that companies had an improved image as a result of hiring people with various types of disabilities. Employers who hired workers with hearing impairments in a coffee shop chain reported that this enhanced their image of caring and inclusivity. Similarly, hearing-impaired workers in the business process outsourcing (BPO) sector helped improve company image and corporate social responsibility.

- **Competitive advantage:** A survey of one hundred customers in the restaurant industry found that restaurants who hired people with vision impairments to be front-line employees gained a competitive advantage over establishments that did not. Another survey found a competitive advantage of including people with disabilities because it created a positive image for guests.

- **Diverse customers:** Employers noticed that more customers with disabilities began shopping at stores with employees who had disabilities. Related to this, employers recognized that people with disabilities represent an important customer base and that there is an opportunity for companies to win brand loyalty among a broad market of customers who value inclusion.

- **Innovation:** Research noted that companies that hire people with disabilities benefited through their ability to be innovative and creative. In the hospitality sector, employees with disabilities helped create innovative services.

Beyond the benefits to business are the ways that helping vulnerable people access good jobs contributes to improving their lives and the lives of their families. In other words, employing people with lived experience is one of the most direct social change actions a business can take. In their paper *The Social Value of a Job*,[24] Robert Quigley and James Baines map out the benefits of work for people and their families. Here's a summary of what they found:

- Money from jobs boosts living standards and provides a way out of poverty or a way to avoid poverty.

- Jobs improve our health and well-being and contribute to lower death rates, improved physical health, lower rates of chronic illness, and reduced use of medicine and the health care system.

- People who have jobs are less likely to be addicted to, or heavily use, tobacco, alcohol, and drugs.

- Jobs improve mental health, resulting in lower rates of death by suicide and from accidents, lower rates of depression and anxiety, and improve self-respect and self-esteem.

- People who have jobs contribute to making their children's lives better and healthier, and children demonstrate lowered rates of chronic illness, enhanced well-being, reduced delinquent behaviour, and improved future job prospects.

Added to this, in our work at impakt we've found that people with jobs are also much less likely to perpetrate family violence and be in the criminal justice system.

I find it so interesting that many of these positive outcomes are exactly what corporations identify as social issues that are priorities for support through corporate donations to charities or corporate social responsibility programs. Over the long term, if more businesses created more good jobs for vulnerable people, their need for supporting charities would diminish. And they'd be creating significant business value for their companies.

CREATING CHANGE FOR GOOD JOBS: HOW TO TAKE ACTION

There are two dimensions to Change for Good jobs: One aspect is the need for much more diversity in hiring and for much more inclusive workplaces. For more information on these important topics, I refer you to organizations such as McKinsey, Catalyst, and Deloitte. I also found the Forbes Insights Survey titled *Fostering Innovation Through a Diverse Workforce* to be a particularly valuable resource.[25] The other aspect is the need to help solve social problems such as homelessness, domestic violence, and low levels of educational attainment by hiring people from BIPOC and other vulnerable communities who are more likely to experience these problems.

The ways in which providing good jobs to vulnerable people benefits companies as well as vulnerable people needs be made more widely known. I've shared some of my own experiences in this area and some of the evidence from others that supports what we've found in creating employment programs for people with lived experience creating employment programs for people who have experienced homelessness or faced other systemic barriers to employment. I'm also happy to share some ideas that I hope will encourage and assist you in creating Change for Good jobs:

i. **Understand the perspectives of vulnerable people.**
   People with disabilities, those who have experienced homelessness, or people new to your country are most likely to have a very different idea about what having a job at your company looks like than you do. Similar to other aspects of Change for Good, the only way to move forward in this area is to meet people where they are. This involves taking the time to understand their previous experiences with employment and introducing them to the work culture and job position at your company.

2. **Tap into the experiences of executives.**

   During our work in creating jobs in large corporations for youth who'd experienced homelessness, we occasionally heard from people in these businesses, including executives, who shared that they had been homeless at an earlier time in their life. People like this with a shared experience have empathy for others and will often be interested in helping out. This may be at an executive level when decisions need to be made or among managers and employees who can participate in planning, act as mentors, or help to develop new programs that reflect their experiences.

3. **Co-create a Change for Good jobs program.**

   Building on what I've suggested above, you should review and revise the full spectrum of your recruitment, onboarding, and retention strategy to reflect the perspective of vulnerable people who could get jobs at your company. Specific pieces for review and input include messages and advertising on job boards, involvement of social service organizations that provide pre-employment and employment-finding services for people with lived experience, questions for job interviews, the onboarding experience, training, and job performance assessments. (We discovered some very basic things that impacted new recruits, including being unfamiliar with public transit, having to purchase work clothes in the two weeks before they received their first paycheque, and being unsure if they were allowed to go to a doctor's appointment.)

4. **Move slowly.**

   Contrary to what I suggested in Chapter 5 about wanting social change to happen more quickly, creating Change for Good jobs isn't easy and shouldn't necessarily happen quickly. It's also important to have the right expectations of timing and success. One time, an HR manager at one of Canada's largest companies told us that she urgently needed to find 12 people for one of their locations in Winnipeg. She told us that if we could provide youth for these jobs, they'd hire them right away. In fact, if we could find *anyone*, they would hire them immediately. I understood the pressure she was under to fill these positions quickly, but it was a signal that our program for transforming the lives of vulnerable youth wasn't a good fit for this company. If your approach is purely transactional, it's best to rely on Indeed or conventional hiring channels.

MORE THAN A QUOTA

Once we were meeting with a hiring manager at a large financial institution to assess their interest in hiring youth who had experienced homelessness. I asked him what his hiring objectives were for the year, and he shared he had a target to hire 24 Black youth. I was so shocked when he said this that I asked, "Did you actually say that you have a target of hiring 24 Black youth?"

I started imagining months of meetings with managers in this bank sitting in their head office trying to decide if they should hire Black youth, how many should be hired, what jobs they might be capable of doing, and where they would find these youth. Finally, somehow, they came to the conclusion that 24 was the right number and that this manager would be responsible for making that happen. They had no idea where to go from there. Perhaps the bigger problem here would have been for the bank to actually achieve their goal of hiring these Black youth without any understanding of what it might take to ensure that they were treated in a way that was fair and equitable.

Creating Change for Good jobs doesn't happen by setting arbitrary goals that aren't backed up with programs that give new hires the support they need to be successful. This bank would have fared much better to have engaged existing Black employees, Black community leaders, and Black youth themselves in helping to identify what jobs would be most suitable and what the best approach would be to hire, onboard, and retain these youth. Success in this area isn't about numbers or meeting quotas. Success happens when companies genuinely believe this is the right thing to do and then operationalize this belief with the input of people inside and outside the business who have lived experience.

Making Change for Good involves making meaningful change to people's lives. The best way to do that is by creating job opportunities and a context for employment that prioritizes marginalized people . The steps I've mapped out in this chapter for creating Change for Good jobs are a good beginning. Beyond this, companies need to expect the unexpected and be flexible and tolerant. One of the best young people we worked with when we developed HireUp came to me and said that he needed a police check before visiting an organization that supports youth who've experienced homelessness. He also said that this could be a problem for him and for us. We told him not to worry and that we'd support him regardless of the results.

CHAPTER 10

Change for Good. Good for Change.

Winston Churchill said you should never waste a good crisis. Since I started impakt in 2001, I've experienced what it's like to be in the "business" of social change during four crises that have had a profound impact on business and society: the Great Recession, the presidency of Donald Trump, the death of George Floyd at the hands of Minneapolis police officer Derek Chauvin, and most recently, the COVID-19 crisis.

What I've seen during each of these crises in terms of how businesses have done more and more towards solving social problems has amazed me. Some of the most important business responses to these crises include very rapid innovation and new approaches to solving problems, extraordinary examples of resiliency and commitment to employees and communities, more cooperation and collaboration, new regulations and policies, and the emergence of new leaders — people who are able to thrive in complex, rapidly evolving and stressful situations. I wrote this book during the novel coronavirus crisis — at a time when much of the progress towards achieving the UN SDGs was erased. Despite the daunting challenges that face the world as a result of the COVID-19, I've never felt such optimism for the potential to solve these problems. Complacent, risk-averse approaches to social change have given way to urgent, innovative action.

I think each of these four challenging crises in recent years have contributed to an increased understanding of the opportunities for businesses to address the problems that created these situations in the first place and help to solve the SDGs. Together, they've contributed to a new imperative for business in society — what I call Change for Good.

First is the Great Recession in 2008–09, which was caused by board-room capitalism in the financial sector. Decisions that were made for the sole purpose of benefiting directors, executives, and shareholders caused massive unemployment. This realization contributed to the existence of a more transparent and accountable form of capitalism that considers the priorities of all stakeholders, not just shareholders.[1]

Second, the presidency of Donald Trump polarized more than just the voting public. Issues that were found to be most polarizing during the Trump administration included abortion, anthem protesting, climate change, and immigration.[2] Many corporations were positioned on one side of the aisle or the other and, more than ever before, their leaders spoke out about where they stood on "hot button" issues, which influenced the decisions of their investors and the choices of consumers.

Third, the Black Lives Matter movement highlighted that many companies were contributing to the perpetuation of systemic racism, and it also created an opportunity for corporations to become advocates for change. This watershed movement was propelled by hashtag activism and, in many cases, by meaningful change in the corporate sector. Companies such as Citibank that were previously leery of taking a stand spoke up against racial injustice and police violence. In Canada, Wes Hall created the BlackNorth Initiative as a business solution to a social problem. The initiative aims to increase the representation of Black people on corporate boards and executive teams.[3]

Finally, the COVID-19 crisis led to people who were already vulnerable becoming even more vulnerable. It also caused people who hadn't been in need before the crisis to line up at food banks. The pandemic amplified the actions of corporations such as Ally Financial that went above and beyond to take care of their employees, and it also shone a light on corporations such as Cargill that were accused of putting their workers in danger. I think the degree to which corporations stepped up to address the needs of their employees and communities will contribute to them having a high level of trust and loyalty for a very long time.

Aspects of each of these illustrate the central paradox of business and social change — that corporations contribute to social problems and can help solve them. For me, they've also created a context for corporations to escape from the Twilight Zone of CSR Lite — to contribute to solving SDGs in ways that are seen as authentic and genuine and to benefit from doing so. In this chapter, I'll be exploring why these four turning points have contributed to a watershed moment for businesses to Change for Good. In each case, I'll share how businesses were complacent in these problems and also how the impact of each crisis contributed to a greater understanding of their social purpose and better approaches to solving social problems.

THE GREAT RECESSION OF 2008 AND CHANGE FOR GOOD GOVERNANCE

The Great Recession of 2008 affected our work at impakt in a very surprising way — it was the most successful year we'd had since I founded the company in 2001. I think one of the reasons for this is because it was so clear to employees, customers, governments, and investors that irresponsible and egregious actions in the financial services sector were responsible for the meltdown.

Milton Friedman's theory that companies fulfill their social responsibility by maximizing the return to their shareholders was proved to be wrong by the long list of companies that were taken over or merged with other institutions, nationalized by governments or central banks, or declared insolvent or liquidated. In the US, these included some of the sector's most venerable institutions including Lehman Brothers, Merrill Lynch, and Bear Sterns.[4]

The Great Recession revealed that the role of business wasn't just its ability to produce desirable products and services and make society stronger through paying taxes, creating a return for shareholders, and giving something back to communities; its role was to create stable, sustainable employment, and this is what was lost most during that time. What began with a crisis in the subprime housing market in the US turned into the most severe recession the world has encountered since the Great

Depression of the 1930s,[5] and the economic downturn led to a global jobs crisis. Global unemployment surged to over 200 million,[6] and it was estimated that 61 million fewer people were employed in 2014 than there would have been had pre-crisis employment growth rates continued.[7]

The rapid growth of artificial intelligence (AI) and other cost-saving technologies contributed to even more instability and uncertainty in the workforce. Was AI going to be a source of employment or unemployment? In 2018, the World Economic Forum estimated that by 2022, AI would create a net total of fifty-eight million new jobs and also displace or eliminate seventy-five million jobs.[8] The areas most impacted by job loss as a result of automation were predicted to be in manufacturing, agriculture, food service, retail, transportation and logistics, and hospitality. These are all areas that have traditionally been a source of employment for newcomers and other vulnerable populations.

Economists found that many of the jobs in these industries were eliminated by employers who used the recession as an opportunity to fire workers and invest in AI and other labour-saving technology.[9] Research has also revealed that employers increased skill requirements for job-vacancy postings in areas that were hit hardest by the recession.[10] By requiring potential employees to have a higher level of education for the same jobs, it effectively reduced the need for workers, created more opportunity for people with higher levels of education, and thereby increased income inequality. In the years following the Great Recession, global economies rebounded in many ways, but also left a world that is more unequal, poorer, and sicker than it would have been had the crisis been less severe.

Ironically, despite actions that I'd characterize as irresponsible and unethical, the "case" for corporate social responsibility had never been stronger. In an environment where cost cutting was ubiquitous, more companies began to recognize the value of maintaining a commitment to CSR.

Harvard Business School professor John Quelch has written extensively about the risks involved in cutting corporate responsibility budgets and the reasons why doing good is the right strategy, even when times are bad such as during a recession: Here's what Quelch said in a *Harvard Business Review* article titled "How Corporate Responsibility Can Survive the Recession"[11]:

1. Critical cross-border global issues require multinational corporations and their CEOs to lead in the search for solutions, recession or not.

2. Recession results in more poverty and exacerbates problems that national governments and NGOs alone cannot solve.

3. A global economic crisis increases distrust of business. Corporations with a strong commitment to corporate responsibility are better able to withstand the downdraft and put the brakes on increased regulation.

4. Employees are attracted to and motivated to stay with socially responsible companies, and want to see commitment to corporate responsibility initiatives continue through tough times.

5. An increasing proportion of consumers are willing to pay price premiums for products and services marketed by companies with proven and sustained track records of doing good.

After the Great Recession, we also began to understand that there are degrees of commitment to social change and that the relative value of social responsibility to business varies considerably. Quelch identified four progressive levels of CR commitment.[12] I've built on his ideas to reflect my experience:

- **Level 1:** Companies that consider corporate responsibility only in terms of corporate philanthropy derive very little value from this approach and have no hesitation reducing donations to charities during times that are challenging for their business.

- **Level 2:** Brands that have become associated with particular social causes and/or charitable organizations are unlikely to discontinue their support for social programs because doing so could result in reputational damage and lower sales. Quelch gives the example of the American Express Red card that donated a percentage of the value of card member purchases to the fight against AIDS. A more recent example is Bell Canada, which has been widely associated with mental health through its annual Bell Let's Talk campaign.

- **Level 3:** Companies that embed corporate social responsibility and sustainability in their daily operations see even more value in maintaining these investments. These include companies that require their suppliers to comply with specific environmental and labour practice standards. For example, Starbucks' commitment to purchasing fair trade coffee or Walmart's requirements for its suppliers to reduce packaging.

- **Level 4:** At the highest level are companies that have built social change into their corporate cultures, mission statements, and daily decision-making. The Johnson & Johnson credo puts the interests of customers, employees, and community ahead of those of shareholders. The priority that Erreka Group places on its people is a defining characteristic of who they are and what they believe in and is reflected in its structure, where most of its workers are also owners of the company.

In my experience, prior to the Great Recession the vast majority of companies practised corporate social responsibility through philanthropy. During the financial crisis, some of the companies maintained their donations to charity but many more reduced spending in this area. The very small number of companies (such as Erreka) that have social change embedded in everything they do continued as they were before the recession. (The list of companies that are seen as social purpose leaders has remained the same for years. I've conducted dozens of workshops where I've asked participants to make a list of 10 companies that they believe are the most socially responsible. Mostly, people provide two to three names and usually they're the same companies: Patagonia, TOMS, and Ben & Jerry's.)

The Great Recession was also a great reset. During that time, a great many people realized that the pursuit of socio-economic status through work had been a dead end and that the loyalty they had expected from their employers had evaporated. As jobs vaporized during the recession and in the years that followed, people's relationship with employment was upended. Work that had been a dependable source of income and a meaningful place of community for millions of people was lost. Even people who didn't lose their jobs during the Great Recession experienced an existential wake-up call. What really mattered? Who did they want to spend their time with? If work wasn't available, or dependable, what would their purpose be?

In terms of business and society, the most important learning from the Great Recession was that decisions that impacted the lives of hundreds of millions of people were being made for the sole benefit of quick returns for corporate directors, executives, and shareholders. Unbridled short-termism had lined the pockets of a handful of executives without any consideration of how this affected employees, customers, suppliers, the government, or the communities. This realization led to improved transparency and accountability in corporate boardrooms and an approach to governance that considers and balances the interests of all stakeholders.

In Germany, for example, management and supervisory boards are now accountable not just to shareholders, but also to stakeholders. In South Africa, stakeholder relationship governance and sustainability reporting are now explicit responsibilities of boards of directors. The country's *Corporate Governance and King III* report states: "Sustainability is the primary moral and economic imperative of the 21st century. It is one of the most important sources of both opportunities and risks for businesses. Nature, society, and business are interconnected in complex ways that should be understood by decision-makers. Most importantly, current incremental changes towards sustainability are not sufficient — we need a fundamental shift in the way companies and directors act and organize themselves."[13]

As I highlighted earlier in the book, in 2019, members of the Business Roundtable, a group of the world's most influential executives, issued a new statement on the purpose of a corporation, arguing that companies should no longer have an exclusive focus on the interests of their shareholders. Instead, they must also invest in their employees, protect the environment, and deal fairly and ethically with their suppliers.[14]

The degree to which corporations embrace and operationalize social change starts in the boardroom. The Great Recession shifted decision-making from being solely about profitability to reflecting the broader interests of society. Change for Good can only happen when the most influential decision-makers in a corporation understand that their business has purpose beyond making money and when their compensation reflects their ability to make a profit and help solve social problems.

THE TRUMP PRESIDENCY AND CHANGE FOR GOOD ACTIVISM

With respect to business and social change, Donald Trump created a new opportunity (perhaps even an imperative) for business leaders to declare which side of the aisle they stood on. This played out in the positions taken by CEOs on social issues and by shareholder activists and in the way consumers boycotted companies based on their politics.

Leaders Take Sides

One of President Trump's first actions after his inauguration in 2017 was to impose a temporary ban on all visitors from seven predominantly Muslim countries. After his executive order on January 27, 2017, nearly one hundred technology companies including Apple, Facebook, Microsoft, Google, Tesla, Uber, and Intel said that President Trump's ban would violate both immigration law and the United States Constitution.[15]

A few months later, he decided to withdraw from the Paris Climate Agreement. "I was elected to represent the citizens of Pittsburgh, not Paris," the president said, drawing support from Republican Party members and condemnation from political leaders, environmentalists, and business executives. Leaders including Elon Musk of Tesla, Jeffrey R. Immelt of General Electric, and Lloyd C. Blankfein of Goldman Sachs said Trump's decision would ultimately harm the economy by ceding the jobs of the future in clean energy and technology to overseas competitors. Musk also resigned from two business-related councils that Trump had established early in his presidency.[16]

In August of the same year, President Trump blamed "many sides" for an outburst of white supremacist violence in Charlottesville, Virginia. In response, some of the most influential chief executive officers in the country (including Indra Nooyi of PepsiCo, Mary T. Barra of General Motors, Virginia M. Rometty of IBM, and Rich Lesser of Boston Consulting Group) stepped down from the Strategic and Policy Forum, an elite group formed to advise the president on economic issues. About the same time, the president's other main business advisory group, the Manufacturing Jobs Initiative, was disintegrating. "There is continuing pressure on CEOs from customers, employees, shareholders and board members to take a position against what's going on and separate themselves from President Trump's councils," said Bill George, the former chief executive of the medical device maker Medtronic and a board member of Goldman Sachs. "These executives cannot live with customers thinking they are in cahoots with someone who supports white supremacists or neo-Nazis."[17]

Other polarizing decisions in the first year of Trump's presidency included the July decision to bar transgender service members from the US military and the decision to end the Deferred Action for Childhood Arrivals (DACA) program that was made in December. After the DACA program was repealed, Microsoft CEO Satya Nadella wrote a LinkedIn post titled "DREAMers Make Our Countries and Communities Stronger," in which he wrote, "As I shared at the White House in June, I am a product of two uniquely American attributes: the ingenuity of

American technology reaching me where I was growing up, fueling my dreams, and the enlightened immigration policy that allowed me to pursue my dreams."[18]

I think there were three reasons why corporate leaders responded to Trump's actions the way they did:

1. Trump's decisions impacted the social welfare of corporations' employees, customers, and communities. The shift from shareholder primacy to stakeholder primacy, as described earlier, meant that the concerns of these groups mattered just as much as the interests of investors.

2. By the time Trump was elected, corporations had begun to understand the importance and value of diversity and inclusion, and were investing heavily in operationalizing these programs. Government policy that was contradictory to these priorities would create new risks. Opportunities for hiring talented people would be compromised and consumer loyalty would be in jeopardy — especially with millennials, who said they would feel more loyal towards their own CEO if they took a stand on a hotly debated issue.[19]

3. The Trump presidency coincided with a shift in how corporate leaders viewed how their companies contributed to society — from being "socially responsible" to having a "social purpose." This new imperative was spelled out in January 2019 by Larry Fink, the founder, chairman, and chief executive officer of BlackRock. Fink acknowledged the pressures companies and their CEOs faced in such a polarized political environment, saying that profit and purpose were inextricably linked and that "companies must demonstrate their commitment to the countries, regions, and communities where they operate, particularly on issues central to the world's future prosperity."[20]

Shareholders Advocate for Change

When George W. Bush was president, I was advising an American Fortune 500 company based in San Francisco. I met with the president and CEO of this company and noticed that one of the most prominent features of his office was a very large autographed picture of President Bush. I asked this executive what he thought was the business value of the company's considerable investment in corporate social responsibility. At first, he really didn't have an answer. After a while, he said that perhaps it could help them "win the war on talent"; that is to say, ensure that the best and brightest young people would want work at his company over his competitors. Then he said that he really only ever thought about what mattered to the company's institutional investors. I'd be willing to bet that, at that time, none of his investors were thinking about anything to do with social change.

There had been a gradual increase in how investors considered a corporation's environmental, social, and governance performance along with its financial results. However, after Larry Fink said that BlackRock would be expecting the companies it invested in to have a social purpose, investors became advocates for social change. When institutional investors recognized there was a risk in owning shares of companies that had poor ESG performance, they became shareholder activists and contributed to more responsible decision-making in the boardroom.

According to Investopedia, "Shareholder activism is a way that shareholders can influence a corporation's behavior by exercising their rights as partial owners." This isn't a new phenomenon. During the Trump era, social activists and institutional investors began joining forces and pushing for boardroom decisions that put ESG at the highest level of priority. For example, in 2019, prominent pension funds, asset managers, and other charitable organizations sent a joint letter to all Fortune 500 companies, calling for greater disclosure of mid-level worker pay practices. In addition, the Interfaith Center for Corporate Responsibility — on behalf of over one hundred investors — spearheaded the submission of more than

10 shareholder proposals focusing on environmental and labour issues for the annual meeting of a single corporation.[21]

An executive order that President Trump signed soon after he took office got widespread attention for fast-tracking oil and gas pipelines and going one step further: it sought a review of laws that allowed investors to challenge environmental, social, and governance issues that affected their investments. Not surprisingly, this drew immediate criticism from shareholder advocacy groups, which saw it as an attempt to scale back investors' efforts to pressure fossil fuel companies about climate change and its related risks.[22]

The CEO I met in San Francisco isn't in that role anymore, but if he were, he would have to listen to people like Jeffrey Ubben, who founded Inclusive Capital Partners, and Lady Lynn Forester de Rothschild of the Coalition for Inclusive Capitalism. The Coalition for Inclusive Capitalism is a global non-profit organization that works with leaders across the private, public, and civic sectors to make capitalism inclusive and ensure that its benefits are more widely and equitably shared. Inclusive Capital Partners is a return-driven environmental and social activist firm that pushes companies in oil, gas, and other sectors to transition quickly to socially beneficial business models. Ubben also went through a personal Change for Good. Prior to founding Inclusive Capital, he was an activist investor at a $16 billion hedge fund he founded in 2000 called ValueAct Capital. His role there was to push companies to make short-term decisions to increase profits, fire workers, and buy back shares. "I'm on a crusade," Ubben said in 2020. "I've got five years to fix the harm I've done."[23]

Consumers Vote with Their Wallets

"Do you have experience working in campaigning within the NGO, charity, or grassroots movement-building space? Have you got a passion for the idea that business can be used to drive positive change in the world? Do issues of social and environmental justice drive you to take action?"

These questions are from a recent Ben & Jerry's recruitment message for the role of Activism Manager — a position that involves translating the company's progressive values into "successful externally-focused activism campaigns that create impact and drive action."[24] Ben & Jerry's has continued to remain, in their words, the most progressive, innovative, and impactful activist company. In 2018, the company launched a new flavour called Pecan Resist to

promote activism in the US. "The company cannot be silent in the face of President Trump's policies that attack and attempt to roll back decades of progress on racial and gender equity, climate change, LGBTQ rights and refugee and immigrant rights — all issues that have been at the core of the company's social mission for 40 years," Ben & Jerry's said in a statement.[25]

Since the days of the Peace Pop, Ben & Jerry's has enabled its "fans" to help make change on issues that matter to the company. During the Trump era, consumers became more motivated than ever to vote for social change with their wallets in a way that reflected their politics. This was revealed in research conducted in 2018 by Morning Consult, which found that 30 percent of people would have a more favourable view of a company if it issued a positive mention of Trump and 32 percent would have a more favourable view of a company if it issued a negative mention of Trump.[26]

Increasingly, activist consumers took action through boycotts when Starbucks challenged the Trump administration's immigration policies and when Uber was seen to support them. Consumer activism also took the form of buycotts, such as when the CEO of the Latin food brand Goya Foods called Donald Trump a "blessed" leader. His comment at the White House sparked a boycott of Goya products, with Latinos citing Trump's treatment of family separations at the southern border and his attempts to deport young "dreamer" immigrants. (Research by Weber Shandwick in 2017 found that buycotts are gaining momentum over the prevalence of boycotts, with 83 percent of consumer activists agreeing that it is more important than ever to show support for companies by buying from them versus participating in boycotts (59 percent).

According to the firm, this is related to a growing body of research that suggests boycotts haven't impacted the revenue of companies such as Amazon, which has grown exponentially despite calls to boycott it over its labour conditions.[27])

Hopefully, we won't have to worry about Donald Trump anymore. However, many countries continue to face a severely polarized political and social context, and it's the combined responsibility of corporate leaders, investors, and consumers to influence change by doing what's morally correct.

Black Lives Matter and Change for Good Transparency

This is the hardest part of this book to write. Despite growing up in a family that was steeped in social justice, I lived in a place of white privilege. Rosedale, the downtown Toronto neighbourhood we lived in, was almost exclusively white and I have no memory of any Black families or other diversity there. In retrospect, I really can't imagine what our neighbours at the time must have thought about the diverse and eclectic mix of people who were coming and going from our house. None of them ever said anything, but I'm sure many of them must have been surprised at the very least.

All this to say, my opinion as someone with no lived experience of racial discrimination is purely limited to the response that I've seen from the corporate sector. Some of the responses from corporations to racial injustice seem genuine. Other actions seem to be intended to either reduce the risk of being seen as insensitive or out of touch with something so important, or as a way to build loyalty and connection with customers for whom increased racial tolerance is a moral imperative or personally relevant. For me, the only thing that matters is the ways in which Black people, and the broader BIPOC community, perceive and are influenced by what corporations are doing to reduce systemic racism.

"There are a lot of brands that specifically love to capitalize on Black culture, Black music, Black aesthetic, but are dead silent when it comes to talking about Black issues and Black struggles in our community," said Jackie Aina, an influencer with more than 3.5 million subscribers on YouTube. "Can you all just say something when Black people are being brutally murdered by cops?"[28] Aina was urging fashion brands like Fashion Nova to weigh in on the nationwide protests that took place after George Floyd was handcuffed and pinned to the ground by police and then was killed in an episode that was captured on video.

Five days after Mr. Floyd's death, Reebok tweeted this message to "the Black community" that said, "Without the Black community Reebok would not exist. America would not exist. We are not asking you to buy our shoes. We are asking you to walk in someone else's. To stand in solidarity. To find our common ground of humanity."[29] As I write this, Reebok (which was acquired by Adidas in 2006) has virtually nothing on their website about Black Lives Matter. Clicking on "About Us" took me to the Customer Service page about "Adidas Group Inquiries," which contains these questions: Where can I find company information about Adidas? What do I do if I want to work at Adidas group or get information on traineeships, internships and graduate programs? Which browsers does the Reebok online shop support? What do I do if my question isn't covered here?[30]

Clicking on "Where can I find company information about Adidas?" took me to "'Own the Game' — Our Strategy 2025." This is a three-hour video that includes Amanda Rajkumar, the company's executive board member of Global Human Resources.[31] Rajkumar's message sounds like a very sincere commitment to diversity and inclusion, and she specifically makes reference to the impact of Black Lives Matter on the company's actions in this area. In addition to declaring the company's strategic commitment to being against discrimination in all forms and standing united against racism, Rajkumar outlines a number of programs that put this commitment into action including:

- Creation of an accelerating inclusion committee headed by the CEO to drive the company's clear commitment to the diversity and inclusion journey with sincerity and with speed.

- Expanding employee listening, celebrating a global day of inclusion, strengthening diverse talent groups, and scaling access to mentoring and development programs.

- Investing $120 million in North America over five years to "social engagement projects for Black and underrepresented communities."

- Introducing mandatory training for all employees including executives through a "creating a culture of inclusion course."

- A target of 35 percent women in leadership positions.

- Ensuring diverse representation among the company's leadership.

Rajkumar reinforces these commitments by saying, "Our ambition is to continue to be a workplace where employees and future employees want to be. A workplace where diversity and inclusion are deeply ingrained in who we are, how we act, how we create and how we innovate — it's the level playing field we need to own the game."

I watched the entire video. (Which probably makes me one of the handful of people on the planet to do so, raising the bigger question of why this company's position on an issue that's so important is so opaque. Adidas is far from being an exception in this area. Too many companies limit their commitment to social change in corporate responsibility reports that virtually no one reads. It is another example of companies doing CSR Lite. Producing an annual CSR report doesn't mean you're helping to change the world; it means you've successfully produced a CSR report — or in this case, a three-hour video.)

The Adidas video is full of action shots of Black athletes, but the voices representing the company's leadership, with the exception of Rajkumar, are exclusively white. It is difficult not to notice that the company's message and its reality, as shown in this important piece of communication, seem inconsistent. Plus, you've got to go quite deep into Adidas communications to get this perspective. Rajkumar's presentation begins 34 minutes into a three-hour video. On the surface, Adidas and Reebok paint a much more diverse picture of their brands.

What does it mean when companies like Adidas show very different sides of who they are in this space? On the one hand, their brand marketing shows a very diverse but also very stereotyped image. On the other hand, I'd imagine that how this company is portraying itself behind the scenes wouldn't resonate nearly as much with BIPOC communities.

Why do brands make it so difficult for people to find out how they are addressing systemic racism in their operations? Perhaps they think that only the most superficial communications will be of interest to BIPOC consumers or that people in these communities will be critical of the actions they are taking. In my experience, people are interested in the details and, in what's been called the golden age of transparency, it feels somehow deceptive to be putting such important information so far from the public's eyes.

As companies like Reebok, Netflix, and Old Navy were standing up for Black Lives Matter, Sharon Chuter, the founder of UOMA Beauty, a cosmetics company that caters to Black women, was skeptical of the messages of support for Black lives coming from corporate brands. In response, she created the #PullUpOrShutUp Challenge, which asked for brands to share the percentage of Black employees they had in leadership positions to test how committed these corporate brands really were to this issue. "Reflection is painful," Chuter said. "The truth hurts, and I just felt like brands didn't want to do it."[32]

Black Lives Matter propelled consumer activism. In 2020, researcher Opinium found that a majority of Americans believed that brands should take a position on Black Lives Matter. An even greater number said they believe companies have a role to play in responding to issues of racial justice and police brutality.[33]

The Black Lives Matter movement was actually started in 2013 following the death of Trayvon Martin, an African-American teenager who was shot while walking to a family friend's house, and the subsequent acquittal of George Zimmerman, the man who shot him. However, it took seven years and a tragedy like the brutal death of George Floyd for corporations to begin to take action.

Companies that want to change for good need to understand where social change needs to happen, take action as soon as possible, and not wait until they are conspicuous by their absence. Adidas has a very solid game plan for beginning to address systemic racism, but they should have put this into play much sooner, and they should be much clearer and transparent about their plans.

COVID-19 AND CHANGE FOR GOOD LIFE

impakt's Change for Good series of conversations wouldn't have been possible without COVID-19. In early 2020, as the pandemic started to have an impact, it became clear that the socio-economic conditions for too many people were getting worse than ever and that people who were vulnerable before were becoming even more vulnerable. Not only that, the organizations that existed to help those people were also becoming vulnerable. In Canada, it was estimated that close to 20 percent of charitable and non-profit organizations who people depend on would be in danger of going out of businesses. And when employment numbers plummeted, people who might have been donors to charitable organizations were now in need of their services — but not able access them because many had already ceased operations.

I wondered what could be done to create a shared community where changemakers could get a glimpse into what leaders from different sectors were doing around the world. That's when we started having Change for Good conversations with people who shared the incredible work they were doing and provided ideas and inspiration for people at a time when they really needed it.

As I write this, we are hopefully in the beginning of the last wave of the pandemic, and I think it's pointless to spend time elaborating on what's already very clear: COVID-19 has impacted people disproportionately according to socio-economic status, gender and race, much of progress that was made towards achieving the Sustainable Development Goals has been erased, and the societal and human cost of illness and loss has been incalculable.

There has also been a remarkable and hopeful counterbalance to this devastating impact. Existing but underutilized technologies, such as Zoom, became a source of community that helped people cope with isolation and were used to deliver vitally important social services, such as learning, mental health counselling, and fitness. New bike lanes that have been debated for years appeared within weeks. We were reminded of what matters most: the value of relationships and family (and the challenges that come along with both). We were also reminded that money is the thing that people worry about most but what matters least. Working from home became normalized, along with the benefits and challenges that came along with this shift. "Buy local or goodbye local" became a new imperative at the same time as we helped companies like Amazon become even more profitable — at the expense of its workers.

The degree to which organizations in all sectors responded to the crisis by developing innovative new approaches to social change and moving quickly to put these ideas into action was unprecedented. And, at the same time as trying to stay afloat, businesses continually adapted to help their customers in any way they could and discovered a new sense of social purpose in how they looked after their employees and contributed to their communities.

Andrea Barrack, who is the global head of sustainability and corporate citizenship at TD, told me that one of the biggest changes she's seen during COVID-19 is that corporations are willing to accept risks in a way we haven't seen before, referring to it as a GEPO (good enough, push on) mentality.[34] Valerie McMurtry, the president and CEO of the Children's Aid Foundation of Canada said, "This is a crisis. We're going to have to take some risks. We're going to have to jump in and go for it. And we're going to have to mend it as we go. But let's just go."[35]

I think making Change for Good depends on doing exactly what Barrack and McMurtry said. For me, this means listening to people who have lived experience that is very different than mine, doing something to support what matters to employees, moving faster than you ever felt was possible, taking more risks, being leaders, and eliminating CSR Lite.

There's a long, and often dark, history of bad things happening when corporations make profit the sole measure of success. There's also never been a time when corporations have had such an opportunity to re-establish the reason why business started in the first place — to contribute to the common good.

Tabatha Bull, the president and chief executive of the Canadian Council for Aboriginal Business, told me what is fundamental to how Indigenous people consider their impact on the world: think seven generations ahead. "For everything I'm doing and everything I'm taking from the land today, how is this going to influence my seventh generation?"[36] Bull says she asks herself. Corporations that consider their actions through this same lens will have more sustainable businesses, have better social change outcomes, and help prevent another pandemic crisis in the future.

During the early days of the pandemic, rock star, writer, speaker, cancer survivor, and tireless humanitarian Bif Naked said this during a Change for Good conversation:

> There are always going to be people in a society that live in a variety of tiers. People who are living cheque to cheque and work hard for very little. There are always going to be people who have multiple barriers and vulnerabilities. COVID-19 created a situation where people who are more fortunate finally noticed what's always been there. All that you can really hope for out of this is that compassion grows with awareness. Moving forward, let's not do it again in an emergency. Let's work on prevention. Let's change the system. Let's do things with a little more passion. Let's do them with deliberation. Let's live loudly.[37]

THAT'S CHANGE FOR GOOD

Nothing can justify the devasting impact of the Great Recession, the Trump presidency, systemic racism, and the COVID-19 crisis. However, in their own ways, each revealed why social change is so important, reinforced the imperative to solve the SDGs, and uncovered new ways for corporations to help solve social problems.

My experience in each of these crises has contributed immensely to the creation of Change for Good. It was during these challenging times that many of the ideas I've shared in this book were incubated, albeit in ways that were not particularly organized or intentional at the time. This includes realizing how important it is to listen to and involve people with lived experience in your targeted areas, why employing vulnerable people is one of the most important acts of social change that a company can take, and why it's so important for corporations to move past CSR Lite.

If the COVID-19 crisis hadn't happened, we never would have started the Change for Good conversation series. It's also likely that I never would have recognized the throughline that connected the small innovations I'd developed over many years. The ideas that I've shared in this book happened organically without me realizing that, unconsciously, I was creating a new system for business to help solve social problems.

CONCLUSION

You Are the Change for Good

My first taste of Change for Good was a Ben & Jerry's Peace Pop in 1988, as I wrote about in the introduction. Seeing Cohen's keynote speech literally changed my life. It's the first thing that comes to mind when I think about how I came to be helping businesses solve social problems, and it was my inspiration for starting impakt.

In his talk, Cohen also shared the story of how the Cherry Garcia flavour came to be. This is recounted on Ben & Jerry's website. Apparently, a customer in Maine sent a postcard to the company's main office in Burlington, Vermont, and it said: "Dear Ben & Jerry's, We're great fans of the Grateful Dead and we're great fans of your ice cream. Why don't you make a cherry flavour and call it Cherry Garcia? You know it will sell because Dead paraphernalia always sells. We are talking good business sense here, plus it will be a real hoot for the fans."

Cherry Garcia made its debut on February 15, 1987, and the company sent the first eight pints to Jerry Garcia, lead guitarist of the Grateful Dead. His wife and publicist called them to say how much he loved it. A few years later, Ben Cohen and Jerry Greenfield were in Burlington opening the week's fan mail. They opened one envelope and a Cherry Garcia pint lid fell out with a note from Jane Williamson, the person who had suggested the flavour. "I'm glad you made the flavor," it said. Ben & Jerry's contacted Jane and invited her to the next shareholders' meeting as the guest of honour. She received a standing ovation along with a year's supply of Ben & Jerry's ice cream.

At the time, I was a big fan of the Grateful Dead and, to be honest, this story was just as great as eating the Peace Pop. What I didn't mention earlier in this book is that social activism has been a part of my life for as long as I can remember and also that music has been central to my experience and inspiration to help make the world a better place.

My mother was the artistic director of the Mariposa Folk Festival and had a strong belief that music was a tool for social change. American folk singer and social rights activist Pete Seeger sang in our living room with a banjo that was inscribed with this message: "This machine surrounds hate and forces it to surrender." I also had the opportunity to hear stories from Utah Phillips, the legendary folk musician, peace and labour activist, and lifelong member of the Industrial Workers of the World (known as the Wobblies). In 1968, Phillips ran for the US Senate on the Peace and Freedom Party ticket and also helped found the Hospitality House homeless shelter and the Peace and Justice Center.

Hearing the stories and music of Black musicians like Muddy Waters, Reverend Gary Davis, and Mississippi John Hurt (who were very old when I was very young) was what resonated most with me. These were people who lived during the time that sharecropping and segregation were still legal. Blues music is rooted in the lived experience of enslaved people of both suffering and hope.

My father was an architect who had a particular interest in affordable housing. His firm Klein & Sears was an innovator in this area, and he believed that more access to affordable housing depended on three ingredients: lower cost, improved quality, and increased speed of construction. Innovation in social change is based on the same ingredients. When considering how to solve social problems, I think it's important to consider the same three things: what is the least expensive way to make the biggest difference in the shortest time? My father also said that the most important thing you can do in life is to make the world just a little bit better than it was before. That's another thing I always remember.

In 1967, when I was nine, my parents took me to a march in Toronto led by activists César Chavez and Dolores Huerta to raise awareness of poor working conditions and low wages in California's grape industry. My mother would never buy grapes from California, and I think that's my first memory of social change related to a specific product.

The first corporate advocacy that I can recall was in the early 1980s from the United Colors of Benetton, which targeted health, politics, and racial justice through provocative advertising campaigns that aligned its brand with social issues. Two particularly memorable ads were the one with a man dying of AIDS surrounded by his grieving family, and the one with three hearts labelled separately as "white," "black," and "yellow" all portraying a "one-world" theme. Benetton has continued to raise awareness of social injustice. More recently, it launched an advertising campaign featuring images of migrants rescued from the Mediterranean accompanied by volunteers. (The charity behind the rescue, SOS Méditerranée, condemned Benetton for using pictures of people in distress and disassociated itself from the campaign.[1])

Those are the moments that stand out to me when I think of where my own Change for Good journey began.

Early in the COVID-19 crisis, my friend and colleague Rem Langan started asking how impakt could help organizations change for good. This led to a series of 17 virtual conversations with me and social change leaders from around the world. These leaders shared their perspectives and ideas on what was needed to help vulnerable people during the crisis and how businesses could improve their impact on society in the future.

Here are some of the most memorable takeaways from these first Change for Good conversations in 2020 that I think will also resonate with you — and help you develop your own Change for Good.

- **Tim Cormode, CEO of Power To Be:** The first conversation I had was with Cormode, who told me that the most important priorities were to invest in leadership, deploy action now, and take all impact measurements off the table. Power To Be is an incredible organization that creates access to nature for people living with cognitive, physical, financial, and social barriers.

- **Markus Lux, senior vice-president of Active Citizenship at Robert Bosch Stiftung:** This is one of Europe's largest foundations associated with a private company. Lux said that the COVID-19 crisis had made tolerance for complexity a common denominator for everyone in the social change space.

- **Naina Batra, chairperson & CEO of AVPN:** AVPN is a Singapore-based network of funders and impact investors. Batra said that today business is not just about profit and, moving forward, it would remain to be seen if this realization will be sustained after the crisis.

- **Bruce MacDonald, president & CEO of Imagine Canada:** He described the special role corporations have to play in helping their employees who have become caregivers and need mental health support. Imagine is an organization that bolsters that work of charities, non-profits, and social entrepreneurs.

- **Tabatha Bull, president & CEO of the Canadian Council for Aboriginal Business:** She shared what's needed for Indigenous business to be successful: increased access to capital, economic reconciliation, more Indigenous suppliers, and leveraging the inherent commitment to sustainability that exists within this community.

- **Daniele Zanotti, president & CEO of United Way of Greater Toronto:** Zanotti shared the four things that he thinks about every day: What is the shortest route between us and action in the community? How are we going to keep our own cash flow so we can distribute cash to the community? Who are the people

I never would have thought of before that I can collaborate with for long-term sustainability? And: Never take "That's not possible" as an answer. Everything is possible.

- **Stephen Huddart, president & CEO of the J.W. McConnnell Family Foundation:** Huddart told me what was needed to address immediate social change needs and also create the conditions for success in the future. These included identifying, collaborating with, and funding existing community-based systems and organizations that can map out and respond to local vulnerabilities; involving people with lived experience in the development of new solutions to social problems; providing no-interest loans for charitable organizations; using new models for impact investing, such as impact bonds that are used to finance outcomes at scale; and giving more now to support social change leaders on the front lines.

- **Manju Menju, CEO and co-founder of NuSocia:** NuSocia is a social impact advisory firm based in India. Menju said businesses need to make long-term meaningful social changes to establish their impression as responsible companies and that companies no longer have an option of not doing this.

- **David "Patch" Patchell-Evans, founder and CEO of GoodLife Fitness:** Patch was the last person I spoke with in 2020. He said that the pandemic had pointed out to people that they are in charge of their own health, not the healthcare system. Patch also talked about how access to fitness should be an essential human right and that too many vulnerable people were ending up in hospital because they lacked access to physical activity needed to stay healthy and survive COVID-19.

The underlying message that these leaders have shared in the Change for Good conversations is that real, genuine change begins with you.

You have to want to make the world a better place as the first step to change for good. The Change for Good approach reflects what's most important to me, and I think the ethos behind it can be helpful to you, too. Finding your path to making the world a better place starts with asking yourself the same questions that we ask businesses that want to solve social problems.

If you want to change for good, some of the questions that I think are most important to ask yourself, include:

- What's most important, being financially successful or contributing to my community?

- How can I best make a difference in helping to change the world in a way that's practical for me and my family?

- How does what I do for work and for the world influence my relationships with friends and family?

- Am I enjoying life to the fullest?

Of course, these are easier questions to ask than to answer, and there are lots of ways to make a difference. For me, there are four things that are most important: spending time with people I like and respect (starting with my family), doing work (large or small) that is helping to change the world, being compensated at a level that's fair and reflects my experience, and having fun. I'm very fortunate to say that I experience most of this most of the time. The biggest variable is the money, but I think it's important to remember that money is the thing that people worry about most but matters least.

Patch says that what's most important is to not let the things that you can't do hold you back from the things you can do. I couldn't agree more, and I hope that after reading this book you won't hold back from making the Change for Good that's right for your company and right for you.

NOTES

Introduction: The Journey to Change for Good

1. Milton Friedman, "A Friedman Doctrine — The Social Responsibility of Business Is to Increase Its Profits," *The New York Times*, September 13, 1970, https://www.nytimes.com/1970/09/13/archives/a-friedman-doctrine-the-social-responsibility-of-business-is-to.html.

2. Matteo Tonello, "The Business Case for Corporate Social Responsibility," Harvard Law School Forum on Corporate Governance, June 26, 2011, https://corpgov.law.harvard.edu/2011/06/26/the-business-case-for-corporate-social-responsibility/.

3. Jennifer C. Chen, M. Dennis, and Robin Roberts, "Corporate Charitable Contributions: A Corporate Social Performance or Legitimacy Strategy?" *Journal of Business Ethics* (2008): 131–44, https://www.jstor.org/stable/25482278?seq=1.

4. Claudia Cahalane, "I Believe They Are Honourable and the Work They Do Is Honourable," *The Guardian*, November 3, 2006, https://www.theguardian.com/business/2006/nov/03/ethicalliving.environment.

5. United Nations, "Resolution Adopted by the General Assembly on 6 July 2017, Work of the Statistical Commission pertaining to the 2030 Agenda for Sustainable Development," July 10, 2017, http://ggim.un.org/documents/a_res_71_313.pdf.

6. Four Seasons, "Four Seasons Hotels and Resorts Announces Enhanced Health and Safety Program at Properties Worldwide," June 18, 2020, https://press .fourseasons.com/news-releases/2020/lead-with-care-program/.

7. World Socialist Web, "Canadian Workers at Cargill Meatpacking Plant Forced Back to Work Despite 935 Infections," May 5, 2020, https://www.wsws .org/en/articles/2020/05/05/alca-m05.html.

Chapter 1: Change for Good Today

1. Paul Klein, "How Creating Opportunities Helps Make Social Change," *Strategy*, January 9, 2020, https://strategyonline.ca/2020/01/09/how-creating-opportunities-helps-make-social-change/.

2. United Nations, Department of Social and Environmental Affairs. Sustainable Development, https://sdgs.un.org/goals.

3. Ibid.

4. NDP Group, "Cycling Industry Sales Growth Accelerates in April, Up 75%, Generating an Unprecedented $1 Billion for the Month, According to NPD," June 16, 2020, https://www.npd.com/wps/portal/npd/us/news/press-releases/2020/cycling-industry-sales-growth-accelerates-in-april.

5. Smartbrief Industry News, "How the Work-from-Home Trend Became a Marketing Opportunity," July 28, 2020, https://www.smartbrief.com/original/2020/07/how-work-home-trend-became-marketing-opportunity.

6. Global E-Learning Industry, *Market Impact Survey COVID-19 & Looming Recession*, October 2020, https://www.reportlinker.com/p03646043/Global-Mobile-Learning-Industry.html?utm_source=GNW.

7. Paul Klein, "Where Is Apple's Social Purpose?" *Forbes*, August 12, 2011, https://www.forbes.com/sites/csr/2011/08/12/where-is-apples-social-purpose/?sh=71302625499d.

8. *Forbes*, "World's Most Valuable Brands," 2020, https://www.forbes.com/the-worlds-most-valuable-brands/#35fabe78119c.

9. *Computerworld*, "Apple's COVID-19 Response Shines Light on Social Responsibility," December 16, 2020, https://www.computerworld.com/article/3601512/apples-covid-19-response-shines-light-on-social-responsibility.html.

10. Ibid.

11. Apple, "Fourth Quarter Results," October 29, 2020, https://www.apple.com/newsroom/2020/10/apple-reports-fourth-quarter-results.

12. Anneken Tappe, "Trump Has the Worst Job Losses on Record Heading into the Election," CNN, October 6, 2020, https://www.cnn.com/2020/10/02/economy/september-2020-jobs-report-election/index.html.

13. Amazon, "Our Impact," aboutamazon.com/impact.

14. Amazon, "Quarterly Results," 2020, https://ir.aboutamazon.com/quarterly-results/default.aspx.

15. *Forbes*, "Jeff Bezos Becomes the First Person Ever Worth $200 Billion," *Forbes*, August 26, 2020, https://www.forbes.com/sites/jonathanponciano/2020/08/26/worlds-richest-billionaire-jeff-bezos-first-200-billion/.

16. Global Finance, "World's Largest Companies 2020," November 30, 2020, https://www.gfmag.com/global-data/economic-data/largest-companies.

17. Saijel Kishan, "Amazon Investors Push for Racial Equity Audit, Worker on Board," BNN Bloomberg, December 18, 2020, https://www.bloomberg.com/news/articles/2020-12-18/amazon-investors-push-for-racial-equity-audit-worker-on-board.

18. Geneva Abdul, "A Canadian 'Buy Local' Effort Fights Amazon on Its Own Turf," *The New York Times*, January 2, 2021, https://www.nytimes.com/2021/01/02/business/not-amazon-canada.html.

19. Erreka Group, https://www.erreka.com/grupo/en/.

20. Peter S. Goodman, "Co-ops in Spain's Basque Region Soften Capitalism's Rough Edges," *The New York Times*, December 29, 2020, https://www.nytimes.com/2020/12/29/business/cooperatives-basque-spain-economy.html.

21. Business Roundtable, "Statement on Events in the Nation's Capital," January 6, 2021, https://www.businessroundtable.org/business-roundtable-statement-on-events-in-the-nations-capital.

22. Frederick E. Allen, "Howard Schultz to Anti-Gay-Marriage Starbucks Shareholder: 'You Can Sell Your Shares,'" *Forbes*, March 22, 2013, https://www.forbes.com/sites/frederickallen/2013/03/22/howard-schultz-to-anti-gay-marriage-starbucks-shareholder-you-can-sell-your-shares/?sh=3a8c9d2f43fa.

23. Paul Klein, "Corporates as Agents of Social Change: The Academic View," *The Guardian*, January 15, 2014, https://www.theguardian.com/sustainable-business/corporates-agents-social-change-academic-view.

24. Living Tradition, "Potlatch," https://umistapotlatch.ca/potlatch-eng.php.

Chapter 2: Change for Good History

1. Wikipedia, "Volkswagen emissions scandal," https://en.wikipedia.org/wiki/ Volkswagen_emissions_scandal.
2. Marta Riera and María Iborra, "Corporate Social Irresponsibility: Review and Conceptual Boundaries," *European Journal of Management and Business Economics* 26, no. 2 (2017): 146–62, https://doi.org/10.1108/EJMBE-07-2017-009.
3. Ancient History Encyclopedia, "Trade in the Roman World," https://www .ancient.eu/article/638/trade-in-the-roman-world/.
4. U. Malmendier, "Roman Shares," in W.N. Goetzmann and K.G. Rouwenhorst, eds., *The Origins of Value: The Financial Innovations that Created Modern Capital Markets* (Oxford University Press, 2005).
5. Ibid
6. Ibid.
7. R. Backhouse, *The Penguin History of Economics* (Penguin, 2002).
8. Business Managed Democracy, "Ancient Romans and Greeks," https://www .herinst.org/BusinessManagedDemocracy/culture/wealth/ancient.html.
9. Harold Whetstone Johnston, *The Private Life of the Romans* (Johnston, Scott, Foresman and Company, 1903, 1932), forumromanum.org.
10. Earl Shoris, *A Nation of Salesmen: The Tyranny of the Market and the Subversion of Culture* (W.W. Norton & Company, 2012), 61.
11. Ibid.
12. S. Ogilvie, "The Economics of Guilds," *The Journal of Economic Perspectives* 28, no. 4 (2014): 169–92, https://doi.org/10.1257/jep.28.4.169.
13. Ancient History Encyclopedia, "Medieval Guilds," https://www.ancient.eu/ Medieval_Guilds.
14. Ibid.
15. R. Backhouse, *The Penguin History of Economics* (Penguin, 2002).
16. Edwin S. Hunt, *The Medieval Super-companies: A Study of the Peruzzi Company of Florence* (Cambridge: Cambridge University Press, 1994), https://doi .org/10.1017/CBO9780511528798.
17. https://www.salesforce.com/company/about-us/.

18. Paul Ginsberg, "What Is the Salesforce 'Ohana'?" May 14, 2018, https://www
    .salesforceben.com/what-is-the-salesforce-ohana/.

19. Richard Branson, "Why You Should Treat Your Company Like Family,"
    LinkedIn, November 20, 2012, https://www.linkedin.com/pulse/20121120154818-
    204068115-why-you-should-treat-your-company-like-family/.

20. Leonardo Davoudi, Christopher McKenna, and Rowena Olegario, "The
    Historical Role of the Corporation in Society," *Journal of the British Academy* 6,
    special issue (2018), https://doi.org/10.5871/jba/006s1.017.

21. A.W. Pettigrew, *Freedom's Debt: The Royal African Company and the Politics of
    the Atlantic Slave Trade, 1672–1752* (University of North Carolina Press, 2013),
    https://uncpress.org/book/9781469629858/freedoms-debt/.

22. A.W. Pettigrew and A.L. Brock, "Leadership and the Social Agendas of the
    Seventeenth-Century English Trading Corporation," in A.W. Pettigrew
    and D.C. Smith, eds., *A History of Socially Responsible Business, c. 1600–1950*
    (London: Palgrave Macmillan, 2017).

23. S. Muthu, "Adam Smith's Critique of International Trading Companies:
    Theorizing 'Globalization' in the Age of Enlightenment," *Political Theory*,
    April 1, 2008, https://doi.org/10.1177/0090591707312430.

24. Leonardo Davoudi, Christopher McKenna, and Rowena Olegario, "The
    Historical Role of the Corporation in Society," *Journal of the British Academy* 6,
    special issue (2018), https://doi.org/10.5871/jba/006s1.017.

25. Andrew Carnegie, "The Gospel of Wealth," *North American Review*, June 1889,
    https://www.carnegie.org/about/our-history/gospelofwealth/.

26. William H. Ordway, "Sanatorium Care of Sick Employees of the Metropolitan
    Life Insurance Company," *Tubercule*, August 1928, https://doi.org/10.1016/
    S0041-3879(28)80127-9.

27. Ibid.

28. National Public Radio, "The Sweet, Social Legacy of Cadbury Chocolate,"
    National Public Radio, October 29, 2010, https://www.npr.org/templates/
    story/story.php?storyId=130558647.

29. Ibid.

30. Triple Pundit, "Kraft Tries to Curb Fears over Cadbury's Future," February 1,
    2010, https://www.triplepundit.com/story/2010/kraft-tries-curb-fears-over-
    cadburys-future/102031.

31. Justmeans, "Bittersweet: How Kraft's Acquisition of Cadbury Ended the Dynasty of a CSR Luminary," March 13, 2011, http://www.justmeans.com/blogs/bittersweet-how-krafts-acquisition-of-cadbury-ended-the-dynasty-of-a-csr-luminary.

32. Mondelēz International, https://www.mondelezinternational.com/News/Progressing-Snacking-Made-Right-Agenda-Towards-2025-ESG-Targets.

33. A.A Berle and G.C. Means, *The Modern Corporation and Private Property* (MacMillan, 1932).

34. Stanford Graduate School of Business, "Theodore Kreps," https://www.gsb.stanford.edu/experience/news-history/history/theodore-kreps.

35. A.B. Carroll and G.W. Beiler, "Landmarks in the Evolution of the Social Audit," *The Academy of Management Journal* 18, no. 3 (September 1975): 589–599.

36. Chester Barnard, *The Functions of the Executive* (Harvard University Press, 1938).

37. Nicoleta Farcane and Eusebiu Bureana, "History of 'Corporate Social Responsibility' Concept," *Annales Universitatis Apulensis Series Oeconomica* 2 (2015): 31–48, doi: 10.29302/oeconomica.2015.17.2.3.

38. Homeless Hub, "What It Means to Be 'Working Poor,'" 2011, https://www.homelesshub.ca/resource/what-it-means-be-%E2%80%98working-poor%E2%80%99.

39. Philip Mattera, "Corporate Research Project," December 7, 2020, https://www.corp-research.org/wal-mart.

40. H.R. Bowen, *Social Responsibilities of the Businessman*, (New York: Harper, 1953).

41. Milton Friedman, "A Friedman Doctrine — The Social Responsibility of Business Is to Increase Its Profits," *The New York Times*, September 13, 1970, https://www.nytimes.com/1970/09/13/archives/a-friedman-doctrine-the-social-responsibility-of-business-is-to.html.

42. Jonathon Soros, "The Friedman Doctrine Revisited," *Democracy*, October 30, 2020, https://democracyjournal.org/arguments/the-friedman-doctrine-revisited/.

43. Peter Brabeck, "The Baby Killer," *War on Want*, 1974, http://archive.babymilkaction.org/pdfs/babykiller.pdf.

44. Changing Markets Foundation, *Based on Science? Revisiting Nestlé's Infant Milk Products and Claims*, 2019, https://changingmarkets.org/portfolio/milking-it/.

45. Nestlé, *Progress Report 2019*, https://www.nestle.com/sites/default/files/2020-03/creating-shared-value-report-2019-en.pdf.

46. Archie B. Carroll, "A History of Corporate Social Responsibility: Concepts and Practice," in A.M. Andrew Crane, D. Matte, J. Moon, and D. Siegel, eds., *The Oxford Handbook of Corporate Social Responsibility*, Oxford University Press, February 2008, https://dl.bsu.by/pluginfile.php/66249/mod_resource/content/1/A_History_of_Corporate_Social_Responsibility.pdf.

47. Business Roundtable, "Statement on the Purpose of a Corporation," 2020, https://s3.amazonaws.com/brt.org/BRT-StatementonthePurposeofaCorporationOctober2020.pdf.

48. McKinsey & Company, "The CEO Moment: Leadership for a New Era," 2020, https://www.mckinsey.com/featured-insights/leadership/the-ceo-moment-leadership-for-a-new-era.

49. Ezquiel Minaya, "New Ranking of Nation's Top Employers' Response to Panedmic," *Forbes*, forbes.com/sites/ezequielminaya/2020/05/26/the-forbes-corporate-responders-new-ranking-of-nations-top-employers-responses-to-pandemic/.

50. Josie Wexler, "Ten Companies to Avoid over Their Response to COVID-19," Ethical Consumer, May 12, 2020, ethicalconsumer.org/covid-19-ethical-consumption/ten-companies-avoid-over-their-response-covid-19.

51. James Gorman, "Committing to Diversity and Inclusion," June 4, 2020, https://www.linkedin.com/pulse/committing-diversity-inclusion-james-gorman/?

52. Morgan Stanley, "Institute for Inclusion," https://www.morganstanley.com/about-us/diversity/institute-for-inclusion.

53. John Harrington, "Seven in 10 People Would Shun Firms that Behaved Badly During COVID-19 Crisis — Research," *PR Week*, May 10, 2020, https://www.prweek.com/article/1682510/seven-10-people-shun-firms-behaved-badly-during-covid-19-crisis-%E2%80%93-research.

54. Guttmann, "Global Consumers Discouraging from Brand Use Due to Poor COVID-19 Response 2020," https://www.statista.com/statistics/1110243/global-consumer-reaction-to-brand-poor-covid19-response/.

55. Just Capital, "The COVID-19 Corporate Response Tracker: How America's Largest Employers Are Treating Stakeholders Amid the Coronavirus Crisis," https://justcapital.com/reports/the-covid-19-corporate-response-tracker-how-americas-largest-employers-are-treating-stakeholders-amid-the-coronavirus-crisis/.

56. Ian Portsmouth, "Podcast 27 Transcript, Corporate Social Responsibility,"

Canadian Business, October 10, 2008, https://www.canadianbusiness.com/leadership/podcast-27-transcript-corporate-social-responsibility/.

Chapter 3: Change for Good Employees

1. Alan Kohll, "One Company Is Taking Care of Employees During COVID-19," *Forbes*, April 6, 2020, https://www.forbes.com/sites/alankohll/2020/04/06/how-one-company-is-taking-care-of-employees-during-covid-19/.
2. Pfizer, "Global Health Fellows and Teams," https://www.pfizer.com/purpose/global-health/unleashing-the-power-of-our-colleagues/global-health-fellows.
3. True Impact, "Pro Bono Impact Case Study: Pfizer Global Health Fellows," 2012, https://cdn2.hubspot.net/hub/35299/file-30904269-pdf/docs/pfizer_ghf_case_study.printed.pdf.
4. Pyxera Global, "PepsiCorps," https://www.pyxeraglobal.org/pepsicorps/.
5. Nature Medicine, "Pfizer Lawsuit Spotlights Ethics of Developing World Clinical Trials," *Nature Medicine*, July 2007, https://www.nature.com/articles/nm0707-763.pdf?
6. PepsiCo, https://www.pepsico.com/about/about-the-company.
7. Deanna L. Pucciarelli and Louis E. Grivetti, "The Medicinal Use of Chocolate in Early North America," *Molecular Nutrition & Food Research*, October 6, 2008, https://onlinelibrary.wiley.com/doi/abs/10.1002/mnfr.200700264.
8. Karen Spaeder, "Side Effects of Eating Too Much Chocolate," Livestrong.com, November 22, 2019, https://www.livestrong.com/article/411407-side-effects-of-eating-too-much-chocolate/.
9. Wikipedia, "Eli Lilly," https://en.wikipedia.org/wiki/Eli_Lilly.
10. Lilly, "Our Impact," https://www.lilly.com/impact/overview.
11. Sam Laprade, "Philanthropy in Ottawa: Tobi Lütke and Fiona McKean Support Community COVID-19 Relief Efforts," *The Ottawa Citizen*, March 9, 2021, https://obj.ca/article/local/philanthropy-ottawa-tobi-lutke-and-fiona-mckean-support-community-covid-19-relief.
12. Andrew Duffy, "Shopify Founder's Charitable Foundation Turns Attention to COVID-19," *The Ottawa Citizen*, April 9, 2020, https://ottawacitizen.com/news/local-news/shopify-founders-charitable-foundation-turns-attention-to-covid-19.

13. Deloitte, *2017 Deloitte Volunteer Survey*, June 2017, https://www2.deloitte. com/content/dam/Deloitte/us/Documents/about-deloitte/us-2017-deloitte-volunteerism-survey.pdf.

14. Matt Gavin, "How to Create Social Change: 4 Business Strategies," Harvard Business School Online, January 24, 2019, https://online.hbs.edu/blog/post/how-can-business-drive-social-change.

15. Marcel Vander Wier, "Offering Choice in CSR Activity Spurs Employee Engagement: Study," *Canadian HR Reporter*, January 9, 2019, https://www.hrreporter.com/focus-areas/culture-and-engagement/offering-choice-in-csr-activity-spurs-employee-engagement-study/283567.

16. The Upside Foundation, "#GivingTuesday Report: Canadians Value Corporate Giving, 70% of Canadians More Likely to Purchase from Companies that Give Back," Ciscon Canada, November 27, 2018, https://www.newswire.ca/news-releases/givingtuesday-report-canadians-value-corporate-giving-70-of-canadians-more-likely-to-purchase-from-companies-that-give-back-701316351.html.

17. Stuart Gentle, "Kenexa Study Finds Tangible Link Between CSR and Bottom Line Business Success," Onrec, June 14, 2011, https://www.onrec.com/news/news-archive/kenexa-study-finds-tangible-link-between-csr-and-bottom-line-business-success.

18. IBM, "IBM Service Corps," https://www.ibm.org/initiatives/ibm-service-corps.

19. Paul Klein and Milinda Martin, "In the Future, Companies Will Survive Only if They Help Solve Social Problems," *Forbes*, December 4, 2014, https://www.forbes.com/sites/forbesleadershipforum/2014/12/04/in-the-future-companies-will-survive-only-if-they-help-solve-big-social-problems/.

Chapter 4: Change for Good Risk

1. Wikipedia, *The Twilight Zone*, https://en.wikipedia.org/wiki/The_Twilight_Zone_(1959_TV_series,_season_1).

2. Annie Bright, "10 of the Most Socially Responsible Companies and Brands to Model in 2021," *Grow Ensemble*, October 23, 2020, https://growensemble.com/socially-responsible-companies.

3. Hannah Durbin, "9 Socially Responsible Companies to Applaud," Classy, March 29, 2021, https://www.classy.org/blog/6-socially-responsible-companies-applaud/.

4. *Slate*, "The Evil List," January 15, 2020, https://slate.com/technology/2020/01/evil-list-tech-companies-dangerous-amazon-facebook-google-palantir.html.

5. United Nations, SDG Goal 5: Achieve gender equality and empower all women and girls," https://www.un.org/sustainabledevelopment/gender-equality/.

6. Newswire, "Hudson's Bay Hosts National Charity Shopping Event in Support of Boys and Girls Clubs of Canada," March 21, 2016, https://www.newswire.ca/news-releases/hudsons-bay-hosts-national-charity-shopping-event-in-support-of-boys-and-girls-clubs-of-canada-572968021.html.

7. United Nations, "The Shadow Pandemic, Violence against women during COVID-19," https://www.unwomen.org/en/news/in-focus/in-focus-gender-equality-in-covid-19-response/violence-against-women-during-covid-19.

8. Business Wire, "Hudson's Bay Foundation Launches Hudson's Bay Charter for Change With a $30 Million Investment to Accelerate Racial Equity in Canada," May 3, 2021, https://www.businesswire.com/news/home/20210503005299/en/Hudson%E2%80%99s-Bay-Foundation-Launches-Hudson%E2%80%99s-Bay-Charter-for-Change-With-a-30-Million-Investment-to-Accelerate-Racial-Equity-in-Canada.

9. Deloitte LLP, *Reputation Matters — Developing Reputational Resilience Ahead of Your Crisis*, 2016, https://www2.deloitte.com/content/dam/Deloitte/at/Documents/risk/deloitte-uk-reputation-matters-june-2016.pdf.

10. Margaret Ormiston, "Cashing in on Moral Credit," *Forbes*, April 23, 2014, https://www.forbes.com/sites/lbsbusinessstrategyreview/2014/04/23/cashing-in-on-moral-credits/?sh=73cf0b553cd9.

11. Paul Conway and Johanna Peetz, "When Does Feeling Moral Actually Make You a Better Person? Conceptual Abstraction Moderates Whether Past Moral Deeds Motivate Consistency or Compensatory Behavior," *Personality and Social Psychology Bulletin*, April 6, 2012, https://journals.sagepub.com/doi/10.1177/0146167212442394.

12. Margaret E. Ormiston and Elaine Wong, "License to Ill: The Effects of Corporate Social Responsibility and CEO Moral Identity on Corporate Social Irresponsibility," *Personnel Psychology*, February 16, 2013, https://onlinelibrary.wiley.com/doi/full/10.1111/peps.12029.

13. Ibid.

14. Reuters Events, "Beyond Petroleum: Why the CSR Community Collaborated in Creating the BP Oil Disaster," August 2, 2010, https://www.reutersevents.com/sustainability/stakeholder-engagement/beyond-petroleum-why-csr-community-collaborated-creating-bp-oil-disaster.

15. Wikipedia, "Deepwater Horizon oil spill," https://en.wikipedia.org/wiki/Deepwater_Horizon_oil_spill.

16. Ibid.

17. BP, "Energy with Purpose," https://www.bp.com/en/global/corporate/sustainability/sustainability-report-quick-read.html.

18. Alina Dizik, "Why Corporate Responsibility Can Backfire," *Chicago Booth Review*, June 2018, https://review.chicagobooth.edu/strategy/2018/article/why-corporate-social-responsibility-can-backfire.

19. Ibid.

20. Colin West and Chen-Bo Zhong, "Moral Cleansing," *Current Opinion in Psychology*, November 23, 2015, https://www.ethicalpsychology.com/2015/11/moral-cleansing.html.

21. Nadra Nittle, "What the Rana Plaza Disaster Changed About Worker Safety," Racked, April 13, 2018, https://www.racked.com/2018/4/13/17230770/rana-plaza-collapse-anniversary-garment-workers-safety.

22. *Wall Street Journal*, "Behind Your Amazon Order," October 23, 2019, https://www.wsj.com/video/series/behind-your-amazon-order/unsafe-factories-in-bangladesh-are-supplying-amazon-sellers/.

23. Anti Corporate Social Responsibility, "CSR Created Risk," http://anticsr.com/csr-created-risk/.

24. Sarah Dean, "Coca-Cola Accused of 'Health Washing' Because a Single Can of Coke Life Maxes the Daily Recommended Amount of SIX Teaspoons of Sugar," *Daily Mail Australia*, March 30, 2015, https://www.dailymail.co.uk/news/article-3018850/Coca-Cola-accused-health-washing-single-Coke-Life-maxes-daily-recommended-SIX-teaspoons-sugar.html.

25. Daily Mail Reporter, "'It's a Free Country . . . Sell Your Shares': Starbucks CEO Blasts Shareholder Who Told Him that Company's Support for Gay Marriage Was Hitting Profits," *Daily Mail*, March 22, 2013, https://www.dailymail.co.uk/news/article-2297856/Howard-Schultz-Starbucks-CEO-spars-anti-gay-marriage-activist-companys-stockholder-meeting.html.

26. Harvard Business Publishing, "Harvard ManageMentor: Business Case Development," https://hbsp.harvard.edu/product/7089-HTM-ENG.

27. Grant Thornton, *Corporate Responsibility: Burden or Opportunity? Grant Thornton's 15th Survey of U.S. Business Leaders*, Grant Thornton in partnership with BusinessWeek Research Services, September 2007.

28. Cone Communications, 2010 Cone Cause Evolotion Study, Cone 2010, https://www.conecomm.com/2010-cone-communications-cause-evolution-study-pdf.

29. Cone Communications, *2006 Millennial Cause Study*, Cone, 2006, https://www.conecomm.com/research-blog/2006-millennial-cause-study/.

30. Paul Klein, "What's Your Return on Integrity?" *Forbes*, June 6, 2011, https://www.forbes.com/sites/csr/2011/06/06/whats-your-return-on-integrity/.

Chapter 5: Change for Good Action

1. impakt, "Change for Good with Tim Cormode: Funding and Philanthropy," https://impaktcorp.com/change-for-good-with-tim-cormode-funding-and-philanthropy/.

2. impakt, "Change for Good with Andrea Barrack, Building a Sustainable Tomorrow," https://impaktcorp.com/change-for-good-with-andrea-barrack-building-a-sustainable-tomorrow/.

3. Paul Klein, "COVID: How Corporations Can Improve Their Impact on Society," *LSE Business Review*, September 15, 2020, https://blogs.lse.ac.uk/businessreview/2020/09/15/covid-how-corporations-can-improve-their-impact-on-society/.

4. Tim Draimin and Paul Klein, "The Other Innovation: Unleashing Canada's Capacity for Good," *Policy Magazine*, May 2017, https://policymagazine.ca/the-other-innovation-unleashing-canadas-capacity-for-good/.

5. Wouter Aghina et al., "Five Trademarks of Agile Organizations," McKinsey, January 2018, https://www.mckinsey.com/business-functions/organization/our-insights/the-five-trademarks-of-agile-organizations.

6. HRZone, "What is Business Agility?" https://www.hrzone.com/hr-glossary/what-is-business-agility.

7. impakt, "Change for Good with Daniele Zanotti: Taking Action in the

Community," April 16, 2020, https://impaktcorp.com/change-for-good-with-daniele-zanotti-taking-action-in-community/.

8. Buisness Roundtable, "Business Roundtable Redefines the Purpose of a Corporation to Promote 'An Economy That Serves All Americans,'" August 2019, https://www.businessroundtable.org/business-roundtable-redefines-the-purpose-of-a-corporation-to-promote-an-economy-that-serves-all-americans.

9. Edelman Trust Barometer 2021, https://www.edelman.com/trust/2021-trust-barometer.

10. KPMG Australia, *Customer Connections: Kindness and Loyalty in Uncertain Times*, April 2020, https://assets.kpmg/content/dam/kpmg/au/pdf/2020/customer-connections-covid-19.pdf.

11. Instagram, https://www.instagram.com/p/B9xEYEvJlH9/?igshid=10f7gs2b5e2qv.

12. Abha Bhattarai, "Walmart, Apple and Olive Garden Are Among Major Employers Updating Sick Leave Policies as Coronavirus Cases Spread," *The Washington Post*, March 10, 2020, https://www.washingtonpost.com/business/2020/03/10/walmart-apple-olive-garden-are-among-major-employers-updating-sick-leave-policies-coronavirus-cases-spread/.

13. KPMG Australia, "COVID-19: Mastering Meaningful and Human Connections with Customers," April 7, 2020, https://home.kpmg/au/en/home/insights/2020/04/coronavirus-covid-19-meaningful-human-connections-with-customers.html.

14. Samuel Stebbins and Grant Suneson, "Amazon, Apple Among the Companies that Are Helping Americans Fight COVID-19," *USA Today*, April 21, 2020, https://www.usatoday.com/story/money/2020/04/21/companies-that-are-helping-americans-fight-covid-19/111565368/.

15. Mike Robuck, "Verizon Takes Aim at Corporate Responsibility with its New Citizen Verizon Initiative," Fierce Telecom, July 14, 2020, https://www.fiercetelecom.com/telecom/verizon-takes-aim-at-corporate-responsibility-citizen-verizon-initiative.

16. *Business Wire*, "Mary Kay Inc. COVID-19 Support Efforts Target Disproportionately Effected Native American Populations Through the Indian Health Service Network," September 9, 2020, https://www.businesswire.com/news/home/20200909005162/en.

17. "Small and Medium Enterprises (SMEs) Finance," World Bank, worldbank.org/en/topic/smefinance.

18. Sarah Perez, "Amazon Creates $5M Relief Fund to Aid Small Businesses in Seattle Impacted by Coronavirus Outbreak," TechCrunch, March 10, 2020, https://techcrunch.com/2020/03/10/amazon-creates-5m-relief-fund-to-aid-small-businesses-in-seattle-impacted-by-coronavirus-outbreak/.

19. Adam Schrader, "Mark Cuban to Reimburse Employees Who Shop Locally Amid Coronavirus Outbreak," *The New York Post*, March 14, 2020, https://nypost.com/2020/03/14/mark-cuban-to-reimburse-employees-who-shop-locally-amid-coronavirus-outbreak/.

20. Target, SAFE Retail, "Considerations for Retail Operations Post COVID-19," https://corporate.target.com/_media/TargetCorp/about/pdf/Target_SAFE_Retail_Considerations-for-Retail-Operations-Post-COVID-19.pdf.

21. Sarah Kaplan and Peter Dey, *Where Are the Directors In a World in Crisis?*, Rotman School of Management, University of Toronto, 2021,https://www.rotman.utoronto.ca/FacultyAndResearch/ResearchCentres/LeeChinInstitute/Sustainability-Research-Resources/360-Governance-Report.

22. Tim Kiladze, "Canada's Corporate Boards Are Trapped in the Past, Must Be Revamped for ESG Era: Governance Expert," *The Globe and Mail*, February 22, 2020, https://www.theglobeandmail.com/business/article-canadas-corporate-boards-are-trapped-in-the-past-must-be-revamped-for/.

23. Better Evaluation, "Describe the Theory of Change," https://www.betterevaluation.org/en/node/5280/.

Chapter 6: Change for Good Responsibility

1. Australian HR Institute, "The History of Employee Assistance Programs and How They've Coped with COVID-19," August 2020, https://www.hrmonline.com.au/employee-wellbeing/history-of-employee-assistance-programs/.

2. William White and David Sharar, *The Evolution of Employee Assistance: A Brief History and Trend Analysis*, EAP Digest, 2003 http://www.williamwhitepapers.com/pr/2003EAPhistorytrendsEAPDigest.pdf.

3. Manulife, "A Brief History of the Employee Assistance Program," http://groupbenefits.manulife.com/Canada/GB_v2.nsf/LookupFiles/EBNQ305EAPHistory/$File/EAPHistory.htm.

4. International Employee Assistance Professionals Association, "About the EA profession and EAPA," https://www.eapassn.org/FAQs.

5. Marc Milot, "A Researcher's Inside Look at the Impact of Employee Assistance Programs," *International Foundation of Employee Benefit Plans*, February 2020, http://hdl.handle.net/10713/14266.

6. Susan M. Heathfield, "Do EAPs Work or Just Make Employers Feel Good?" The Balance Careers, April 27, 2019, https://www.thebalancecareers.com/do-eaps-work-or-just-make-employers-feel-good-1917971.

7. Wine to Water, https://www.winetowater.org/.

8. Michelle Lent Hirsch, "Americas Company Towns, Then and Now," *Smithsonian Magazine*, September 4, 2015.

9. Carol Sanford, "Are Corporations Outsourcing Responsibility?" *The Economist*, April 24, 2013, https://carolsanford.com/2013/04/are-corporations-outsourcing-responsibility/.

10. Judith S. Gooding et al. "Family Support and Family-Centered Care in the Neonatal Intensive Care Unit: Origins, Advances, Impact," *Seminars in Perinatology*, February 2011, https://pubmed.ncbi.nlm.nih.gov/21255703/.

11. impakt Corporation, "Ronald McDonald House Charities of Canada: Social Purpose," June 2015.

12. Starbucks, "'I Want to Grow': Hundreds of Young Adults Interview, Get Hired for Jobs at Dallas Opportunity Fair," May 19, 2017, https://stories.starbucks.com/stories/2017/dallas-opportunity-fair/.

13. Hyundai, "2016 Hyundai Motor Energizing Project for Taxi Drivers," March 29, 2016, https://www.hyundai.com/worldwide/en/company/newsroom/2016-hyundai-motor-energizing-project-for-taxi-drivers-0000015794.

14. Warby Parker, https://ca.warbyparker.com/history.

15. Ibid.

16. Haile Lesavage, "What Corporate Responsibility Means to Warby Parker in 2020," *Retail Brew*, August 18, 2020, https://www.morningbrew.com/retail/stories/2020/08/18/corporate-responsibility-means-warby-parker-2020.

17. Paul Klein, "Ten Ways for Mining Companies to Work Better with Indigenous People," *Forbes*, February 29, 2012, https://www.forbes.com/sites/csr/2012/02/29/ten-ways-for-mining-companies-to-work-better-with-indigenous-people/.

18. Wolff Olins x CitizenMe, *Radical Everyone*, 2017, https://radicaleveryone
.wolffolins.com/assets/pdf/RadicalEveryone.pdf.

19. David Gelles, "The Moral Voice of Corporate America," *The New York Times*,
August 19, 2017, https://www.nytimes.com/2017/08/19/business/moral-voice-
ceos.html.

20. Lee Hyo-sik, "Active Seniors," *The Korea Times*, September 8, 2013, http://www
.koreatimes.co.kr/www/news/biz/2016/04/335_142407.html.

21. Patricia Tomasi, "Researchers Hope to Move New Depression Treatment
Technique — rTMS — From the Margin to the Mainstream,"
Theravive, December 11, 2018, https://www.theravive.com/today/post/
researchers-hope-to-move-new-depression-treatment-technique-rtms-from-
the-margin-to-the-mainstream-0003340.aspx.

Chapter 7: Change for Good Investing

1. impakt, "Change for Good with Esther Pan Sloane," October 7, 2020, https://
impaktcorp.com/change-for-good-with-esther-pan-sloane-the-partnership-
conference/.

2. Mark Rendell, "Fund Aims to Help Alberta's Indigenous Women Start
Businesses," *The Globe and Mail*, June 20, 2017, https://www.theglobeandmail
.com/report-on-business/small-business/sb-money/fund-aims-to-help-
albertas-indigenous-women-start-businesses/article35399084/.

3. Indian Business Corporation, *Indigenous Business Women*, 2019, http://www
.indianbc.ca/news.php.

4. Giving USA, "Giving USA 2020," June 16, 2020, https://givingusa.org/
giving-usa-2020-charitable-giving-showed-solid-growth-climbing-to-449-64-
billion-in-2019-one-of-the-highest-years-for-giving-on-record/.

5. Chief Executives for Corporate Purpose, *Giving in Numbers 2020 Edition*,
2020, https://cecp.co/home/resources/giving-in-numbers/.

6. Global Impact Investing Network, *2020 Annual Impact Investor Survey*, June
2020, https://thegiin.org/research/publication/impinv-survey-2020.

7. CECP, *Investing with Purpose*, November 2016, https://cecp.co/wp-content/
uploads/2016/11/2016_InvestingWithPurpose-Press_Release_Final.pdf.

8. Hazel Bradford, "Global Impact Investment Market Going Strong Despite

Pandemic — GIIN," *Pensions & Investments,* June 11, 2020, https://www
.pionline.com/esg/global-impact-investment-market-going-strong-despite-
pandemic-giin.

9. Gunnar Friede, Timo Busch, and Alexander Bassen, "ESG and Financial
    Performance: Aggregated Evidence from More than 2000 Empirical Studies,"
    Journal of Sustainable Finance & Investment 5, no. 4 (2015): 210–33, ?doi:
    10.1080/20430795.2015.1118917.

10. CECP, *Investing with Purpose,* 2016, https://cecp.co/wp-content/
    uploads/2016/11/cecp_iwp_interactive_Final.pdf.

11. Campbell Soup Company, "Campbell to Acquire Plum Organics, A Leading
    Premium, Organic Kids Nutrition Company," May 23, 2013, https://www
    .campbellsoupcompany.com/newsroom/press-releases/campbell-to-acquire-
    plum-organics-a-leading-premium-organic-kids-nutrition-company/.

12. Cisco, "DFJ and Cisco Announce Husk Power Systems as Winner of Global
    Business Plan Competition," July 1, 2009, https://newsroom.cisco.com/press-
    release-content?type=webcontent&articleId=5010736.

13. Ron Day, "Fortune 500 Consumer Brands Re-up with Closed Loop's
    Infrastructure Fund, Which Loans Money to Support Recycling Technology,"
    Karma, July 27, 2020, https://karmaimpact.com/closed-loop-fund-hits-phase-
    2-as-3m-coke-others-roll-loans-forward/.

14. PRNewswire, "Roshan and Vodafone Sign Strategic Partner Market
    Agreement," December 8, 2011, https://www.prnewswire.com/news-releases/
    roshan-and-vodafone-sign-strategic-partner-market-agreement-135258168.html.

15. AT&T, "AT&T Aspire Accelerator," https://about.att.com/csr/
    aspireaccelerator.

16. Corporate Citizenship, *The Game Changers: Corporate Foundations in a Changing
    World,* December 2016, https://corporate-citizenship.com/our-insights/game-
    changers-corporate-foundations-changing-world/.

17. *Impact Investing,* "Reach for Change and IKEA Foundation: New
    Partnership to Impact 84,000 Children in Ethiopia," April 30, 2017, https://
    impactinvestingconferences.com/reach-for-change-and-ikea-foundation-new-
    partnership-to-impact-84000-children-in-ethiopia/.

18. TELUS, "TELUS Launches New $100 Million Social Impact Fund to Invest
    in New Sustainable Businesses with Bold Ideas to Drive Social Change,"

November 2020, https://www.telus.com/en/about/news-and-events/media-releases/telus-launches-new-100-million-social-impact-fund.

19. Ibid.

20. TELUS, https://www.telus.com/en/about.

Chapter 8: Change for Good Experience

1. Baljeet Sandhu, "Building Opportunities for Inclusive Leadership," *Stanford Social Innovation Review*, December 28, 2016, https://ssir.org/articles/entry/building_opportunities_for_inclusive_leadership#.

2. Sherry Arnstein, "A Ladder of Citizen Participation," *JAIP*, July 1969, https://lithgow-schmidt.dk/sherry-arnstein/ladder-of-citizen-participation_en.pdf.

3. Ibid.

4. Canadian Association of People Who Use Drugs (CAPUD), *Collective Voices, Effecting Change: Final Report of National Meeting of Peer-Run Organizations of People Who Use Drugs*, 2014, https://static1.squarespace.com/static/53015f40e4b0c6ad9e406a13/t/53972833e4b0240065925810/1402415155682/CollectiveVoices+Report+FINAL+30May14.pdf.

5. BC Centre for Disease Control, "Peer Engagement," http://www.bccdc.ca/our-services/programs/peer-engagement.

6. Balijeet Sandhu, *The Value of Lived Experience in Social Change*, July 2017, http://thelivedexperience.org/report/.

7. Tata Steel, "CSR Policy — Tata Steel India," September 2014, https://www.tatasteel.com/media/1879/csr-policy-version-20.pdf.

8. Roger Martin, "Yes, Short-Termism Really Is a Problem," *Harvard Business Review*, October 9, 2015, https://hbr.org/2015/10/yes-short-termism-really-is-a-problem.

9. Lived Experience Advisory Council, *Nothing About Us Without Us: Seven Principles for Leadership and Inclusion of People with Lived Experience of Homelessness*, The Homeless Hub Press, 2016, https://www.homelesshub.ca/sites/default/files/attachments/LEAC-7principles-final.pdf.

Chapter 9: Change for Good Jobs

1. Reggie Wade, "Nike to Tie Exec Pay to Progress in Deepening Diversity and Helping Environment," Yahoo!, March 11, 2021, https://finance.yahoo.com/news/nike-to-tie-exec-pay-to-progress-in-deepening-diversity-and-helping-environment-160416343.html.
2. Nike, Inc., "NIKE, Inc. and National Urban League Are Championing Employment and Home Ownership for the Black Community," March 2021, https://news.nike.com/news/nike-x-national-urban-league-black-community-commitment-march-2021.
3. Nike, Inc., *FY20 Nike, Inc. Impact Report*, https://purpose-cms-preprod01.s3.amazonaws.com/wp-content/uploads/2021/04/26225049/FY20_NIKE_Inc_Impact_Report2.pdf.
4. Edelman, *Earned Brand 2018*, October 2018, https://www.edelman.com/earned-brand.
5. Edelman, *Special Report: Brand Trust in 2020*, June 2020, https://www.edelman.com/sites/g/files/aatuss191/files/2020-06/2020%20Edelman%20Trust%20Barometer%20Specl%20Rept%20Brand%20Trust%20in%202020.pdf.
6. Fernano Duarte, "Black Lives Matter: Do Companies Really Support the Cause?" BBC, June 12, 2020, https://www.bbc.com/worklife/article/20200612-black-lives-matter-do-companies-really-support-the-cause.
7. Ibid.
8. AgentsC, *Equity Matters: A Snapshot of Canadian Non-Profit Perspectives During the COVID-19 Era*, July 2020, shorturl.at/gkzJ3.
9. Rocío Lorenzo et al., "How Diverse Leadership Teams Boost Innovation," BCG, January 23, 2018, https://www.bcg.com/en-us/publications/2018/how-diverse-leadership-teams-boost-innovation.
10. Sundiatu Dixon-Fyle et al., *Diversity Wins: How Inclusion Matters*, McKinsey & Company, May 2020, https://www.mckinsey.com/featured-insights/diversity-and-inclusion/diversity-wins-how-inclusion-matters.
11. Ibid.
12. Hays Talent Solutions, *2018 Hays Asia Diversity and Inclusion Report*, 2018, https://cloud.email.hays.com/hts-asia-diversityinclusion18.

13. Accenture, "The Secret to Boosting Employee Engagement for Millennials and Gen Z," July 2019, https://www.accenture.com/nl-en/blogs/insights/the-secret-to-boosting-employee-engagement-for-millennials-and-gen-z.

14. Peter Economy, "The (Millennial) Workplace of the Future Is Almost Here," Inc., January 15, 2019, https://www.inc.com/peter-economy/the-millennial-workplace-of-future-is-almost-here-these-3-things-are-about-to-change-big-time.html.

15. United Nations Department of Economics and Social Affairs, "Sustainable Development," https://sdgs.un.org/goals/goal1.

16. Arif Jetha, "The Future of Work Will Hit Vulnerable People the Hardest: U of T Expert," University of Toronto News, March 9, 2020, https://www.utoronto.ca/news/future-work-will-hit-vulnerable-people-hardest-u-t-expert.

17. Law Commission of Ontario, "Quick Facts about Vulnerable Workers and Precarious Work," March 3, 2017, https://www.lco-cdo.org/wp-content/uploads/2012/08/vulnerable-workers-interim-report-quick-facts.pdf.

18. Ibid.

19. BDC, "Labour Shortage: Here to Stay," https://www.bdc.ca/en/about/analysis-research/labour-shortage.

20. RBC, *Diversity and Inclusion, We're Not Doing Enough*, http://www.rbc.com/6degrees/_assets-custom/pdf/6Degrees_EN.pdf.

21. Francis Churchill, "Two in Five Employers Unaware Hiring Homeless People is Legal," *People Management*, February 20, 2020, https://www.peoplemanagement.co.uk/news/articles/two-in-five-employers-think-hiring-homeless-people-is-illegal#gref.

22. Refreshing a Career, "Employing Homeless People," https://www.refreshingacareer.com/employers/benefits/employing-homeless-people/.

23. Sally Lindsay et al, "A Systematic Review of the Benefits of Hiring People with Disabilities," *Journal of Occupational Rehabilitation* (2018): 1–22, https://tspace.library.utoronto.ca/bitstream/1807/93886/3/A%20systematic%20review%20benefits_TSpace.pdf.

24. Robert Quigley and James Baines, *The Social Value of a Job*, Wellington: Ministry for Primary Industries, 2014, https://www.mpi.govt.nz/dmsdocument/5266/direct.

25. Forbes Insights, *Fostering Innovation Through a Diverse Workforce*, 2011,

https://images.forbes.com/forbesinsights/StudyPDFs/Innovation_Through_
Diversity.pdf.

Chapter 10: Change for Good. Good for Change.

1. United Nations Conference on Trade and Development, *Corporate Governance in the Wake of the Financial Crisis*, 2010, https://unctad.org/system/files/official-document/diaeed2010z_en.pdf.

2. Morning Consult, *CSR & Political Activism in the Trump Era*, 2018, https://morningconsult.com/form/csr-political-activism/.

3. Greg Dalgetty, "Newsmaker: Failure is not an option," *Investment Executive*, August 21, 2020, https://www.investmentexecutive.com/newspaper_/news-newspaper/newsmaker-failure-is-not-an-option-image-tk/.

4. Wikipedia, "List of banks acquired or bankrupted during the Great Recession," https://en.wikipedia.org/wiki/List_of_banks_acquired_or_bankrupted_during_the_Great_Recession.

5. Frederic S. Mishkin, "Over the Cliff: From the Subprime to the Global Financial Crisis," *Journal of Economic Perspectives*, December 2010, https://www.nber.org/papers/w16609.

6. ILO, *Global Employment Trends 2014: The Risk of a Jobless Recovery*, International Labour Organization, 2014, https://www.ilo.org/wcmsp5/groups/public/---dgreports/---dcomm/---publ/documents/publication/wcms_233953.pdf.

7. Ibid.

8. World Economic Forum, *The Future of Jobs Report 2018*, 2018, http://www3.weforum.org/docs/WEF_Future_of_Jobs_2018.pdf.

9. Annie Lowrey, "The Great Recession Is Still With Us," *The Atlantic*, December 1, 2017, https://www.theatlantic.com/business/archive/2017/12/great-recession-still-with-us/547268/.

10. Brad Hershbein and Lisa B. Kahn, *Do Recessions Accelerate Routine-Biased Technological Change?*, National Bureau of Economics Research, October 2016, https://www.nber.org/system/files/working_papers/w22762/w22762.pdf.

11. John Quelch, "How Corporate Responsibility Can Survive the Recession," *Harvard Business Review*, September 22, 2019, https://hbr.org/2009/09/how-corporate-responsibility-c.

12. Ibid.

13. KPMG, *Corporate Governance and King III*, 2014, https://assets.kpmg/content/dam/kpmg/pdf/2016/07/Corporate-Governance-and-King-III.pdf.

14. Business Roundtable, "Statement on the Purpose of a Corporation," August 2019, https://opportunity.businessroundtable.org/ourcommitment/.

15. David Streitfeld, "Tech Opposition to Trump Propelled by Employees, Not Executives," *The New York Times*, February 6, 2017, https://www.nytimes.com/2017/02/06/business/trump-travel-ban-apple-google-facebook.html.

16. Michale D. Shear, "Trump Will Withdraw U.S. From Paris Climate Agreement," *The New York Times*, June 1, 2017, https://www.nytimes.com/2017/06/01/climate/trump-paris-climate-agreement.html.

17. David Gelles et al., "Inside the C.E.O. Rebellion Against Trump's Advisory Councils," *The New York Times*, August 16, 2017, https://www.nytimes.com/2017/08/16/business/trumps-council-ceos.html.

18. Satya Nadella, "DREAMers Make Our Countries and Communities Stronger," LinkedIn, August 31, 2017, https://www.linkedin.com/pulse/dreamers-make-our-country-communities-stronger-satya-nadella/.

19. Weber Shandwick, "Millennial Demand for CEO Activism Surges," July 24, 2017, https://www.webershandwick.com/news/millennial-demand-for-ceo-activism-surges/.

20. BlackRock, "Larry Fink's 2019 Letter to CEOs — Profit & Purpose," 2019, https://www.blackrock.com/americas-offshore/en/2019-larry-fink-ceo-letter.

21. James E. Langston, Cleary Gottlieb Steen and Hamilton LLP, "Shareholder Activism in 2020: New Risks and Opportunities for Boards," Harvard Law School Forum on Corporate Governance, January 24, 2020, https://corpgov.law.harvard.edu/2020/01/24/shareholder-activism-in-2020-new-risks-and-opportunities-for-boards/.

22. Marco Poggio, "Trump Order Takes Aim at Shareholders Pushing Companies to Address Climate Risks," The Climate Docket, April 17, 2019, https://www.climatedocket.com/2019/04/17/shareholder-climate-resolutions-trump/.

23. ImpactAlpha, "Jeffrey Ubben, Inclusive Capital Partners," September 18, 2020, https://impactalpha.com/agent-of-impact-jeffrey-ubben/.

24. Ben & Jerry's, https://www.benandjerrys.ca/en/whats-new/could-you-be-our-

new-activism-manager#:~:text=At%20Ben%20%26%20Jerry's%20we%20have,
spirit%20into%20everything%20we%20do.

25. Zlati Meyer, "Ben & Jerry's Launches Donald Trump-Inspired Ice Cream
    Flavor, Pecan Resist," *USA Today*, October 30, 2018, https://www.usatoday.com/
    story/money/2018/10/30/ben-and-jerrys-ice-cream-flavor-pecan-resist-
    trump/1811714002/.

26. Morning Consult, *CSR & Political Activism in the Trump Era*, 2018, https://
    morningconsult.com/form/csr-political-activism/.

27. Weber Shandwick, *Battle of the Wallets: The Changing Landscape of Consumer
    Activism*, 2017, https://www.webershandwick.com/wp-content/uploads/2018/05/
    Battle_of_the_Wallets.pdf.

28. Jackie Aina, YouTube, May 28, 2020, https://twitter.com/omariannee/
    status/1266127149712449537?s=20.

29. Reebok, Twitter, May 30, 2020, https://twitter.com/Reebok/
    status/1266792697941164032.

30. Reebok, "Customer Service," https://www.reebok.ca/en/company.html.

31. Adidas, "'Own the Game, Our Strategy 2025," https://www.adidas-group.com/
    en/strategy/summary/.

32. Sally Ho, "'Empty Words': Companies Touting Black Lives Matter Accused of
    Hypocrisy," KOMONEWS, June 11, 2020, https://komonews.com/news/local/
    empty-words-companies-touting-black-lives-matter-accused-of.

33. Opinium, "US Brand & Marketing Study: Responding to Black Lives
    Matter," July 9, 2020, https://www.opinium.com/us-brand-marketing-study-
    responding-to-black-lives-matter/.

34. impakt, "Change for Good with Andrea Barrack," May 7, 2020, https://
    impaktcorp.com/change-for-good-with-andrea-barrack-building-a-
    sustainable-tomorrow/.

35. impakt, "Change for Good with Valerie McMurtry," May 7, 2020, April 9, 2020,
    https://impaktcorp.com/change-for-good-with-valerie-mcmurtry-supporting-
    vulnerable-populations/.

36. impakt, "Change for Good with Tabatha Bull," April 30, https://impaktcorp
    .com/change-for-good-with-tabatha-bull-seven-generations-ahead/.

37. impakt, "Change for Good with Bif Naked," May 19, 2020, https://impaktcorp
    .com/change-for-good-with-bif-naked-creativity-lived-experience/.

Conclusion: You Are the Change for Good

1. BBC News, "Italy Migrants: Benetton Criticised Over Ad Campaign," June 20, 2018, https://www.bbc.com/news/world-europe-44545860.

ACKNOWLEDGEMENTS

The ways in which I've been able to help businesses contribute to social change would not have happened without Larry Enkin's guidance and friendship. Larry's been encouraging me to write a book for many years. Like many things he's suggested to me, I should have listened to him and done this a lot sooner.

I appreciate the input of many people who contributed to some of the ideas I've shared in this book. These include Tim Draimin, Gilad Lang, Eric Solomon, Esther Pan Sloane, Upkar Arora, and Mide Akerewusi.

Preston Aitken, Sam Bennett, Nicole Bryck, Cameron, Elizabeth Castrillon Jimenez, Jesse Donaldson, Amir Fleischmann, Elana Hazghia, Olivia Larkin, Lesley McMillan, Julie Middleton, Andrea O'Reilly, Alex Schneidman, Julie-Anne Starling, Péter Sós, and Maya Stevens-Uninsky are some of the talented people who I've collaborated with at impakt over the years. I also appreciate the contributions of impakt's social purpose leaders: Rem Langan, Jon Packer, Magdalena Kowalska, and Clifford Moss.

In 2019, we launched the Impakt Foundation for Social Change. I deeply value the guidance and support of the people on our board of directors, including Fatemeh Alhosseini, Rem Langan, Jon Packer, Noni Rabinovitch, Stuart Svonkin, and our executive director, Martina Ambiri.

I've also had the opportunity to collaborate with and learn from a number of academics who have each made significant contributions to better understanding the relationship between business and society. These include Andrew Crane, Jay Handelman, Peter Madsen, and Dirk Matten.

I always appreciate and look forward to speaking with my colleagues at the Global Wellness Institute's Social Impact Initiative: Wendy Bosalavage, Brian Brazeau, Sallie Fraenkel, Monique Iacobacci, Isabelle Houde, Gilad Lang, Andrea Leja, and Cassandre Tissot.

I worked closely with Peter Ross at the Toronto Symphony Orchestra — he's the best boss I have ever had. I had the privilege of helping John Kim Bell establish the National Aboriginal Achievement Awards and the opportunity to listen to and learn from Aboriginal people across Canada. I learned an immense amount about social change strategy and communications from Mark Sarner, founder and president of Manifest Communications. Jon Packer and I have been talking about the meaning of life, work, and creativity for years. We haven't figured out too much, but these conversations are always so enjoyable. Tim Cormode is a social change leader who inspires me to believe that everything is possible.

This book wouldn't have happened if we hadn't convened the Change for Good leadership series in 2020. I'm very grateful to the social change leaders who shared their ideas for how to continue having an impact during COVID-19 and what "building back better" would look like for the social change sector after the pandemic. Big thanks go to Andrea Barrack, Naina Batra, Tabatha Bull, Tim Cormode, David "Patch" Patchell-Evans, Pamela Fuselli, Jenn Harper, Stephen Huddart, Gilad Lang, Markus Lux, Bruce MacDonald, Valerie McMurtry, Manju Menon, Bif Naked, Craig Ryan, Mark Tewksbury, and Daniele Zanotti.

Finally, I appreciate the support of Jennifer Smith at ECW Press and editor Anam Ahmed, who helped to turn what I wrote into a book that I hope will create much more Change for Good.

ABOUT THE AUTHOR

Paul Klein is a globally recognized authority on helping businesses solve social problems. In 2001, Paul founded impakt, a B Corp that has helped corporations including De Beers, Home Depot Canada, John Deere, McCain Foods, McKesson, Nestlé, National Bank, Petro-Canada, Pfizer, RONA, Shoppers Drug Mart, Scotiabank, Sobeys, Starbucks, TD, Walmart, TELUS International, GoodLife Fitness, and 3M improve the value and impact of their investments in social change. Paul has also helped non-profit organizations to understand their social purpose and improve their impact on society.

In 2019, Paul established the Impakt Foundation for Social Change, a registered charitable organization with a mission of helping people in need find pathways to employment.

Paul serves on the Advisory Council of the Centre of Excellence for Responsible Business at the Schulich School of Business, the Advisory Board of Urban Matters, and he is a member of the Global Wellness Institute's Social Impact Initiative. Paul also writes extensively about the intersection of business and social change for publications including *Advertising Age*, *Canadian Business*, *Forbes*, the *Financial Post*, the *Globe and Mail*, the *Guardian*, the *Stanford Social Innovation Review*, and the *LSE Business Review*.

INDEX

Mondelēz International, 47
Mondragon Corporation, 28–29
moral cleansing, 88
moral licensing and moral credits, 85, 86–87
Morgan Stanley company, 56
motorcycle transportation, 149–50
Mountain Equipment Co-op (MEC), 18–20
music, and social change, 219
Muthu, Sankar, 44

Nadella, Satya, 205–6
Nairn, Iain, 83
National Aboriginal Achievement Foundation (now known as Indspire), 3, 4
National Urban League, 179
Native Americans, COVID-19's impact, 116
   See also Indigenous people
natural resource businesses, 3
Nestlé, 8, 52–53, 122
newcomers to Canada, 177, 184–85, 187
Newman's Own, 53
New York State Common Retirement Fund on Amazon, 27
Nike, 115, 179–80
non-profits. *See* charities
Not-amazon.co (or Not Amazon), 27–28
"nothing about us without us," 164, 165
novel coronavirus. *See* COVID-19 pandemic
NuSocia, 222

ohana (or Ohana), 42
oil and gas industry, 139–40, 207
oil spills, 85–86
Olins, Wolff, 140
1% for Peace campaign, 1
100,000 Opportunities Initiative and 100,000 Opportunity Youth, 134–35
Orange Door Project, 103

Ormiston, Margaret, 85
Osanloo, Michael, 47
"The Other Innovation: Unleashing Canada's Capacity for Good" (Klein and Draimin), 109–11

pace of change
   and agents of change, 118–19
   in businesses, 104, 106–7, 113
   and COVID pandemic, 106–7, 108, 111–17
   description, 107–8
   in employment of vulnerable people, 194–95
   examples, 111, 112–17
   social change, 104–5, 106, 108–9, 122
   tool for, 117–22
Pan Sloane, Esther, 148–52, 154
participation by citizens, ladder as guide, 164–65
partnerships, 5–6, 32, 143
Patagonia, 19, 63
Patchell-Evans, David "Patch," 17, 222, 223
Patterson, Kathie, 65
Peace River (Alberta), 139–40
people in need. *See* vulnerable people
people with disabilities, employment, 190–91
PepsiCo and PepsiCorps, 66–68
Petro-Canada CareMakers Foundation, 13, 100–101
Pettigrew, William, 43
Pfizer, 54, 65–66, 67, 100
PGA of America, 56
Philadelphia (US), racist incident, 135
philanthropic activities, in early modern period, 43–45
philanthropic donations
   as CSR Lite, 90
   and Great Recession, 201, 202
   vs. impact investing, 154–55
   as investment, 147–48, 151–52
Phillips, Utah, 219